Always Near

Always Near

Daily Moments with God

JESSICA MILLER KELLEY, EDITOR

First edition
Published by Westminster John Knox Press
Louisville, Kentucky

26 27 28 29 30 31 32 33 34 35—10 9 8 7 6 5 4 3 2 1

Book design by Ann DeVilbiss
Cover design by Mary Ann Smith

Library of Congress Cataloging-in-Publication Data

Names: Kelley, Jessica Miller editor
Title: Always near : daily moments with God / Jessica Miller Kelley, editor.
Description: First edition. | Louisville, Kentucky : Westminster John Knox Press, [2026] | Summary: "Features devotions for every day of the year and offers timely insights for the seasons as well as biblical wisdom for daily living. Each day's reflection is grounded in Scripture and offers a prayer to guide your daily walk with God"-- Provided by publisher.
Identifiers: LCCN 2026006391 (print) | LCCN 2026006392 (ebook) | ISBN 9780664269357 | ISBN 9781646984602 ebook
Subjects: LCSH: Devotional calendars
Classification: LCC BV4811 .A498 2026 (print) | LCC BV4811 (ebook)
LC record available at https://lccn.loc.gov/2026006391
LC ebook record available at https://lccn.loc.gov/2026006392

PRINTED IN THE UNITED STATES OF AMERICA

♾ The paper used in this publication meets the minimum requirements of the American National Standard for Information Sciences–Permanence of Paper for Printed Library Materials, ANSI Z39.48-1992.

O Lord, you have searched me and known me.
You know when I sit down and when I rise up;
you discern my thoughts from far away.
You search out my path and my lying down,
and are acquainted with all my ways.
Even before a word is on my tongue,
O Lord, you know it completely.
You hem me in, behind and before,
and lay your hand upon me.
Such knowledge is too wonderful for me;
it is so high that I cannot attain it.

Where can I go from your spirit?
Or where can I flee from your presence?
If I ascend to heaven, you are there;
if I make my bed in Sheol, you are there.
If I take the wings of the morning
and settle at the farthest limits of the sea,
even there your hand shall lead me,
and your right hand shall hold me fast.

—Psalm 139:1–10

JANUARY 1

ECCLESIASTES 3:1–13

Welcoming All Experiences

For everything there is a season, and a time for every matter under heaven.

Ecclesiastes 3:1

As a new year begins, the writer of Ecclesiastes invites us to consider the cyclical and balanced nature of life, in which a full range of human experiences finds a place and time. The author of this text is clear that there are times for joyous experiences like dancing, laughing, and building; and there are times for painful experiences like mourning, weeping, and tearing down.

In a world that seems to overvalue success and denigrate failure, this passage from Ecclesiastes provides a powerful corrective. God has made all experiences beautiful in their time, including those experiences we would rather escape. There are simply times when weeping is the only and most appropriate response. Our tears can be a beautiful testament to the heart's ability to express grief when what we've loved is lost.

As we begin a new year, may we welcome all the experiences awaiting us, embracing *both* joy and struggle as part of the beauty and gift of our lives.

God, help us to welcome all experiences into our lives knowing that you make all things beautiful in their time. Amen.

Laurie Milito

JANUARY 2

ISAIAH 60:1–6

Seeing with New Eyes

Lift up your eyes and look around;
they all gather together, they come to you.

Isaiah 60:4a

To those in the darkness of the Babylonian exile, the prophet Isaiah spoke a powerful word of hope. Into the darkness of their fear and uncertainty, Isaiah proclaimed that the light of God's glory was rising.

Many of us live in our own modern-day exiles. We are abandoned by others, excluded from political systems, denied access to education, or cut off from our own bodies due to disability or illness. Into our thick darkness, we hear the distant voice of Isaiah proclaiming that the light of God's glory still rises.

This glory, though, can be easy to miss. Knowing this, Isaiah counseled his disheartened people to "lift up [their] eyes and look around." Seeing God's glory requires us to search beyond our own situations to find where God is at work. When we witness God's glory shining in the world around us, something wondrous happens: our hearts "shall thrill and rejoice" (v. 5). So lift your eyes and look around. What do you see?

Lord, help us to see your glory in others so that others may see your light in us. Amen.

Laurie Milito

JANUARY 3

EPHESIANS 3:8–12

Revealing the Wisdom of God

So that through the church the wisdom of God in its rich variety might now be made known.

Ephesians 3:10a

It is through the church, Paul tells the Ephesians, that God's plan is worked out. Importantly, this plan requires rich variety. God's generous love flows through this assortment, expressing the wisdom of God to the world. Too often, however, we create a hierarchy of gifts and fail to appreciate the wisdom that flows from the least of these.

In one of my former congregations, there was a talented lay preacher whose wife was a brilliant musician. Their gifts were widely celebrated. Their only child, a sweet boy with developmental disabilities, often helped the greeters at the door on Sundays. When the family moved away, we mourned the loss of this talented couple. Many were surprised, however, to find themselves also mourning the loss of their young son, whose enthusiasm and smile at the church door warmed the hearts of all who entered. The wisdom of God expressed through this child was as significant as what God expressed through his parents' gifts.

God, thank you for the rich variety of gifts that allow your wisdom to be made known. Amen.

Laurie Milito

JANUARY 4

ACTS 8:14–17

Hands of Blessing

Then Peter and John laid their hands on them, and they received the Holy Spirit.

Acts 8:17

During their mission to Samaria, Peter and John prayed and laid hands on the new converts who had previously been baptized by Philip, and they received the Holy Spirit. By evangelizing to the Samaritans, an ethnic group historically at odds with the Jews, Peter and John gave us a model of a church eager to reach out to outsiders, following the Spirit's leading. We are reminded, once more, that the Holy Spirit is a Spirit of inclusion, unifying God's people across difference.

The children in my church are often the ones moved by the Spirit to reach across boundaries. For example, when one of our members with schizophrenia, "Sam," had trouble sitting still in the pew, they had an idea. They boxed up little puzzles and hung them in bags at the back of the church. When they noticed Sam becoming agitated, they would bring him a puzzle and work on it together. While adult members sometimes felt annoyed by Sam, the children's inclusiveness promoted a Spirit of loving acceptance.

God, may our churches be inspired by a spirit of inclusion and love as we share life together. Amen.

Laurie Milito

JANUARY 5

MATTHEW 2:1–6

Searching Hearts

In the time of King Herod, after Jesus was born in Bethlehem of Judea, wise men from the East came to Jerusalem.

Matthew 2:1

In search of a king, wise men from the East came to Jerusalem. These foreigners were not steeped in the teachings of the Torah. Rather, they received their divine direction from their study of the movement of the stars in the heavens. They were the original spiritual seekers, following the light without knowing its destination but open to its possibilities.

For those of us raised in the church and immersed in its teachings, our ability to wonder and seek after new epiphanies might be somewhat truncated. We seek revelation in our tradition but may be reluctant to also search our experience. Perhaps we need to set aside the doctrines to which we cling in order to again become simple seekers, willing to be led to the manger and open to what we might see there. For the magi and for us, it is the presence of Christ, not the knowledge of great religious truths, that finally satisfies our seeking hearts.

God of starlight, lead us to seek out your presence hidden in ordinary sight. Amen.

Laurie Milito

JANUARY 6

MATTHEW 2:7–12

Finding Another Way Home

And having been warned in a dream not to return to Herod, they left for their own country by another road.

Matthew 2:12

Following the star to where the Christ child was, the magi worshiped him. However, they soon learned that the promise embodied in this child did not remove the dangers of the world. In some ways, the danger was heightened. Warned in a dream not to go back to Herod, the magi had no choice but to find another way home.

The presence of Christ in our lives does not remove life's dangers either. I learned this for myself when I went into labor with my first child. Filled with the joy of new life, I was devastated when a long labor ended in stillbirth. As I left the hospital afterward, I could not go home in the same way. I was forever changed. I felt the poignancy and fragility of life in ways that woke me up to the blessing and promise of life itself. I would cherish the two children I went on to have in deeper ways than I might have otherwise.

God, help us to face life's dangers knowing the promise of your presence is unfailing. Amen.

Laurie Milito

JANUARY 7

LUKE 3:15–17, 21–22

Loved from the Start

And a voice came from heaven, "You are my Son, the Beloved; with you I am well pleased."

Luke 3:22b

Baptism marked the beginning of Jesus' public ministry. In Luke, the Gospel writer was careful to point out that Jesus' baptism happened "when all the people were baptized" (v. 21). It is possible, then, to see Jesus' baptism as an act of solidarity with the people he was preparing to serve. At the river's edge, Jesus identified with the troubled and downtrodden as he would throughout his ministry.

Because Jesus identified with the common people, God declared his pleasure in the actions of his Son. That profound declaration of God's love propelled Jesus through the darkest moments of his life. It is a declaration we, too, make whenever we baptize in his name. Our life together in Christ has these twin blessings: we exist in community as one body of believers and we find our energy for service from the experience and joy of God's deep love for each one of us.

God of the journey, loved from the start, may we each find our purpose in loving others as you have loved us. Amen.

Laurie Milito

JANUARY 8

HEBREWS 11:1–2

Extraordinary Faith

Now faith is the assurance of things hoped for, the conviction of things not seen.

Hebrews 11:1

Hebrews 11 has been called the "faith chapter." In it, we discover some characteristics of extraordinary faith through the examples of some of the great men and women of the Bible. These faithful servants sought out and trusted God, and as a result, they pleased God and were rewarded for their faith. They approached God with obedience and perseverance and *by faith* received God's approval along with the strength to accomplish humanly impossible things.

There are many other stories of ordinary, nameless people in the Bible who had extraordinary faith in the face of their own overwhelming circumstances. A little Israelite maid had great courage. The healing miracles of Jesus show other characteristics of faith, including humility, persistence, penitence, expectation, and confidence. These faithful ones also sought out God, trusted God, pleased God, and *by faith* were rewarded with what they asked.

Our faith manifests itself in unique ways as well. Think of some of the characteristics of your faith. How is it extraordinary?

Strengthen our faith, O Lord, that we might please you more and more. Amen.

Xavia Arndt Sheffield

JANUARY 9

2 Kings 5:2–4

Courageous Faith

"If only my lord were with the prophet who is in Samaria! He would cure him of his leprosy."

2 Kings 5:3

We are told only two things about this young girl: she was taken captive from the land of Israel by King Aram's army, and she became a slave to Naaman's wife. But in spite of her lowly status and insignificance, her eyes of faith perceived hope and the possibility that Naaman could be cured of his leprosy.

She had been taught about the healing God of Israel. She also knew of the prophet Elisha and how he had healed many. And she had tremendous courage in speaking up on behalf of her master. She believed God, through the prophet, would cure him. And when Naaman did what Elisha told him to do, "his flesh was restored like the flesh of a young boy, and he was clean" (v. 14).

We can have faith, but if we lack the courage to act on it, the power of faith remains hidden. What is the character of your faith—is it full of fear or courage?

Lord, give us courage to always trust you enough to act on our faith. Amen.

Xavia Arndt Sheffield

JANUARY 10

MATTHEW 8:5–13

Humble Faith

The centurion answered, "Lord, I am not worthy to have you come under my roof; but only speak the word, and my servant will be healed."

Matthew 8:8

The centurion was not a follower of Jesus but an officer in the Roman army, a Gentile. He had a great need the day he approached Jesus, not for himself, but for his beloved servant, who lay paralyzed. When he asked for help, Jesus said he would go and cure him. But the centurion added that he was not worthy to have the Master enter his house. He believed Jesus could but speak the word and the servant would be healed from a distance.

One characteristic of this man's faith was humility. He confessed his unworthiness as well as his trust in the outcome. And Jesus put the emphasis on *his* faith with this amazing response: "Truly I tell you, in no one in Israel have I found such faith" (v. 10). After Jesus said to him, "'Go; let it be done for you according to your faith.' And the servant was healed in that hour" (v. 13).

Is humility one of the characteristics of your faith?

Lord, help us supplement our faith with true humility. Amen.

Xavia Arndt Sheffield

JANUARY 11

MATTHEW 15:21–28

Persistent Faith

Just then a Canaanite woman from that region came out and started shouting, "Have mercy on me, Lord, Son of David; my daughter is tormented by a demon."

Matthew 15:22

This Canaanite mother was a Gentile. And if her faith was anything, it was persistent. She shouted to let people know of her dilemma. She knelt at Jesus' feet and begged him to rid her daughter of a demon. She engaged Jesus in an argument. She knew Jesus was the Messiah, and she knew the Messiah could heal her daughter. This was a mother's love in action.

Jesus ignored her at first, being harsh and even offensive in his response to her. But she would not be deterred. She argued that she, too, was somehow worthy of God's mercy, whatever Jesus' position. Her persistent faith brought about a reversal in Jesus, perhaps a preliminary sign of what was to come for the Gentiles, and Jesus answered her: "Woman, great is your faith! Let it be done for you as you wish" (v. 28). Her daughter was healed instantly.

Is your faith persistent? Do you believe God's mercy is also for you?

Lord, help us have persistent faith to not give up on ourselves or on you. Amen.

Xavia Arndt Sheffield

JANUARY 12

LUKE 23:39–43

Penitent Faith

Then he said, "Jesus, remember me when you come into your kingdom."

Luke 23:42

Most of the conversation in this story was between the two criminals who were crucified with Jesus. One cynically taunted Jesus and asked, "Are you not the Messiah? Save yourself and us!" (v. 39). But the other rebuked the first and said they deserved the sentence they were getting, but Jesus did not, because he had not done anything wrong. This dying man was acknowledging his own guilt and asking for forgiveness. He asked Jesus to remember him, and Jesus extended mercy to one of the wretched outcasts of that society.

Jesus' last words to another human being were the *assurance* of salvation. He replied, "Truly I tell you, today you will be with me in Paradise" (v. 43). The penitent criminal was given far more than what he asked.

Jesus' answer tells us that we are also welcome in his kingdom, in spite of *our* sin. Does your faith carry with it the fear of God and the recognition of your need for penitence?

Help us, Lord, to confess our sin before you this day. Amen.

Xavia Arndt Sheffield

JANUARY 13

MARK 5:25–34

Expectant Faith

"If I but touch his clothes, I will be made well."

Mark 5:28

This woman had been suffering a long time and was sure that if she could just get close enough to Jesus to simply touch his clothes, she would be made well. She expected it. She didn't even have to face him or talk to him. She pushed her way through the crowd, touched Jesus' cloak, and was immediately healed.

Jesus sought out the one who touched the cloak. Jesus wanted to affirm her faith and did so by saying to her, "Daughter, your faith has made you well; go in peace, and be healed of your disease" (v. 34). Jesus did not take the credit; instead, he said that her faith was the real source of her healing. And by calling her daughter, Jesus included her as a member of God's family.

Does your faith hold the expectation that God will heal you? Or do you come to God with a "maybe" or a "we'll see" attitude?

Lord, help us come to you with the expectation of your healing touch. Amen.

Xavia Arndt Sheffield

JANUARY 14

MATTHEW 9:27–31

Confident Faith

When he entered the house, the blind men came to him; and Jesus said to them, "Do you believe that I am able to do this?" They said to him, "Yes, Lord."

Matthew 9:28

In this story, we are introduced to two blind men as they followed Jesus, crying, "Have mercy on us, Son of David" (v. 27). This title shows that they recognized Jesus as the Messiah and that they had faith the Messiah could work miracles. When Jesus questioned them further by asking, "Do you believe that I am able to do this?" Without hesitation, they confidently replied, "Yes, Lord" (v. 28).

Healing the blind was one of the characteristic activities of Jesus and was interpreted as a messianic sign. In the Near East, eye diseases were as repulsive as leprosy, but in spite of this, Jesus' method of healing them was to touch their eyes. As Jesus did this, he said, "According to your faith let it be done to you" (v. 29). And their eyes were opened.

Confidence is a significant characteristic of faith. These two blind men had confidence in Jesus' power. And just as Jesus healed their eyes, he can also heal us wherever we need healing.

Lord, give us confident faith. Amen.

Xavia Arndt Sheffield

JANUARY 15

EPHESIANS 3:14–19

Hallowed Be Thy Name

I pray that, according to the riches of his glory, he may grant that you may be strengthened in your inner being with power through his Spirit.

Ephesians 3:16

I am a Presbyterian, and when Presbyterians worship, we usually stand to sing and sit to pray and listen for God's word. We rarely kneel or "bow [our] knees before the Father," as the apostle Paul describes his posture toward the God of the universe (v. 14).

A few years ago, while forest fires raged in a nearby area, Christians in my city were invited to join with the Muslim community in prayer for rain. We gathered outside in a park, took off our shoes, and stood, kneeled, and bowed our heads on the dry grass of God's earth. I didn't understand the words that the imam prayed, but as I joined in the humbling postures of prayer, I comprehended in a new way the breadth and length and height and depth of the God of all people. I was in awe of the power of God's love to bring us together in prayer and concern for those who were in trouble.

Hallowed be your name, O God. May we be strengthened in our inner beings as we are rooted and grounded in your love. Amen.

Amanda Currie

JANUARY 16

PSALM 14:4–7

Thy Kingdom Come, Thy Will Be Done

Have they no knowledge, all the evildoers
who eat up my people as they eat bread?

Psalm 14:4

In today's psalm, the writer is despairing because of the injustice and suffering that he sees in his community. Oppressors are taking advantage of the poor, and "the evildoers . . . eat up my people as they eat bread."

We may relate to the psalmist's cry of despair when we observe the poor treatment of indigenous peoples throughout the world, the horror of human trafficking, or the persecution of so many people based on race, religion, gender, or sexual orientation. How long, O Lord?

The psalmist believes, however, that "God is with the company of the righteous" and that although many "would confound the plans of the poor, . . . the LORD is their refuge" (vv. 5–6). He looks toward a future in which the people will be delivered and they will rejoice!

We cannot give up in despair but must continue to pray and cooperate with God in building a world of peace, justice, and love for all people.

God of hope, thy kingdom come. Thy will be done on earth as in heaven. Amen.

Amanda Currie

JANUARY 17

JOHN 6:1–14

Give Us This Day Our Daily Bread

Then Jesus took the loaves, and when he had given thanks, he distributed them to those who were seated; so also the fish, as much as they wanted.

John 6:11

In an effort to improve my health, I've been counting calories. I have learned that I have access to more than enough bread and other foods. The challenge for me is not in getting enough but in avoiding eating too much! Of course, not everyone lives with such abundance, but most of those reading this devotional will probably admit that they have plenty.

And yet we often act as if resources are scarce. We worry about the future and hoard what we have "just in case." When we see people in need, we are hesitant to help, lest our resources be depleted.

The Gospel gives us the example of the boy with five loaves and two fish. He has some food (perhaps a little more than he needs), and he decides to share. As Jesus prays and passes it around, something happens, and it turns out to be more than enough.

Perhaps Jesus can do the same with our offerings. Certainly we have a little more than we need. So why not try?

Generous God, thank you for our daily bread. Help us to share with those who are hungry. Amen.

Amanda Currie

JANUARY 18

PSALM 14:1–3

Forgive Us Our Sins as We Forgive

They have all gone astray, they are all alike perverse.

Psalm 14:3

As people of faith, sometimes we observe our secular society and declare that our agnostic or atheistic neighbors are fools or corrupt sinners. Everyone around us seems to be living for their own wealth and pleasure. They do not care about God's law of love and mercy.

The psalmist reminds us today that even as we judge our neighbors, God judges us all. "The LORD looks down from heaven on humankind to see if there are any who are wise, who seek after God" but finds that we "have all gone astray, [we] are all alike perverse; there is no one who does good, no, not one" (vv. 2–3).

The good news is that God's grace and mercy is for every one of us; that in Jesus Christ, we are forgiven; and that by the Holy Spirit, we are empowered to love and begin to do some good. Remembering the psalm, can we choose to show the same mercy, love, and patience to others that God shows to us?

Forgiving God, we are so grateful for your mercy. Give us the grace to love and forgive others in your way. Amen.

Amanda Currie

JANUARY 19

2 Samuel 11:1–5

Lead Us Not into Temptation

So David sent messengers to get her, and she came to him, and he lay with her.

2 Samuel 11:4

When I think about temptation, I think of that inner struggle when we know that an action is wrong but we are tempted by our desire for comfort, pleasure, or power to do it anyway. What strikes me about King David's temptation to sleep with Bathsheba is that he doesn't seem to struggle against his sexual appetite. As soon as he notices the beautiful woman, he decides that he should have her. He doesn't think about her desires or marital status at all.

Most of us recognize adultery as wrong. But what are the temptations that we succumb to regularly because we do not consider the consequences of our actions? Does our goal of finding the best deal on products we buy contribute to the suffering of underpaid workers in the local store or a faraway country? Does our desire for the comfort and convenience of a gas-guzzling vehicle impact the future of our planet and generations to come?

God of justice and love, help us to examine our goals and our actions so that we are not led into temptation but into your ways of goodness and grace. Amen.

Amanda Currie

JANUARY 20

2 SAMUEL 11:6–15

Deliver Us from Evil

"Set Uriah in the forefront of the hardest fighting, and then draw back from him, so that he may be struck down and die."

2 Samuel 11:15

King David got another man's wife pregnant, so naturally, he tried to cover it up. If Uriah thought the child was his own, David would be off the hook. But no matter what he tried, he couldn't get Uriah to come home from battle to sleep with his wife. He decided his only option was to send Uriah out into the worst of the fighting so that he would be killed.

Can you think of anything else David could have done? Would admitting his wrongdoing be a possibility? It's easy for us to say. We can't even imagine doing something as evil as what David did to Bathsheba and Uriah.

But we also make mistakes and do wrong things. We hurt one another by our actions or inactions. It can be just as difficult for us to admit what we have done and deal with the consequences. Trying to cover it up will only dig us deeper into the pit of our misdeeds. We need the courage to choose another way.

God of grace, deliver us from evil. Give us the courage to humble ourselves, admit our sin, and begin the process of healing and reconciliation. Amen.

Amanda Currie

JANUARY 21

EPHESIANS 3:20–21

Thine Is the Kingdom, the Power, and the Glory

To him be glory in the church and in Christ Jesus to all generations, forever and ever.

Ephesians 3:21

I am a pretty competent person and not bad at my job of being a minister. Like others who share their gifts in the church's ministry, I receive a fair amount of thanks and praise for what I do. Although the encouragement is wonderful, I have to be careful not to start thinking that I am actually worthy of such praise! Without the Spirit's gifting and God's help, neither I, nor you, would be able to accomplish anything in our ministries. That means that the glory must go to God.

If you are doing what you do (preaching or hospitality or evangelism or teaching or prayer) through your own strength and competence, then you can do more! Ask for God's help. Look for God's direction. Let the Spirit of God fill you, and remember what the apostle Paul tells us—that God, by the Spirit's power, "is able to accomplish abundantly far more than all we can ask or imagine" (v. 20).

Awesome God, to you be glory in the church and in Christ Jesus to all generations. Yours is the kingdom, the power, and the glory. Amen.

Amanda Currie

JANUARY 22

LUKE 3:1–2

God's in the Details

In the fifteenth year of the reign of Emperor Tiberius, when Pontius Pilate was governor of Judea . . . the word of God came to John son of Zechariah in the wilderness.

Luke 3:1–2

As I work among people in our care community who are losing their ability to see, hear, remember, walk, use their hands, I imagine it could seem like a small jump for these friends to then think that God has forgotten them. I can't tell you how often I've been asked by those I serve in long-term care: "Why am I still here?" Their cries echo the Good Friday cry of Christ, "My God, my God, why have you forsaken me?" (Ps. 22:1).

Today's often-skipped-over verses in Luke set the advent of Christ in an exact context of history. As Luke names names, he reminds us that God does not come to us in general but in the real details of our lives. The good news is that God cares and seeks to break into our real time and even our very own experiences of suffering.

Thank you for caring for us by name, God of grace. Prepare us to find you in the cries of our lives. Amen.

Andrew Yee

JANUARY 23

LUKE 3:3–4

Transformed by Forgiveness

As it is written in the book of the words of the prophet Isaiah,
"The voice of one crying out in the wilderness:
'Prepare the way of the Lord,
make his paths straight.'"

Luke 3:4

When I was twenty-one years old, I attended a company party and was served cognac. Not liking the taste, I drank it mainly to get rid of it. But my boss kept pouring more into my glass. The alcohol hit me as I walked to my grandmother's apartment to stay the night, and I felt worse as the night wore on. Finally, I threw up all over my grandmother's couch. Knowing that I was embarrassed and sick and that I had learned an important lesson, my grandmother helped me clean up and gave me some Sprite to help calm my stomach. She never mentioned the incident to anyone.

The forgiveness my grandmother showed me that night will forever stay with me. I know that the patience and restraint I find to keep from rubbing things in people's noses comes from my grandmother and that experience. I'm so grateful for her forgiveness and love.

Forgiving God, prepare our hearts so that, being honest about our brokenness, we might be fertile enough to find joy in your forgiveness! Amen.

Andrew Yee

JANUARY 24

LUKE 3:5–6

The Joy of Finding Equality

"Every valley shall be filled,
and every mountain and hill shall be made low,
and the crooked shall be made straight,
and the rough ways made smooth;
and all flesh shall see the salvation of God."

Luke 3:5–6

What a bold statement! So how *really* will "all flesh" see God's salvation? When I look at our world, I see a lot of people who don't feel the least bit saved. Someone dies of hunger every few seconds—do they feel saved? How about those who can never seem to escape financial debt—do they feel saved? What about people of color, Muslims, and LGBTQIA people whom some insist on scapegoating for the ills of the world—do they feel saved?

Might our focus verses today suggest that God's salvation somehow includes us seeing each other and the world with some kind of equality? The cross showed how blind we can be in this world when only some feel more blessed, more powerful, or more chosen. Maybe if we can learn to see everyone as a valuable child of God, we can take a genuine step closer to all flesh seeing God's salvation.

God of all, may each small action we do in the way of Christ prepare us to see how you intend to save us. Amen.

Andrew Yee

JANUARY 25

MALACHI 3:1–4

Now Is the Time to Prepare

He will sit as a refiner and purifier of silver, and he will purify the descendants of Levi and refine them like gold and silver, until they present offerings to the LORD in righteousness.

Malachi 3:3

When my grandmother passed away recently, I felt so grateful for all she had taught me in spite of our language barrier. (She knew very little English, and I knew very little Chinese.) My grandmother possessed an incredibly strong faith. She saw opportunities to live in faith in the midst of brokenness, found ways to feed people during times of famine, prayed with her frightened daughter during invasions and wars, and raised three insightful children alone after my grandfather's premature death.

As I reflect in gratitude on how she influenced me to be who I am today, I also realize the importance of our earthly time. We are not meant to just wait for a heavenly afterlife. Every gifted moment and circumstance is an opportunity to be refined and purified to live in God's righteousness. Unless we practice generosity now, can we ever know the generosity of heaven? Unless we practice forgiveness now, can we ever hope to know the radical forgiveness of God?

Great Purifier, refine and purify us now so that we might realize even greater beauty. Amen.

Andrew Yee

JANUARY 26

PHILIPPIANS 1:3–11

Preparing to Live in Grace

For all of you share in God's grace with me.

Philippians 1:7b

Do you ever have trouble receiving gifts freely, instead feeling urges to give a gift in return? This propensity highlights a culture not based on free receiving but on payment and debt. It's not easy to receive freely. American culture, in particular, encourages independence and self-reliance—considering us failures if we are anything less than that. No wonder it is so difficult for people coming into our nursing homes to start receiving help that they might need, when all their lives they've been the cooks, the drivers, the caregivers, and the difference makers.

Christ invites us to a different life, as Paul shares here, to a life not of payment and debt but of God's grace. Can we imagine a life where we might encourage and allow our caregivers to live out their call and where we receive their offerings to us as grace? Verse 6 reminds us that God created us to practice a life of grace, both freely giving and receiving, until our time is finished and complete.

Gracious God, forgive our tendency to focus on debts so that we might live lives of grace. Amen.

Andrew Yee

JANUARY 27

John 19:26–27

Preparing Our Hearts for Something Bigger

When Jesus saw his mother and the disciple whom he loved standing beside her, he said to his mother, "Woman, here is your son."

John 19:26

Chuck lost his wife of sixty-five years a few months ago. As you can imagine, he experienced tremendous grief, pain, and alienation. The grief seemed to consume his life. Later he also felt guilt at even considering moving on to some sort of happier existence.

When Jesus was dying on the cross and said one of his last words to his mother and his beloved disciple, what if he didn't really mean to emphasize a break in their relationship as much as to commend his mother to something larger? Yes, she was his mother, but he didn't own her—she belonged to their Creator. Yes, he cared for her, but he was giving that responsibility to someone who could do it better. Yes, he loved his mother—and maybe this commending was the best way to love her within his new circumstances.

God of life, even in the midst of times of grief, prepare our hearts to imagine Advent hope! Amen.

Andrew Yee

JANUARY 28

PSALM 139:1–18

Preparing to See a Person

O LORD, you have searched me and known me.
You know when I sit down and when I rise up;
you discern my thoughts from far away.
You search out my path and my lying down,
and are acquainted with all my ways.

Psalm 139:1–3

As my own dad's Alzheimer's progresses, I realize that each of us can be consumed with loss. Alzheimer's talk always seems to focus on loss of brain function, and we frequently say, "He is only a shell of who he used to be."

Our challenge today might be to stop thinking about loss for a moment as we ask: Are we more than our ability to think? Does our memory loss lessen God's love for us and God's desire to know us intimately?

Jesus consistently displayed an amazing ability to see the person behind whatever losses he or she had experienced. I want to live like Jesus lived—to not let the losses get in the way of me having a relationship with my dad and the chance to know him in a different way. I may not be able to cure my dad's disease, but I *can* value him truly.

Omniscient God, in our fascination to know disease, prepare our hearts to really know and see the person going through the disease. Amen.

Andrew Yee

JANUARY 29

Micah 6:1–8

The Gift of Humility

He has told you, O mortal, what is good;
and what does the Lord require of you
but to do justice, and to love kindness,
and to walk humbly with your God?

Micah 6:8

Giving a gift can be a way of demonstrating appreciation to those we love. A gift can also be an expression of guilty regret for wrongdoing. For example, we may bring flowers as an act of reconciliation with someone we have wronged.

In today's text, Micah speaks to a people who believe the greatest gift they have to offer is their possessions. Burnt offerings? Young calves? Thousands of rams? (vv. 6–7). It seems there is nothing they aren't willing to sacrifice in payment for their wrongdoing.

However, what God asks in exchange for their transgressions is a willingness to live life in a new way. This way of life calls them away from patterns of injustice and pride to a life of justice and humility. Nothing—literally, no *thing*—can take the place of these gifts in the eyes of our God.

O God, may I offer you the gifts of doing justice, loving kindness, and walking humbly. Amen.

Kathy Wolf Reed

JANUARY 30

Matthew 5:1–12

Humbled in Our Mourning

"Blessed are those who mourn, for they will be comforted."

Matthew 5:4

The experience of grief has the power to humble even the greatest among us. When we mourn the loss of a life, job, or marriage, we experience a loss of control in our lives. Grief can feel like standing in the ocean. At times, our feet are firmly planted in the sand and we feel grounded. Then a wave comes crashing in and drags the sands out from under us.

Jesus knew what it meant to mourn. He wept over the death of his friend Lazarus. He cried out to God from the cross. It is this same Jesus who preaches and promises, in Matthew's Gospel, that those who mourn will receive comfort from a God who, in all humility, stands with us in our pain.

Dear Jesus, be with us as we face our grief. Amen.

Kathy Wolf Reed

JANUARY 31

1 Corinthians 1:18–31

Strength in Humility

But God chose what is foolish in the world to shame the wise; God chose what is weak in the world to shame the strong.

1 Corinthians 1:27

So much of what Jesus showed us about God seems counterintuitive. The faithful of Jesus' day waited for the King of Kings to enter into their midst and certainly didn't expect this king to make his entrance in a lowly stable. As Jesus' ministry unfolded, many assumed he would assert his power with force. Instead, they encountered a servant Lord who preached about peace.

The gospel of Jesus Christ continues to challenge each of us to consider new definitions of what it means to be powerful, strong, and wise. Worshiping a God who calls us to identify our weaknesses, rely on grace, and pray for those who persecute us may seem like foolishness. But for those who have heard the good news of Christ's love for us, we discover daily the strength that comes from a life of humble servanthood.

May I find true strength by humbling myself before you and others. Amen.

Kathy Wolf Reed

FEBRUARY 1

MATTHEW 5:1–12

Humbled by Mercy

"Blessed are the merciful, for they will receive mercy."

Matthew 5:7

It is one thing to be the giver of mercy; it is quite another thing to be the recipient of mercy.

When we offer mercy to others, we acknowledge their needs. Sometimes, we offer physical kindnesses, such as clean water, food, or clothing. Other times, we extend emotional or spiritual mercies via empathy, forgiveness, and grace. In many ways, we find ourselves strengthened and renewed when we fulfill God's call to be merciful to our neighbors.

However, it takes humility to become the one on the receiving end of mercy. When we open ourselves to receive forgiveness and compassion from others, we admit our need for grace. We put away any sense of self-reliance and acknowledge the very real centrality of God in our lives.

May I offer mercy to others as freely as it is offered to me in the grace of Jesus Christ. Amen.

Kathy Wolf Reed

FEBRUARY 2

Psalm 15

How Might I Be Humble?

O Lord, who may abide in your tent?
Who may dwell on your holy hill?
Those who walk blamelessly, and do what is right,
and speak the truth from their heart.

Psalm 15:1–2

Most people of faith say they want to become closer to God. Some seek this relationship through prayer, Bible study, and worship, hoping these practices will draw them nearer to the presence of the Holy.

In today's text, the psalmist offers a glimpse of some practices that lead us to God. As it turns out, those who seek to "do what is right" have quite the task before them. The psalmist is specific: don't speak maliciously about others, don't be mean to your friends or neighbors, don't charge people interest when you lend them money, and don't take a bribe that will hurt an innocent person (v. 3).

If we are to take our relationship with God seriously, we must take all the intricacies of our relationships with others seriously. Those who truly wish to humble themselves before the Lord must be honest with themselves and others before they can hope to dwell on God's holy hill.

Let my words and actions be a reflection of the God I humbly serve. Amen.

Kathy Wolf Reed

FEBRUARY 3

1 Corinthians 1:18–31

Humble Fools

For the message about the cross is foolishness to those who are perishing, but to us who are being saved it is the power of God.

1 Corinthians 1:18

We live in a world that is constantly telling us power comes from having more possessions, more control, and more success. The more we accumulate, the more we become lost in the illusion that we are self-sufficient. Thank goodness for the cross, which serves as a reminder of the sacrificial nature of our faith and our God. The crucifixion of Jesus Christ was the ultimate act of humility

Paul writes "to us who are *being* saved" (v. 18, emphasis mine). Note that the verb is presented passively. We are not saving ourselves as we attempt to build careers, families, and bank accounts. No, in fact, we are *being* saved. The cross reminds us of the One from whom our salvation comes. Jesus died and rose again so that we might have hope for a life beyond the brokenness of the world. In moments when we find ourselves lost in the world's messages about what we should have or be, may the message of the cross humble us.

Loving God, may I remember Christ's ultimate act of humility. Amen.

Kathy Wolf Reed

FEBRUARY 4

MATTHEW 5:1–12

The Humility of the Saints

"Blessed are you when people revile you and persecute you and utter all kinds of evil against you falsely on my account. Rejoice and be glad, for your reward is great in heaven, for in the same way they persecuted the prophets who were before you."

Matthew 5:11–12

Today's text acknowledges what we likely already know to be true: the path of righteousness and humility is not an easy path. Jesus warns his followers that the message they bear will not be popular. Those in power will be threatened by Jesus. Those with great wealth will not take kindly to ones who claim treasure dwells in heaven. Those who take pride in their accomplishments will despise ones who value humility above all else.

To prepare for the difficult journey ahead, Jesus reminds disciples that they are not the first to struggle for the sake of the gospel. Long before the birth of Jesus, "they persecuted the prophets who were before you."Preaching the truth of sacrificial humility has never been a popular message to the ones who seek power in this world. However, the witness of those before us strengthens our resolve to live lives pleasing to God.

Gracious God, give us strength for the journey. Amen.

Kathy Wolf Reed

FEBRUARY 5

Isaiah 58:1–9

Repentance

Is not this the fast that I choose:
to loose the bonds of injustice,
to undo the thongs of the yoke,
to let the oppressed go free,
and to break every yoke?

Isaiah 58:6

In C. S. Lewis's novel *The Screwtape Letters* (Harper One, 2001), an elder demon counsels his young protégé demon to encourage people to be falsely proud of their humility. It was easiest to ensnare people in sin who thought that they could avoid this trap.

It seems that the men and women to whom Isaiah spoke in this passage have fallen into exactly that sin trap of making public displays of their piety. The people fasted in sackcloth and ashes, and they prided themselves on their humble repentance. But God had other ideas.

God would have none of their false pride. God would not hear a hypocritical prayer. Instead God would send a prophet messenger to deliver God's word that uncovers sin and saves those who turn to what is holy.

O God, may we have ears to hear your call and eyes to see our motivations. Amen.

Andrew Taylor-Troutman

FEBRUARY 6

ISAIAH 58:1–9

Healing Light

Then your light shall break forth like the dawn,
and your healing shall spring up quickly.

Isaiah 58:8a

The poetry of Isaiah 58 uses various images to proclaim a beautiful assurance of faith. For instance, dawn is a powerful symbol of hope. Yet we must not sentimentalize this passage. The preceding verses in Isaiah speak of real and painful realities, such as oppression and poverty. Clearly there were profound reasons that God's light and healing were needed.

The core drama played out throughout the book of Isaiah is that God's word meets with humankind's refusal to sustain faithfulness. Who will overcome this lack of understanding? In many a passage of Isaiah, the question remains tragically unanswered. Yet God continues to be faithful, breaking through sin with signs of redemption.

Gracious Redeemer, may healing and hope for the world inspire our repentance. Amen.

Andrew Taylor-Troutman

FEBRUARY 7

PSALM 112:1–9

Safe

They rise in the darkness as a light for the upright; they are gracious, merciful, and righteous.

Psalm 112:4

The words "rise in the darkness" immediately call to mind the sound of my young daughter crying out from a nightmare. In the darkness of our home, I shuffle down the hall to the crib and take her in my arms. "You are *safe*," I say quietly.

As her father, I am keenly aware that the world is often unsafe. Life itself can be a nightmare. When I awake in the night, anxious for myself and for my children's future, I call to mind another verse from Psalm 112: "They are not afraid of evil tidings; their hearts are firm, secure in the LORD" (v. 7). I also lean on Jesus' message: "Do not be afraid" (Matt. 14:27).

O God, who neither slumbers nor sleeps, keep your children mindful of your love. Amen.

Andrew Taylor-Troutman

FEBRUARY 8

1 Corinthians 2:1–12

Words of Wisdom

But we speak God's wisdom, secret and hidden, which God decreed before the ages for our glory.

1 Corinthians 2:7

When a child is baptized in our church, we gift the family with a small wooden cross made from leftover sanctuary floorboards. As this young one grows and matures in faith, we pray that Christ will be that child's foundation.

Children are not only the treasured future of the church but also our teachers.

One Saturday, I explained to a four-year-old what would happen during her baptism the following day. I showed her the baptismal font and where she would stand. I explained what I would say and do. Then I asked if she understood.

"When I'm baptized," she replied, "God will be here." She spoke God's wisdom.

Our Savior, may we glimpse your mystery with faith like a child. Amen.

Andrew Taylor-Troutman

FEBRUARY 9

1 CORINTHIANS 2:1–12

Knowing

Now we have received not the spirit of the world, but the Spirit that is from God, so that we may understand the gifts bestowed on us by God.

1 Corinthians 2:12

"Immortal, Invisible, God Only Wise" is a stirring hymn of praise that basically describes how God is a mystery. The hymn confirms that there is truly much we cannot know. As Paul reminds us, God has prepared "what no eye has seen, nor ear heard, nor the human heart conceived" (v. 9).

Yet we try to solve holy mysteries throughout our lives. When my children were first born, they clenched my finger with their fists, as if they wanted to hold onto what they could, to grasp a new truth.

As we grow up, by the grace of God we receive what we cannot know.

And sometimes we grow older still. A wise friend says that she hopes to die with her hands open. Instead of holding on, she prays to be ready to receive the Spirit of God. Her words echo Paul's hopes: "I will know fully, even as I have been fully known" (13:12).

Immortal, invisible God, reveal your grace as the assurance of our faith. Amen.

Andrew Taylor-Troutman

FEBRUARY 10

MATTHEW 5:13–20

Particle and Wave

"You are the light of the world. A city built on a hill cannot be hid."

Matthew 5:14

Jesus says that we are the light of the world. This means that our actions or "good works" should be seen by others (v. 16). Yet we also believe that *Jesus* is the light of the world (John 8:12; 9:5). How can both of these statements be true? Just *who* is the light?

A physicist will tell you that light is both particle and wave, meaning that light is a paradox—two seeming contradictions that are nevertheless both true. Physicist Niels Bohr surmised that the opposite of a profound truth may be yet another profound truth.

Many spiritual truths are also paradoxical. Jesus is "the light [that] shines in the darkness" (1:5). When we look to Jesus as the model for walking in the light, we reflect his brightness in our words and actions.

Lord of light, may we reflect your glory to others. Amen.

Andrew Taylor-Troutman

FEBRUARY 11

MATTHEW 5:13–20

Righteousness

For I tell you, unless your righteousness exceeds that of the scribes and Pharisees, you will never enter the kingdom of heaven.

Matthew 5:20

Every day, I fulfill many different roles: pastor, author, father, spouse, brother, and friend. But none of these roles make me "righteous." Reading this passage, I am reminded that righteousness entails a right relationship with God.

My younger son is named Asa. On his third birthday, he came bounding into my bedroom early in the morning. I sleepily smiled at him and said, "Today, son, you are three!"

He grinned back, "Today, Daddy, I am Asa."

Asa reminded me that my righteousness is born of being a child of God.

Jesus was right when he said, "Truly I tell you, unless you change and become like children, you will never enter the kingdom of heaven" (18:3).

Thank you, God, that we are, first of all, your children. Amen.

Andrew Taylor-Troutman

FEBRUARY 12

Joel 2:1–2, 12–17

It's Urgent

Yet even now, says the Lord,
return to me with all your heart.

Joel 2:12

"Even now, return to me." It reads like a text message sent from one heartbroken lover to another. It's urgent, and it's meant for us. Joel is the messenger, but the message is God's. The time for us to return to God is now. No matter that Joel's writing may be more than 2,800 years old. The divine call, the cry of mercy, the promise of steadfast love is undiminished by centuries and stronger than death.

What are you doing until Easter? What are you doing that could possibly be more important than returning to God wholeheartedly? How will you make the journey back to the One who calls you to come back? Will you run, or crawl, or pray your way there? Will you forgive or give? Will you blow the finest song your trumpet can play or quit doing that unhealthy thing you keep meaning to give up for good anyway? The point is: God will have you back—yesterday. The return is yours to make. And the time to get moving is now.

On my way—so sorry I wandered off. Love, please take me back. Amen.

Rachel M. Srubas

FEBRUARY 13

2 CORINTHIANS 5:20B–6:10

Beloved as You Are

We are treated as impostors, and yet are true; as unknown, and yet are well known.

2 Corinthians 6:8–9

In God's eyes, you're the real deal, the whole and holy enchilada. Almost everybody else perceives you partially, as a parent or a child, a worker or a widow, a sibling, a consumer, a type, "one of those," a collage made of glimpses and impressions, some of them mistaken. Nobody sees through God's eyes but God, who sees you well and truly even when you can't clearly see yourself. Maybe you had to dance backward in heels just to get to the same place as others who are less capable, and that has left you doubting your authenticity, your right to do the work that's really yours to do. Or maybe you believed them when they told you who you should be, yet you wound up being your actual self, the one God sees and loves, but you have some trouble accepting this.

Child of God, grown-up of God, unrepeatable you, they may project their unfounded expectations on you, but you're not here to fulfill those. You're here to be true, to be known, and to be loved as you are.

Creator of all life, including my life, let me see myself as you see me: beloved. Amen.

Rachel M. Srubas

FEBRUARY 14

PSALM 51:1–17

Humility without Humiliation

You desire truth in the inward being;
therefore teach me wisdom in my secret heart.

Psalm 51:6

Psalm 51, the penitential psalm for Ash Wednesday, is a tough read for Christians who understand the damaging effects of shame, especially shame in the name of religion. The psalm's images—God having crushed the bones of one who was a sinner at conception, who is then cleansed to become "whiter than snow"—are hugely problematic for people who refute violent theologies and refuse to equate whiteness with rightness.

Psalm 51 itself may seem to need redemption. But in its midst, there comes a connection between God's desire for each person's honest self-awareness and the human need to be made wise deep within. Verse 6, our focus verse today, is a treasure to be salvaged from the toxic poetry of self-loathing. It can serve as a lens through which to seek and find God, who wants us to know ourselves as we truly are. Lent leads us inward toward honesty and humility without humiliation. These are sacred gifts and practices that then lead us outward, to share with others the joy of our salvation and theirs.

Sustain in me, O God, a spirit willing to be made wise. Amen.

Rachel M. Srubas

FEBRUARY 15

1 Peter 3:18–22

This Baptized Life

And baptism . . . now saves you . . . through the resurrection of Jesus Christ.

1 Peter 3:21

Who do you say you are? Are you the roles you play? The job you do? Who do people say you are? What's baptism got to do with your identity? Your baptism may have been a pretty ritual at church that you were too young to remember later. Along the way, you may have been formed in a faith community that equipped you sincerely to say, *I am a beloved child of God and everything else I am flows from that, the way baptismal water flows from a font and saving grace flows from the heart of God.*

Whoever you are, or have been told you are, or believed yourself to be, one thing's for sure: you are more than your occupations and obligations, more than what the sociologists say about your generation. You are created unrepeatably in God's own image. You are exquisitely fashioned yet undeniably fallible. You are redeemed by a risen Savior and sustained by a Holy Spirit who breathes life into you even now.

Risen Jesus, thank you for bringing your disciples to God and giving us this baptized life to live together. Amen.

Rachel M. Srubas

FEBRUARY 16

MARK 1:9–15

The Terrain of Transformation

And the Spirit immediately drove him out into the wilderness.

Mark 1:12

By *wilderness*, Mark means the Judean wilderness, the stretch of uninhabited desert between Jerusalem and Jericho on the western shore of the Dead Sea. But *wilderness* also refers to the terrain of personal transformation to which we're sometimes driven because God is at our backs, sending us into hard places where we run headlong into truths about ourselves. Some of these we'd prefer not to face, as we'd also rather skip the trials that test and ultimately teach us how near the reign of God has come.

When we're in that rocky crisis of self-recognition, that desert of stark revelation, we can do one of three things: run back unchanged to the safety of familiar patterns and places; give in to our most devilish compulsions and damaging coping mechanisms; or—and this is the way of Jesus—pray hard, strengthened by the sometimes stinging but steadfastly supportive Spirit of the living God.

Through the wearying climbs and at the low points, God of the desert, accompany us. Help us face ourselves and become more wholeheartedly your people. Amen.

Rachel M. Srubas

FEBRUARY 17

ROMANS 4:13–25

A Reckoning

It will be reckoned to us who believe.

Romans 4:24

A woman waits in an oncologist's office, wondering if her cancer has advanced. She'll ask the doctor, though deep down, she knows what her body is saying.

She's a knowing woman. She knows herself and everyone to be beloved of God. She knows she loves and is loved by her sisters, her daughters and son, her daughters-in-law, her grandchildren, nieces, friends, and me, the person writing this devotion. I'm drawing strength from her faith in order to encourage yours.

I may not know you, but I know you love and are beloved. I know there will one day come a reckoning. The God who gives life to the dead will see us and all the saints through to the other side of our questions, our cancers and cures, the answers we hope for, the deaths we fear. All our everyday prayers and small acts of courage, even our failings, will add up to our faith in God. Our faith, by grace alone and no achievement of our own, will be reckoned to us as righteousness.

In spite of pain and bad news, I believe in you and your promises, O God. Amen.

Rachel M. Srubas

FEBRUARY 18

MARK 9:2–9

Listen to Jesus

And there appeared to them Elijah with Moses, who were talking with Jesus.

Mark 9:4

The transfiguration story proclaims who Jesus is and what his disciples are to do: "This is my Son, the Beloved," says the divine voice from the overshadowing cloud. "*Listen* to him!"(v. 7, emphasis added). Earlier in the story, Elijah and Moses, monumental icons of Hebrew prophecy and law, appear, *talking* with Jesus.

Listening and talking to Jesus are essential practices of Christian faith and prayer. Most of us do more talking than listening when we pray, though none of us, it's fair to say, is possessed of Moses' or Elijah's way with words. Often, like Peter up on that high mountain with James, John, and Jesus, we don't know what to say. God knows we need to listen to Jesus. The commandment that we do so couldn't come more forcefully. Let's make this an attentive Lent. Let's go to the Scriptures and our prayers. Let's practice faithful Christian service, open to the new wisdom we'll gain and the transformation we'll undergo if we listen to the Beloved One calling us to make our way back to God.

Most High God, open my ears to hear and respond to the voice of Jesus. Amen.

Rachel M. Srubas

FEBRUARY 19

Jeremiah 32:1–3a, 6–15

God's Providence Is Sure!

For thus says the Lord of hosts, the God of Israel: Houses and fields and vineyards shall again be bought in this land.

Jeremiah 32:15

Jeremiah gets an unusual message from the Lord: Invest in property from which you are about to be exiled. Do all that is legally required to take ownership of the family land from which you will be sent. Jeremiah cannot know if he will ever occupy the place for which he will hold the deed, but in an act of radical trust, he buys it.

No doubt Jeremiah's contemporaries thought him foolish. And yet Jeremiah does not hesitate to do as God asks. Buying land about to be plundered takes an unwavering faith in the long arc of God's providence, a confidence that God will bring about a good ending in spite of the present upheaval.

Where might God be calling us to invest in a promised divine future? Are there desolate places where God intends to bring about new life, places where God wants us to put a stake in the ground so that we can participate in a beautiful rebuilding?

God of new life, help us to trust your salvation story. Show us where and how you want us to invest in a flourishing future for your people. Amen.

Jill Duffield

FEBRUARY 20

Psalm 91:1–6, 14–16

God Protects Us

Those who love me, I will deliver;
I will protect those who know my name.

Psalm 91:14

The imagery in the psalm provides a vivid reminder of God's close and caring presence. We are sheltered beneath the wings of the Almighty. So precious are we to the Lord that the holy stands watch over and around us, keeping us from destruction and despair. Can you remember a time when you called out to God in need and heard God's compassionate response, perhaps made known to you through others' kindness or an unexpected turn of events?

God's promised protection invites us to deep and abiding confidence that we are never alone or abandoned. Such assurance enables us to experience the peace that surpasses understanding, no matter our struggles and challenges. While we cannot escape our human finitude and the pain it entails, we can cling in love to the One who hovers over us, granting us rest, relief, and respite. When we call on God, God hears and answers us, honoring our deepest longing with attentive listening and never-failing faithfulness.

Lord of all, thank you for protecting us under the shadow of your wings. Help us to feel your close presence and be at peace. Amen.

Jill Duffield

FEBRUARY 21

PSALM 146

Don't Trust in Earthly Powers

Happy are those whose help is the God of Jacob,
whose hope is in the LORD their God,
who made heaven and earth,
the sea, and all that is in them;
who keeps faith forever.

Psalm 146:5–6

The temptation to rely on transitory powers for security feels relentless. Advertisements bombard us from every direction, telling us that if we have the right car, make smart investments, or take the miracle supplement, we can rest secure with no worries. The psalmist reminds the faithful that no earthly power can provide for our needs. All earthly kingdoms come to an end. Only those who trust in God can be assured of their well-being. Only God's reign lasts forever.

Our challenge comes in silencing the voices that tell us otherwise. As we go about our day today, how might our choices reflect our belief that God is truly in charge, always doing a new, good thing on which we can depend? Consider when you have experienced God's unmistakable care, remember, and give thanks, allowing those memories to shape your choices and move you forward in faithful confidence.

God, you watch over us. We praise you for all the ways you provide for us daily. Amen.

Jill Duffield

FEBRUARY 22

1 Timothy 6:6–19

The Gain of Godliness and Contentment

Of course, there is great gain in godliness combined with contentment.

1 Timothy 6:6

Contentment can be elusive in a culture that tells us we always need more. We often compare ourselves to others and, in that assessment, feel as if we are less than or lacking. But this passage reminds us to focus not on what we think is missing in our lives but rather on all that God has so generously provided. "If we have food and clothing, we will be content with these," the writer of 1 Timothy 6:8 admonishes believers.

Know what is enough and be content. Such a stance frees our energy from striving for things that do not truly satisfy and frees us to pursue godliness, righteousness, faith, love, endurance, and gentleness. Imagine what Christians might do if they turned aside consumerism and leaned into growing in faith, lavishly sharing love rather than building bigger barns. If we trust God to provide and are content, we could pursue godliness and, in turn, increase in contentment.

Lord of all, you tell us where to focus and what truly matters. Help us to grow in faith, increase in contentment, and be generous in love. Amen.

Jill Duffield

FEBRUARY 23

Luke 6:19–31

Receiving and Believing God's Word

"He said to him, 'If they do not listen to Moses and the prophets, neither will they be convinced even if someone rises from the dead.'"

Luke 16:31

Occasionally I wonder if God gets frustrated with us. If I pay attention to my own prayers, I sometimes get frustrated with myself! I whine. I ask for that which I know is not faithful. I neglect to listen. When I catch myself in this selfish loop and stop for a moment, often a Bible verse comes into my consciousness.

I hear the prophet Micah, perhaps, that God "has told you, O mortal, what is good; do justice, and to love kindness, and to walk humbly with your God" (Mic. 6:8). Or maybe, "Be still, and know that I am God!" (Ps. 46:10). Like the rich man in this story, I can act as if I am unaware of what God wills, ignorant of what God commands. However, the reality, when I have ears to hear, is that, repeatedly and consistently, God provides not only the law and the prophets but also the Spirit and the person of Jesus to form my living and guide my choices.

Loving God, you give us all we need to follow your way and do your will. Today, give us ears to hear and faith to act on your loving commandments. Amen.

Jill Duffield

FEBRUARY 24

Habakkuk 1:1–4; 2:1–4

The Lord Answers Us

Then the Lord answered me and said:
Write the vision;
make it plain on the tablets,
so that a runner may read it.

Habakkuk 2:2

These verses are a call and a response. The writer of Habakkuk cries out to God, wondering when, and if, God will answer. There is a sense of expectation that gets heightened when Habakkuk takes a stand, literally, looking actively for the word of the Lord. The prophet is not disappointed when God resoundingly gives Habakkuk a vision, one writ so clearly and so large that even someone running past cannot fail to see it.

When we feel as if we are crying to God and not hearing a response, when we wonder why the unethical and unfaithful seem to prosper, when we long to have unequivocal divine direction, what do we do? Perhaps we might take a cue from Habakkuk and take a stand, scan the horizon, get quiet, and listen intently, expecting that when we ask, we will receive, and when we seek, we will find. Then get ready to write, legibly, largely, for all the world to see.

Almighty God, you do not turn away from us when we call out to you. Give us ears to hear your word and courage to heed it. Amen.

Jill Duffield

FEBRUARY 25

PSALM 37:1–9

Delight in the Lord

Take delight in the LORD,
and he will give you the desires of your heart.

Psalm 37:4

The psalmist offers tangible advice for those struggling to know how to keep the faith in hard times. Each verse instructs us: first about what not to do and then about what to do. Do not fret. Trust the Lord. Take delight in the Lord. Commit your way to the Lord. Be still. Finally, a reminder we all likely need: refrain from anger and forsake wrath.

We know, of course, the value of these admonishments. We know, too, that practicing them is much more difficult than acknowledging their worth. When we are in the throes of struggle, things like trust and delight are hard to will ourselves to believe and practice. Could we, though, take small steps in the direction of trust, delight, commitment, and stillness? Spiritual practices such as reading a daily devotion, taking a prayer walk, or attending worship give us space and opportunity to take a breath, attend to God's presence, and perhaps even experience delight in the middle of hard times.

Loving God, remind us to take the time to recognize your presence and delight in your grace that comes in surprising ways. Amen.

Jill Duffield

FEBRUARY 26

GENESIS 24:42–48

Choosing to Give More

"I said to her, 'Please let me drink.' She quickly let down her jar from her shoulder, and said, 'Drink, and I will also water your camels.'"

Genesis 24:45–46

In a beautiful commercial from Thailand, a young boy is caught stealing medicine for his mother until a stranger intervenes, buys the medicine, and throws in a bag of veggie soup. Thirty years later, the stranger lies unconscious in a hospital bed, his family unable to pay the bills until a doctor intervenes and pays them. It turns out that the doctor was the boy the stranger had helped.

Truth is, we never know what future we are creating when we choose to give.

Abraham's servant requested only water for himself, and yet Rebekah also chose to water his camels and give him a place to stay. For Rebekah to water ten camels, she had to go up and down the well's steps many times, with many jars of water. It is this act of kindness that reveals her to be the agent of God's promised future.

Today, someone is going to ask something of you: your time, your money, your advocacy, maybe just that you *see* them. Choose to give more.

God, fill us with your Spirit that we might give more than has been asked. Amen.

Patrick D. Heery

FEBRUARY 27

GENESIS 24:58–67

Choosing Consent

And they called Rebekah, and said to her, "Will you go with this man?" She said, "I will."

Genesis 24:58

According to Amnesty International, one out of every three women on the planet has been beaten, raped, or otherwise abused. Turn on the television, and you'll be confronted with images of women in subordinate and objectifying poses. Listen to what passes for political discourse, and you'll hear openly violent and misogynistic language excused as "locker room talk." Watch legislation, and you'll note threats to women's health care, divorce rights, freedom of expression, reproductive options, and ability to work for equal pay in a chosen career.

Couched in this biblical story of an arranged marriage, however, is the seed of an alternative vision: Rebekah speaks for herself. She chooses whom (and if) she marries. While her actual power is likely limited by economic and patriarchal forces, this text offers an unexpected glimpse of the power of consent. It produces a love so great that it can even soften the grief of a mother's passing.

Today, let us labor for choice—ours and others'.

O Liberator, set us free to choose our future—never at the expense of another's. Amen.

Patrick D. Heery

FEBRUARY 28

PSALM 45:10–17

Choosing a New Family

Hear, O daughter, consider and incline your ear;
forget your people and your father's house.

Psalm 45:10

This text is troubling. Why isn't the *man* asked to abandon his family and homeland? Why does this woman's purpose appear to be only to produce sons?

Such questions cannot be ignored, but read in the context of Rebekah's story, we may have in this royal wedding song a witness to the power of chosen families. In fact, this invitation is not unlike the call given to Abram (not yet Abraham): "Go from your country and your kindred and your father's house to the land that I will show you" (Gen. 12:1).

God sometimes uproots us so that God can plant us elsewhere.

Birth families can be wonderful—or they can be awful (or, for some of us, simply unknown or far away). Maybe, right now, you're in a place broken by abuse, or divided by divergent values, or gutted by lack of meaning. The power of the chosen family is that we get to decide who's going to be in our life.

God, pull up these dry roots, strangled by creeping vines, and plant us where we can grow. Amen.

Patrick D. Heery

FEBRUARY 29

SONG OF SONGS 2:8–13

Choosing Passion

My beloved speaks and says to me:
"Arise, my love, my fair one,
and come away;
for now the winter is past,
the rain is over and gone."

Song of Solomon 2:10–11

The Song of Songs, also known as the Song of Solomon, is a hymn of love, sensual and exuberant—shocking perhaps to some, liberating for others. It is as much a woman's testimony to love as it is a man's. It drips with imagery of Eden. Above all, it is an apologia for passion.

The woman declares, "Love is strong as death, passion fierce as the grave. Its flashes are flashes of fire, a raging flame" (8:6). This word *passion* is the same one used elsewhere to describe God's passion for God's children and their reciprocal devotion to God.

With these lovers, we are invited now to come away from the winter of our orderly philosophies and revel in the springtime of God's emergence.

Faith must be more than an idea. It requires the flames of passion. Today, let us fall in love. With God. With life. With another human. With all of it.

O God, sing to us again of your fierce love. Let it shake us, remake us. Amen.

Patrick D. Heery

MARCH 1

ZECHARIAH 9:9–12

Choosing Hope

I will set your prisoners free from the waterless pit.
Return to your stronghold, O prisoners of hope.

Zechariah 9:11–12

Psychiatrist Jonathan Shay recalls in his book *Achilles in Vietnam* (Simon and Schuster, 1995) a veteran still haunted by fear of ambush: "I haven't really slept for twenty years. I lie down, but I don't sleep. I'm always watching the door, the window, then back to the door. I get up at least five times to walk my perimeter, sometimes it's ten or fifteen times" (xiv).

In today's passage, the prophet Zechariah is speaking to another kind of post-traumatic stress disorder—to people who have finally returned home from exile and yet still feel like prisoners. Prisoners of the past, of grief, of disappointed dreams, of fear. And he invites them to become instead "prisoners of hope."

It is a choice we cannot make on our own, but with help, we can confront and break the prisons of our past—not by battling our inner turmoil, but by loving and caring for it, as if a child in pain. That's precisely what Jesus did for us.

God, make us prisoners of hope; make us free within even while we are caged without. Amen.

Patrick D. Heery

MARCH 2

PSALM 145:8–14

Choosing to Bless God

All your works shall give thanks to you, O LORD,
and all your faithful shall bless you.

Psalm 145:10

I recently began keeping a gratitude journal. Each night, I write down all the things from that day for which I am grateful. It could be a kind word, or a minute extra to linger in bed, or an opportunity to care for someone hurting, or a warm walk with my wife. I say thanks to God.

It's not that the bad stuff goes away; it's that, in naming the good stuff, I find greater strength to combat the disappointments and frustrations of life. In blessing God, I oddly find myself blessed in turn.

The psalm you have just read is a special one, appearing in the Jewish prayer book more frequently than any other psalm. The Talmud instructs the faithful to repeat this prayer three times each day in order to "be sure that he is a child of the world to come" (*Berakot*, 4b).

Today, I invite you to bless, praise, and thank God. Though life can be full of grief, there is beauty and goodness still. Become their child.

O Gracious God, I thank you. I thank you. Amen.

Patrick D. Heery

MARCH 3

ROMANS 7:15–25

Choosing Christ

I do not do what I want, but I do the very thing I hate.

Romans 7:15

In 2010, Jason Sadler came up with a great idea. He was going to send one million free T-shirts to Africa. Jason had never been to Africa. He had never spoken with anyone from Africa. But he had love in his heart and wanted to give to those in need. Instead, he ended up threatening to put local merchants out of business, upend entire economies, and provide a bunch of shirts no one needed or wanted.

Like Jason, we want to do good, but as Paul makes clear, evil still prevails. We simply do not have the power to overcome sin on our own.

Thankfully, says Paul, we are not on our own. The solution isn't trying harder; it's accepting the help of Christ. It's turning to the body of Christ, listening and partnering. It's embracing Christ's model of self-emptying. And even after we've done all that, it's trusting that God will use our flawed actions for good.

God, help us uproot our "good" ideas and listen instead—to you and to your children, with whom we seek to partner. Amen.

Patrick D. Heery

MARCH 4

MATTHEW 11:25–30

Chosen

"Come to me, all you that are weary and are carrying heavy burdens, and I will give you rest."

Matthew 11:28

As a young monk, Martin Luther tried everything to come close to God. He stayed up all night, praying and reading Scripture, forsaking sleep. He whipped himself. He fasted. He exposed himself to the freezing cold. And none of it worked.

Years later, after meditating on Scripture, Luther had a flash of insight: salvation wasn't something to be earned; it was a *gift* of grace, through faith. Luther writes that he felt as if he were born again.

We don't choose grace. Grace chooses us.

Of all the choices we can make in the days ahead, the most important is the choice to let go of our striving, to release from our backs all the burdens we think we must carry and humble ourselves, as if infants, to be fed by God.

What we receive will change us. It will lead to a different kind of life, a different kind of yoke. Instead of striving, and competing, and building ourselves up, we shall have the peace and solidarity of love.

God of grace, help us let go. Amen.

Patrick D. Heery

MARCH 5

EXODUS 17:1–7

Be Renewed

"I will be standing there in front of you on the rock at Horeb. Strike the rock, and water will come out of it, so that the people may drink." Moses did so, in the sight of the elders of Israel.

Exodus 17:6

Sin creates a very desperate resistance in us that makes us pull away from all that God desires for us. Our resistance leaves us suffering from a deep need for the things only God can give us.

Yet even in the midst of our resistance, God calls out to us. God knows our deepest longings for life, vitality, hope, and fulfillment. Although we do not always understand what we undergo, God has mapped a purposeful plan for us. How do we know this? We find out from stories, such as today's Scripture from Exodus.

In this story from Exodus, God overcomes the sinful resistance of the people when they doubt God's care for them. Instead of meeting their doubt with punishment, God once again meets the needs of the people—in this case, the need for water. Moses strikes water from the rock, as God commands, satisfying the people's thirst for sustenance and hope.

Restore us, O God of our salvation, to a place overflowing in the celebration of your love. Amen.

Tyesha S. Rice

MARCH 6

PSALM 95

Rejoice

O come, let us worship and bow down,
let us kneel before the LORD, our Maker!
For he is our God,
and we are the people of his pasture,
and the sheep of his hand.

Psalm 95:6–7

In Psalm 95, God calls us to acknowledge God's presence and rejoice! The season of Lent offers a time to stop indulging our self-centeredness and self-righteousness. God beckons us to a new sense that God has delivered us from the bitter reality of sin. Christ has loved us into redemption!

Psalm 95 was probably used in a worship setting. These verses are a sort of hymn for professing the community's faith and celebrating God's work. Thousands of years later we speak this psalm to give thanks for God's spirit of hope and renewal.

Thank you, O God who has moved us to rejoice and sustains us daily. Amen.

Tyesha S. Rice

MARCH 7

JOHN 4:5–42

Thirst No More

Jesus answered her, "If you know the gift of God, and who it is that is saying to you, 'Give me a drink,' you would have asked him, and he would have given you living water."

John 4:10

The Samaritan woman's thirst demonstrates our desire to be fulfilled. She came to a place where she customarily drew water.

Her encounter with Jesus began as a normal interaction with a stranger asking for water to quench an ordinary thirst. But Jesus offered her more—an abundance of life she had yet to embrace and accept. The overflowing wholeness of God's quenching power intrigued and nurtured her.

Imagine what a transformation she enjoyed in those quickening moments with Jesus. Jesus' promise of living water made her want to be where Christ could renew and sustain her through true resurrection power!

Precious God, please grant us new life. Amen.

Tyesha S. Rice

MARCH 8

JOHN 4:5–42

Cultivate Love

Jesus said to her, "I am he, the one who is speaking to you."

John 4:26

True love is not temporary or shallow but abiding and refreshing. When Christ proclaimed the promise of salvation to the Samaritan woman, he encouraged her to replace every broken moment with the hope only Christ can give. Today's words from verse 26 offer affirmation that the Samaritan woman found that all she needed was in Christ.

Once the Samaritan woman was persuaded that Jesus is the Messiah, she did not hesitate to run to the city to share the good news with people and bring them to Jesus.

Loving God, continue to walk with us as we journey daily. Amen.

Tyesha S. Rice

MARCH 9

JOHN 4:5–42

A Ripe Harvest

Then the woman left her water jar and went back to the city. She said to the people, "Come and see a man who told me everything I have ever done! He cannot be the Messiah, can he?"

John 4:28–29

No one is excluded from the love of God. Once we realize that there is nothing we can do to earn the love of God, we humbly accept salvation for the gift that it is. When the Samaritan woman declared all that Christ had told her, she shared what she learned with others.

Christ also encourages and empowers us to live in his ways. The world is hungry for a food that feeds the soul, God's Word. Let us be bold in the journey, primed for the undertaking, and open to labor. God has already completed great work in us. It is up to us to allow God to continue to use us for God's purpose.

Thank you, Lord, for the harvest. Please equip us as we labor to your glory. Amen.

Tyesha S. Rice

MARCH 10

JOHN 4:5–42

Declare God's Word

So when the Samaritans came to him, they asked him to stay with them; and he stayed there two days. And many more believed because of his word.

John 4:40–41

We demonstrate God's message through both our words and our actions. It is not sufficient to merely speak about what God has done; we must also spend time living out God's message of love for others.

Having received the good news from Jesus, the Samaritan woman proclaims it to her people. They invite Jesus to stay with them. He does so for two days, together with his disciples. In the process, the Samaritans discover Jesus for themselves. With both her words and deeds, the Samaritan woman passes on her faith and extends God's love.

Holy God, may we continue daily in the active hope of life in Christ. Amen.

Tyesha S. Rice

MARCH 11

ROMANS 5:1–11

Glorify God

Therefore, since we are justified by faith, we have peace with God through our Lord Jesus Christ, through whom we have obtained access to this grace in which we stand; and we boast in our hope of sharing the glory of God.

Romans 5:1–2

In this passage, Paul emphasizes the hope that is offered to those whom God has justified. Christ has granted us the gift of salvation. We experience God's goodness, and we rejoice in the Lord. The comfort of knowing that God is with us sustains us in daily living. We could never earn God's love nor glorify God enough.

God is worthy of all honor, and we must dedicate our daily lives to God. God has paid a price through Christ we could not afford and offered a gift we truly do not deserve; salvation is priceless! The sustaining glory of God's spirit empowers us.

God of glory, we honor you daily and dedicate our lives to you now and always. Amen.

Tyesha S. Rice

MARCH 12

PSALM 19

When Words Matter

Let the words of my mouth and the meditation
of my heart
be acceptable to you,
O LORD, my rock and my redeemer.

Psalm 19:14

The legendary line about "sticks and stones" does not hold up in daily life, does it? All of us have been hurt by somebody else's words, and, sadly, others have been hurt by our words. The advice to "think before speaking" is sound, with the problem being we do not always adhere to that wisdom. How many of us have suffered with "foot-and-mouth disease" where we seem to follow the instructions to "open mouth, insert foot!" Oh, the regrets from things we have said! If we could only take back hurtful words spoken in anger or in haste or in spite.

The psalmist knew. He knew how important it is to put the two together: meditation and words. "As we think, so are we" is an age-old wise saying. The psalmist put this in a prayer, a prayer that preachers often quote as they stand to deliver a sermon but that all of us could benefit from praying every day.

O God, teach us to weigh our words on the scale of kindness and love and human feelings. Amen.

Thomas D. Campbell

MARCH 13

PSALM 19

Delightful Laws

The precepts of the LORD are right,
rejoicing the heart.

Psalm 19:8a

I much prefer God's grace over God's law. So why do I feel so good every time I read Psalm 19:7–10? Is it the majestic poetry? Is it the joyful rhythm of the passages?

These verses ring a positive note. They are "reviving" to the soul. They make "wise the simple." They send one away "rejoicing." They are "enlightening" to the eyes. They endure forever. How precious are they? More than gold, more than honey! They are "perfect," "sure," "right," "clear," and "pure." Why do these verses lift us up while talking about the laws of God?

The psalmist knew what we know: that we need boundaries, we need guidelines, we need limits, for our good, for our safety, for the good of humankind. Don't be careless with your language. Don't kill. Don't steal. Don't commit adultery. Don't dishonor the Sabbath. Psalm 19 helps us to see the Ten Commandments in a brighter perspective, inviting us to see God's law as the gift that it is.

Lord of the ages, your laws have protected people from one another and from themselves. Help us to exercise wisdom and fairness with today's laws. Amen.

Thomas D. Campbell

MARCH 14

JOHN 2:13–22

Gentle Jesus, Meek and Mild?

After he was raised from the dead, his disciples remembered that he had said this.

John 2:22

I wish I knew more of what Jesus was teaching the day he stormed through the temple and threw the moneychangers and sheep and cattle out. Since it is John's Gospel, we can be sure that there is more to this story than meets the eye. One thing all of us can relate to is the last verse of this story: "After he was raised from the dead, his disciples remembered that he had said this; and they believed the scripture and the word that Jesus had spoken." How true!

How often have we thought, "Now I get it! Now I understand what my parents or my teacher or my pastor said years ago." It was once said that "happiness is not experienced; it is remembered." So are wise sayings. We may not "get it" at the moment, but give us time, like a few months or years or decades! It was later, much later, after the crucifixion and resurrection, that the disciples looked back and remembered what Jesus had said about himself and the temple and those other matters.

O God, thank you for the teachings of Jesus. We are still trying to understand them all. Continue to impress us with your Spirit and with the importance of his words. Amen.

Thomas D. Campbell

MARCH 15

EXODUS 20:1–17

The Invisible Commandment

You shall not covet.

Exodus 20:17

I have discovered a commandment that I can violate and nobody will know it! Yes, of course, God will know, but I'm talking about fellow human beings here. On all the other nine commandments, somebody else knows or can find out. But with the tenth commandment, I am home free! A friend once said, "I don't covet. I want what my neighbor has, and I want my neighbor to have something better!" Well, that may be a way out, but still I am visibly without sin, in the eyes of others. I can covet all day and nobody will know.

But we are aware that the sin of covetousness sometimes is not satisfied to stay in isolation. It desires company. It wants to produce! Some of the other nine commandments are committed precisely because of covetousness gone awry, out of control. Covetousness is not happy unless it infects people and causes havoc out in the world. Instead, let us practice contentment in all things.

God of the ages, increase our gratitude for the way things are in our lives, for the things we see and experience every day, both good and bad. Amen.

Thomas D. Campbell

MARCH 16

PSALM 107:1–3, 17–22

God's Steadfast Love

O give thanks to the LORD, for he is good;
for his steadfast love endures forever.

Psalm 107:1

The words *steadfast love* in the first verse of Psalm 107 appear again in verses 8, 15, 21, 31, and 43 of the same chapter, as well in Psalms 89 and 108. Here it is such a strong statement: steadfast love, enduring forever. What a foundation to stand on! What a faith to live by! No wonder we return often to this resounding statement of praise and reassurance! We preach it. We teach it. And what a blessing it is to live it.

Some of the psalms are very personal. Many of them are hymns and songs of praise. They do not come from poets hoping to be published some day. Instead, they arise from the personal experiences of their different authors. When we read the different verses from the Psalms, we can be assured that the authors were writing out of personal, emotional, spiritual, and life-changing experiences. Reading the poetry of our hymns and highlighting the powerful testimonies from the Psalms give us daily encouragement and, yes, power to make it through these days, thanks to God's steadfast love.

God, thank you for inspiring the psalmists. Inspire us with their words and your Spirit. Amen.

Thomas D. Campbell

MARCH 17

JOHN 3:14–21

Loving the Light

And this is the judgment, that the light has come into the world.

John 3:19a

Verses 19–21 of John 3 include the word *light* five times. Jesus is comparing light to darkness, saying that those who do evil prefer the shadows so that their deeds will not be exposed. The righteous have no need to fear the light and gladly step into the light of Christ.

A minister told of driving along a highway at night and remembering he had to make a call. This was in the time before cell phones, so he stopped and stepped into a phone booth at a gas station, quarters in hand. It was dark outside. Once inside the phone booth, he closed the door. The inside light came on. He likened this to prayer. You go into your quiet place to pray. You close the door. The light comes on as you enter the presence of Jesus, the Light of the World. These days we need a quiet place, a place where the light comes on, stamping out the shadows in our lives.

O God, your Son came as the Light of the World. Thank you for bringing strong, fresh light into our world. Amen.

Thomas D. Campbell

MARCH 18

PSALM 107:17–22

Lenten Blues

Some were sick through their sinful ways,
and because of their iniquities endured affliction.

Psalm 107:17

The season of Lent offers many opportunities for self-reflection and self-correction. The writer of Psalm 107 obviously felt the pangs of hunger, thirst, gloom, misery, sin, distress, and affliction. As these matters are brought to mind, we can see the importance of the season and the value of making crucial decisions about our lives. What to give up? What to change? What to improve? As we reflect and try to correct, we know that our efforts are all built on the fact that we are sinners who are saved by grace.

A church where I was pastor, St. Matthew Church, had a men's softball team one summer. They had their team name proudly emblazoned on their jerseys: "the St. Matthew Sinners," which raised some discussion among the other churches. As we travel through Lent, we do so fully aware of our sin and fully aware that later in that psalm the writer said when they cried to the Lord, "he saved them from their distress . . . and delivered them from destruction" (vv. 19–20).

O God, thank you for helping us acknowledge our sinful selves, and thank you for the healing that comes with your forgiveness. Amen.

Thomas D. Campbell

MARCH 19

Psalm 1

Happy Are Those?

Happy are those
who do not follow the advice of the wicked,
or take the path that sinners tread,
or sit in the seat of scoffers;
but their delight is in the law of the LORD,
and on his law they meditate day and night.

Psalm 1:1–2

Misery often has roots in unfulfilled expectations. People disappoint us. So do jobs. Online purchases. Most painful of all is when our expectations of God disintegrate. One phone call shatters our world. There is no healing. All our prayers seem fruitless. *Happy are those who delight in the law of the* LORD. Is this an invitation to shattered expectations? Faithfulness is not rewarded with bliss. The story of Jesus confirms it; the cross lays bare the lie at the heart of the prosperity gospel.

So what do we do with this psalm? Perhaps there is a clue in the contrast between the green plants and the insubstantial chaff. One endures; one does not. Maybe happiness is not about prosperity at all. Maybe it is about *groundedness*—the equanimity that flows from knowing we are connected to a source stronger and more resilient than anything that seeks to harm or destroy it.

Divine Source, flow through me and keep me grounded. Amen.

Laura Alary

MARCH 20

PSALM 1

Garden of Redemption

They are like trees
planted by streams of water,
which yield their fruit in its season,
and their leaves do not wither.

Psalm 1:3

My daughter has been tending to her heart garden—a project she began one summer as a living memorial to children lost to the residential school system in Canada, to their families, and to those who survived. The garden includes plants of symbolic significance to indigenous people and hundreds of stones, each one painted with the name of a child who died in one of the church-run schools. My daughter noticed that many of the names on official records had been anglicized—the children's indigenous names stripped away along with so much of their identity.

What was done to these children again calls into question the connection the psalm makes between faithfulness and flourishing. But what if we exchange the image of the individual tree for the vision of a garden as collective space? Prosperity can never be limited to a privileged few. Truly delighting in God means tending to the health of the whole community. Just imagine the garden that could thrive!

O God, may our delight in your ways produce a harvest that all can enjoy. Amen.

Laura Alary

MARCH 21

PROVERBS 31:10–18

Are You Still Awake?

She rises while it is still night
and provides food for her household
. . . .
Her lamp does not go out at night.
Proverbs 31:15a, 18b

One of the hardest things about being a parent is the loss of sleep: years of nursing babies through the night, sitting up with sick children, watching the clock and listening for the footsteps of teens who have been out too late. Not sleeping may be an occupational hazard for parents, but it makes me cranky, and I do not celebrate it.

This proverbial woman who burns the midnight oil to maintain her perfect household makes me want to growl, "Just turn out your light and go to bed!" Is she a driven overachiever? Or a so-called godly mother who pours herself out in service to her family? Both are idols. Worshiping them lures too many women into the dual trap of perfectionism and self-sacrifice. So I am wary of her but also intrigued. Like Woman Wisdom, she is strong, generous, shrewd, and practical—the sort of woman I would vote for if she ran for public office. Torn between admiration and suspicion, I can only watch to see what she does next.

Gracious God, help me remember that you call me not to perfection but to faithfulness. Amen.

Laura Alary

MARCH 22

PROVERBS 31:19–31

Off the Pedestal

Strength and dignity are her clothing,
and she laughs at the time to come.
She opens her mouth with wisdom,
and the teaching of kindness is on her tongue.

Proverbs 31:25–26

Here she is again—the capable wife. Now she is laughing at the time to come. This kind of confidence eludes me. There are not sufficient canned goods and toilet paper on earth to make me feel secure enough to laugh in the face of an uncertain future. But maybe her merriment bubbles up from the calm center of someone who has learned to make what plans she can and then release what she cannot control. That would make her wise indeed.

Again I notice the family resemblance between her and Woman Wisdom in Proverbs 1. Both are outspoken and active in public. Both temper boldness with kindness and concern for the vulnerable. Both seek public justice, not simply domestic bliss. Both speak words of wisdom and are associated with torah—the ways of God. Perhaps this capable woman also embodies the divine spirit that calls us to a better way of being in the world. If that is the case, even I might choose her as a beloved companion and life partner—if she would let me sleep in sometimes.

Holy Wisdom, be my beloved companion. Amen.

Laura Alary

MARCH 23

MARK 9:30–32

The Oldest Pear Tree

"The Son of Man is to be betrayed into human hands, and they will kill him, and three days after being killed, he will rise again."

Mark 9:31

Four hundred years ago a pear sapling crossed the Atlantic from England to America, where it was lovingly planted and tended. *The Very Oldest Pear Tree* (Albert Whitman, 2020) by Nancy Sanders follows the fortunes and misfortunes of the tree as a nation takes shape around it. Not only does the tree live through momentous political and social changes, it also survives fires, hurricanes, and vandalism, including having most of its branches chopped off.

This horrified my daughter, who could not comprehend *why* anyone would want to harm such a precious tree. But as the disciples discovered when Jesus bluntly told them he would be handed over to be destroyed, sometimes there are no answers—only grief and incredulity. When attempts to graft back its branches failed, the old pear tree proved astonishingly resilient, sprouting new shoots that eventually produced fruit of their own. What a symbol for the Christian story: betrayed and destroyed by human hands, that old pear tree was rooted in a source of life more powerful than anyone had imagined.

Source of life, I trust in you. Amen.

Laura Alary

MARCH 24

Mark 9:30–32

Afraid to Ask

But they did not understand what he was saying and were afraid to ask him.

Mark 9:32

I am hardly in the door before my daughter's questions begin: What is for supper? Is there meat in it? How were the animals treated? Why did I bring so many plastic bags home from my last trip to the grocery store? My head is starting to ache. I just want to drink my coffee. I know the truth will make demands on me, and I am not ready for that right now. In my own small way, I feel for the disciples. When Jesus tells them yet again of the suffering that is coming, they do not understand but are afraid to ask questions. Why? I suspect they avoid the question because they fear the answer and what it will require of them.

Pondering this, I put down my mug and ask my daughter to show me her vegan cookbook. We choose a recipe, and I promise to bring reusable glass jars the next time I visit the bulk food store. It is only one tiny step. But I wonder what else might change if we stopped hiding behind silence and dared to face good questions and scary truths.

Strong Spirit, give us courage to seek and speak the truth. Amen.

Laura Alary

MARCH 25

MARK 9:33–37

Welcome the Child

"Whoever welcomes one such child in my name welcomes me, and whoever welcomes me welcomes not me but the one who sent me."

Mark 9:37

During the COVID-19 pandemic, I met Christ in the train station. He was wearing a mask—a public health requirement—but the security guards who approached him did not realize it at first. When he turned around and saw them he said, "No worries. I always wear a mask. We want to protect our families, right? Well, the way I see it, *everyone* is my family."

When Jesus overheard his friends bickering about who was the greatest, he could see their priorities: status, prestige, power. No wonder they had such trouble grasping what it meant to follow him. So he brought a child into their midst. This was more than a reminder to make room for the vulnerable. Look, Jesus seems to say. This is *your* child, *your* family, *your* flesh and blood. This child is *you.* And *me.* Now look closer. Do you see God in this child? Do you see that we are all one? This is how you must see all the time—and the seeing will determine the way you choose to live.

May I see the face of Christ in everyone I meet, and may they see the face of Christ in me. Amen.

Laura Alary

MARCH 26

ACTS 10:34–43

No Play Day

"We are witnesses to all that he did both in Judea and in Jerusalem. They put him to death by hanging him on a tree."

Acts 10:39

When I was growing up in the 1950s, Good Friday was a "no play day." In respect for the hours Jesus spent on the cross, my mother expected me to tone down my usual play habits. She took time during Good Friday afternoon to tell me the story of Jesus. In our home, there was never a celebration of Easter without first recalling human failing, God's love, and Jesus' passion.

Truth be told, the cross has always been a part of the story of our salvation. Even in his pivotal sermon introducing the gospel to Cornelius, the apostle Peter doesn't mince words: "They put him to death by hanging him on a tree." Later, Paul will say much the same in 1 Corinthians 1:23: "But we proclaim Christ crucified."

Holy God, may we honor Jesus' life and remember his death. Amen.

Steve Aschmann

MARCH 27

JOHN 20:1–18

A Dark Weekend

Early on the first day of the week, while it was still dark, Mary Magdalene came to the tomb and saw that the stone had been removed from the tomb.

John 20:1

The life of Jesus had been snuffed out. Death looked to be a winner. The fearful disciples laid low on Friday and Saturday. But one solitary figure, Mary Magdalene, stirred in the shadows along the pathway to his tomb on Sunday morning. It was dark because of the early hour but darker still because Mary had stood at the foot of his cross.

Mary discovered that she was not alone. God was up in that darkness, working through the night. God was not in hiding or afraid. God was preparing to unleash the Light and usher in the Easter dawn.

Lord God, in the heart of the deepest darkness, may we find your Spirit at work. Amen.

Steve Aschmann

MARCH 28

PSALM 118:1–2, 14–24

The Difference God Makes

O give thanks to the LORD, for he is good;
his steadfast love endures forever!

Psalm 118:1

With an uplifting spirit of celebration, joy, and thanksgiving, the 118th Psalm has touched the community of faith like few other hymns in the book of Psalms.

Psalm 118 holds a special connection to Holy Week. Jesus' disciples vocalized the stanzas with exuberance on Palm Sunday. They also sang the words with a spirit of gratitude on Maundy Thursday, just before leaving for the Garden of Gethsemane.

The church includes Psalm 118 as a lectionary reading for every Easter Sunday.

With enthusiasm, the psalmist reminds us that despite the troubles and threats that surround us, the Lord "is good; his steadfast love endures forever!"

Good and loving God, may our faith radiate the joy, enthusiasm, and gratitude of the psalmist. Amen.

Steve Aschmann

MARCH 29

ACTS 10:34–43

No Partiality

Then Peter began to speak to them: "I truly understand that God shows no partiality."

Acts 10:34

Familiar Holy Week rituals foster a comfortable atmosphere, especially for older adults. Each year, I look forward to waving the palms, breaking bread on Maundy Thursday, reading the Scriptures, quietly praying on Good Friday, and shouting "Hallelujah!" on Easter morning.

Still, I wonder whether repetitive worship patterns actually cloak the bold spirit of our God, who is unpredictable and full of surprises. After all, our God is the One who speaks from a cross and leaps from an empty tomb!

In today's reading, God calls on disciples like Peter to be daring and unconventional. Peter ultimately grasps God's message and embraces and baptizes Cornelius and his family. All people, old and young, Jews and Gentiles, even Romans, qualify to be a part of Christ's family. The apostle Peter speaks for all of us and to all of us: "I truly understand that God shows no partiality."

O God, may we live in the spirit of Peter, knowing that those who are different from us bear your image. Amen.

Steve Aschmann

MARCH 30

Luke 19:28–40

On the Jerusalem Road

He answered, "I tell you, if these were silent, the stones would shout out."

Luke 19:40

Last year on Palm Sunday, I sang "Hosanna" and joyfully processed with children and families through the streets of Asheville, North Carolina. Yet I also asked myself how I might have reacted on the Jerusalem road long ago. Would I have waved branches, spread my jacket on the roadbed, and treated Jesus like royalty? Or would I have grumbled and plotted his demise?

Jesus believed in himself as Israel's long-anticipated Messiah who offered peace and wholeness. There was no reason for anyone to hold back or to keep silent—even the stones along the wayside were invited to speak up.

Certainly, Jerusalem's opinion had consequences and our reactions matter, but the key opinion comes from the One who made the stones shout. Hosanna to the king!

Eternal God, this Holy Week, may we embrace Jesus' peace and salvation. Amen.

Steve Aschmann

MARCH 31

Psalm 118:1–2, 14–24

Our Cornerstone

The stone that the builders rejected
has become the chief cornerstone.
This is the Lord's doing;
it is marvelous in our eyes.

Psalm 118:22–23

If you live long enough, you will experience the sting and pain of rejection. I have a box overflowing with humbling rejection letters to prove it!

Our psalmist himself experienced the pain of rejection when he was judged unworthy and treated like a flawed building stone. However, God did not view the psalmist in this light. God saw character, possibilities, and someone who could be relied on. Because of God's loving kindness and work, the psalmist's circumstances changed. Our psalmist celebrates this reversal of fortune in verses 22–23.

Jesus' life mirrored that of the psalmist. Jesus was the stone that the builders had rejected. Yet Jesus was raised up to be our chief cornerstone, the rock upon which we build our lives. In our faith journeys, we discover that God is a better architect who knows a bit more about construction materials than mere mortals.

Holy God, may your Son be the sure foundation,
upon which we construct our lives. Amen.

Steve Aschmann

APRIL 1

1 Corinthians 15:19–26

The First Fruit

But in fact Christ has been raised from the dead, the first fruits of those who have died.

1 Corinthians 15:20

Farmers in ancient Israel always presented the very first fruits of their harvest to God. No produce from the crop could be consumed until the farmers gave these offerings to their Lord. What a bold act of faith! The farmers didn't even know what quantity or quality their crop would provide.

Paul draws on this old practice to teach the community of faith in Corinth about the resurrection. Paul invites us to place our trust in God's benevolent power and believe. The focus on Easter Sunday naturally falls on Jesus, but the joyful celebrations should include all who belong to him. Easter is not merely the celebration of Jesus' resurrection; it is a prelude—the first fruits—of our own resurrection.

May we live without fear, finding in Christ the way to eternal life. Amen.

Steve Aschmann

APRIL 2

Acts 5:27–32

We Must Obey God

But Peter and the apostles answered, "We must obey God rather than any human authority."

Acts 5:29

Jesus' apostles had been imprisoned for preaching about Jesus. That night, an angel opened the jail doors and told the apostles, "Go, stand in the temple and tell the people the whole message about this life" (v. 20). So they did.

When the religious council discovered the apostles missing, they were furious and puzzled. The apostles were found in the temple, preaching. When brought before the high priest, they were chastised: "We gave you strict orders not to teach in this name." The apostles replied, "We must obey God rather than any human authority" (vv. 28–29).

The religious authorities could have put the apostles to death. However, an old Pharisee, Gamaliel, stood up and recommended no action be taken against them. "If this plan or undertaking is of human origin, it will fail; but if it is of God . . . you may even be found fighting against God" (v. 39).

As we go about our daily lives, let us seek ways to use our wisdom, like Gamaliel, to council against rash actions.

Lord, help me today to discern and obey your will. Amen.

Quentin A. Holmes

APRIL 3

ACTS 5:27–32

We Are Witnesses to These Things

"And we are witnesses to these things, and so is the Holy Spirit whom God has given to those who obey him."

Acts 5:32

Peter told the Jewish authorities that God had raised Jesus and exalted him and that repentance and forgiveness came through Jesus. The authorities didn't wish to hear this message. Peter persisted by declaring that the disciples were witness to these things and received the Holy Spirit.

This story unfolded about two thousand years ago, but we today are faced with a similar challenge of witnessing to our faith. We must be Christian in actions, not just in name. Our behavior toward others and toward the earth itself bears witness to what it is we truly believe. Love, kindness, and mercy all reflect the love of Jesus in our lives.

Peter and the apostles didn't do their work without the Holy Spirit. Neither do we. The Holy Spirit is always present, giving strength and power to those who follow Christ.

O Lord, may my words and my actions reflect thy love. Amen.

Quentin A. Holmes

APRIL 4

PSALM 118:14–29

This Is the Day the Lord Has Made

This is the day that the LORD has made;
let us rejoice and be glad in it.

Psalm 118:24

The Psalms are some of the oldest parts of the Bible. They give us words to express the highs and lows of life such as joy, despair, and even anger at God.

For example, today's Psalm verse reflects Israel's delight at being delivered from death to life during the exodus and after the Babylonian exile. The Lord delivered them from death to life. Each day was a gift from God; rejoicing was a fitting response for such a marvelous gift.

The psalmist invites us to rejoice that God has made this day. None of us knows our "length of days" (Prov. 3:2). As an older adult in the last third of my life, I feel deeply grateful for each new day.

Dear God, today is the day that you have made. Help me to rejoice and be glad in it. Amen.

Quentin A. Holmes

APRIL 5

PSALM 118:14–29

God's Love Endures Forever

O give thanks to the LORD, for he is good,
for his steadfast love endures forever.

Psalm 118:29

Psalm 118 was used corporately during Passover celebrations. The words *salvation* and *victory* in verses 14 and 15 echo the song used by Moses after the people escaped by crossing through the sea during the exodus.

This psalm is also deeply personal. In verse 18, problems are seen as a form of refining or testing. Victory over struggles does not come from relying on human strength but by relying on God. Righteousness comes from entrusting our life and future to God.

Psalm 118 provides life-giving wisdom for both communities and individuals. The psalmist tells us to trust in God, for God's love endures. What good news in this Easter season!

God, give us the wisdom to rely on your love. Amen.

Quentin A. Holmes

APRIL 6

Revelation 1:4–8

Grace and Peace to You

Blessed is the one who reads aloud the words of the prophecy, and blessed are those who hear and who keep what is written in it; for the time is near.

Revelation 1:3

Revelation is unlike any other book in the New Testament. The writer of Revelation, John of Patmos, was given a vision from Jesus Christ. Ordinary words will not suffice to describe his vision. Only imagery will do.

You and I have been schooled in scientific thought. We use logic and human reasoning to create order out of our experiences and the earthly realm about us. However, God is not limited to human ways. When we seek to interpret the meaning behind John of Patmos's vision, we run the risk of missing the main point. The imagery itself is God making it known that Jesus Christ is the faithful witness, the firstborn from the dead. John of Patmos's revelation is a visual message of grace and peace from Jesus Christ.

O Lord, help us to accept thy grace and peace. Amen.

Quentin A. Holmes

APRIL 7

JOHN 20:19–31

Peace Be with You

When it was evening on that day, the first day of the week, and the doors of the house where the disciples had met were locked for fear of the Jews, Jesus came and stood among them and said, "Peace be with you."

John 20:19

Today, the evening news often brings accounts of strife, discord, and violent acts. All too often, strife breeds even more strife. As Christians, we believe that there is another way.

Today's reading recounts the first appearance of Jesus after his crucifixion. Jesus' disciples gathered together behind locked doors, locked for fear of the Jewish authorities. The world as they knew it was no more. Suddenly, Jesus appeared in the room, showed them his wounds, and granted them peace.

They received peace from Jesus, peace in the midst of their grief and fears about the future.

Jesus did not rail against the Jewish authorities with hate. He responded with peace and instructed his followers to continue on with his work.

Dear God, grant us thy peace. Amen.

Quentin A. Holmes

APRIL 8

John 20:19–31

I Am Sending You

Jesus said to them again, "Peace be with you. As the father has sent me, so I send you."

John 20:21

After his crucifixion and resurrection, the risen Jesus appeared, charging his frightened disciples to go forth and continue his work. "As the father has sent me, so I send you." Jesus breathed the Holy Spirit into them to empower them.

Faced with change and disruption, we often feel sorry for ourselves. Our focus turns inward, and we feel very frightened. Jesus has a prescription for this: go forth and help others as Jesus has done! We, too, have the Holy Spirit to empower us.

I have discovered that simply going forward and trying to help others works. God provides a way forward, and that way is far better than anything I could ever have imagined. Thanks be to God!

O Lord, grant us the wisdom to go forward with your work, especially during times of change and disruption. Amen.

Quentin A. Holmes

APRIL 9

ACTS 3:12–19

Pointing the Praise in the Right Direction

> *"You Israelites, why do you wonder at this, or why do you stare at us, as though by our own power or piety we had made him walk?"*
>
> Acts 3:12b

Although there's no *I* in *team*, we've all seen the athlete or employee who takes all the credit for the team's success. He'll sing his own praises for as long as anyone will listen, and she'll steal the glory for what her staff members did. In return, he gets a multimillion-dollar contract, and she gets a promotion, taking her closer to the top.

It's the complete opposite in the life of people of faith. We know that in order to be great, we must become small. We put ourselves last in order for others to be first. Most of all, we point the praise in the right direction for anything we accomplish. Any and all credit goes to the source, the One who gifted us with life to begin with and blessed us with any talents or success we've been able to achieve.

Mighty source of all, thank you for the life and gifts you have blessed me with. May I always point the praise in your direction, for any and all things I achieve. Amen.

Claire McGarry

APRIL 10

ACTS 3:12–19

Where There's a Will

". . . and you killed the Author of life, whom God raised from the dead."

Acts 3:15a

In 2012, at the age of twenty, Canadian Emily Hime took over an orphanage in Haiti. Running *Maison Ke Kontan* (Happy Heart House) on a shoestring budget put Hime on a financial roller coaster, with the orphanage on the verge of closing multiple times. Each time, one generous donor or another would step forward and save the day. It is clear that Hime has been called to help those in need. With defeat not an option, she finds a way to overcome with God's help.

When God's only son was rejected and crucified, it looked as if God's will was defeated. It seemed that all was lost, causing many to lose hope. Then Christ was resurrected, and hope was restored. The resurrection of Christ is not just a one-time event. It's a recurring miracle that happens every time we lose hope only to have God intervene, creating a way that resurrects hope in our lives and in our hearts.

Sovereign Rescuer, inspire me to help those in need. When I face hardships of any kind, remind me that when it's your will, you'll always resurrect hope in me and in those I help. Amen.

Claire McGarry

APRIL 11

Psalm 4

Free Falling

Offer right sacrifices,
and put your trust in the Lord.

Psalm 4:5

In training to become a resident advisor (RA) in college, they made us take turns doing trust falls for group bonding. We'd form two rows, turn and face each other, and extend our arms. Then, one person would climb up on a table, turn his or her back to us, and fall into our arms. It was a scary experience in both regards: falling and catching. But the more we did it, the better we got at both. Eventually, we were able to do the exercise with complete trust in one another.

Trusting God can be just as intimidating, especially when something really matters. That's when it feels we have further to fall. But just like we repeated that exercise in RA training, the more we practice trusting God, the better we'll get at doing so. Eventually, we'll reach a point where no matter how high the obstacle, we're willing to let go and free-fall, confident our Savior will catch us.

Ever-present Savior, increase my trust in you so that I'm willing to free-fall into your grace, no matter how high the starting point. Amen.

Claire McGarry

APRIL 12

PSALM 4

Guiding Light

"Let the light of your face shine on us, O LORD!"

Psalm 4:6b

Our home has an open floor plan with a cathedral ceiling in the foyer. There's a lamp there I turn on each night. It's amazing how it casts its glow throughout the house, up and down. If anyone has to get up in the middle of the night, there's no fear of tripping. Yet I forget to turn it off each morning. It's not evident it's still on when the sunlight pours in, drowning it out.

This reminds me of how so many of us are with God. When circumstances turn dark, we look to God to light the way. Yet when all is resolved, that holy presence goes unnoticed. Our need isn't as great, so the light gets drowned out by the busyness of life and our own self-sufficiency. What's critical to remember is that although the bulb in the lamp at my house burns out and needs to be replaced, ours is an eternal God whose light never dies. Our goal should be to walk in that light, in bad times and in good.

Luminous God, open my eyes to your guiding light in bad times and in good. Amen.

Claire McGarry

APRIL 13

1 John 3:1–7

Blessing the World

Beloved, we are God's children now; what we will be has not yet been revealed.

1 John 3:2

My MOSAIC Moms group meets once a month to talk about the intersections between motherhood and faith. The discussion at our most recent gathering was about what gifts our children will possess and bless the world with when they grow up. Despite most of our kids being in their teens, we're unsure. There's still so much more for them to experience and discover. We know it will be a complete joy to watch it all play out.

We're all God's children, and God delights in watching our stories unfold. No matter our age, careers, or accomplishments, what we will be still isn't known. We're constantly being made new in God's love, ever growing, ever changing. The more we open ourselves up to God's grace, the more we're led to bless the world in new and exciting ways.

Creator of us all, help me understand that my life is still incomplete. Open my heart to all the ways you want to grow me so that I can further bless the world in new and exciting ways. Amen.

Claire McGarry

APRIL 14

LUKE 24:36B–48

Astounding Joy

While in their joy they were disbelieving and still wondering . . .

Luke 24:41

One day, I got sucked into the YouTube rabbit hole and watched video after video of adorable little kids being told their moms were going to have another baby. Each and every time, the kids were completely dumbfounded—not by jealousy but by sheer excitement. Whether they cried tears of joy, jumped up and down, or threw themselves at their mom with elation, they all said the same thing: "I can't believe it! I just can't believe it!" The news was just too wonderful and too astounding to be fully grasped.

None of the apostles cried, jumped up and down, or threw themselves at Jesus when he appeared to them after the resurrection, but they most certainly couldn't fully grasp that he was standing before them, in the flesh. It was just too wonderful and too astounding to be believed!

Resurrected Christ, the news of your resurrection is so incredible and wondrous, we still grapple with understanding it fully. Open my mind and heart to all that it means, for me and the world. Amen.

Claire McGarry

APRIL 15

LUKE 24:36B–48

Opened Minds

Then he opened their minds to understand the scriptures.

Luke 24:45

Have you ever had the experience where you give your spouse or kids advice, and they brush it off as if you don't know what you're talking about? Then, days later, someone else says the same exact thing, and suddenly your spouse or kids think it's a great idea? When we call them on it, they claim they have no idea what we're talking about. Sadly, we know it's because they've tuned us out. It takes a new source to open their minds.

Jesus was with his disciples for three years, teaching them about the Scriptures and God's love. Even though they knew he was the Messiah and the greatest teacher ever known, their minds weren't open wide enough to truly understand all that he was teaching. It wasn't until he opened their minds after his resurrection and the Holy Spirit came upon them (Acts 2:4) that they could truly comprehend the magnitude and magnificence of God's holy word.

Magnificent Teacher, open my mind to the wonders of your great love and holy teachings. Amen.

Claire McGarry

APRIL 16

PSALM 133:1–3

How Very Good and Pleasant!

How very good and pleasant it is
when kindred live together in unity!

Psalm 133:1

In Israel, during the time of Jesus, most Jewish families made an annual pilgrimage to Jerusalem. Each festival held special significance, but getting to Jerusalem was important. The pilgrimage began with family groups from a village or region; these small walking groups merged with others until a large celebratory community formed. Singing the psalms of accent (Pss. 120–34) transformed strangers into spiritual companions. Psalm 133 was sung when the pilgrims first caught sight of Jerusalem. It celebrated spiritual community and joy at journey's end. Jesus' disciples likely shared such an experience as pilgrims walking to Jerusalem. Yet, as profound as was their pilgrimage, their time in Jerusalem changed them forever.

For contemporary believers, the events of Holy Week are often framed as a pilgrimage. I wonder: After your pilgrimage through Holy Week, is your community spiritually united and joyful on Easter morning? Are you aware of your contribution to such unity and joy?

Kind God, thank you for this pilgrimage in faith. Help me receive the grace you send me today. May I always be open to your transforming Spirit. Amen.

Kay E. Huggins

APRIL 17

John 20:19–23

So, I Send You

Jesus said to them again, "Peace be with you. As the Father has sent me, so I send you."

John 20:21

Often Easter accounts have a singular focus: Jesus. Not so in John's account; the disciples are dynamically included. By God's power, Jesus passed through death to a new and glorious life. Jesus greeted his friends with "Peace be with you" and immediately challenged them to pass through their fears and despair into a glorious participation in living resurrection. Jesus sent his disciples into this new way of living with three resources: peace, Spirit, and his own ministry of forgiveness. He desired that they experience the power of resurrection while they were alive.

Easter's glory extends from Jesus to his disciples to every subsequent believer. Today, take time to consider the role of these three aspects of resurrection living in your life. Ask yourself: Am I seeking peace and unity among family, friends, colleagues, and community? Am I open to the Holy Spirit's leadership? Am I diligent in forgiving as Christ forgave?

Christ Jesus, send me into resurrection living this day. May I offer your peace, follow the Holy Spirit's guidance, and freely forgive those you bring to me today. Amen.

Kay E. Huggins

APRIL 18

JOHN 20:24–25

I Will Not Believe!

"Unless I see the mark of the nails in his hands, and put my finger in the mark of the nails and my hand in his side, I will not believe."

John 20:25

Were you ever the one who wasn't there? It is never easy to miss an important communal experience. Thus Thomas's adamant statement makes sense: "Unless . . . I will not believe." Nevertheless, when it comes to deepening our faith, we are called to go beyond personal experience. We are encouraged to trust the wisdom of our community, to rest on the fulfilled promises others experienced, and to learn from the Bible and church history.

It takes humility to accept the faithful testimony of others without demanding verifying evidence. Yet there is something poignant about Thomas. He seems too alone and too resistant to even the possibility of the miracle. Perhaps Thomas is that part of us we wish were more trusting. What would you say to a Thomas today? What do you say to that resistant, unbelieving voice within you?

Dear God, help me as I encounter Thomas today—whether in a friend or a stranger or deep within myself. Keep me alert to Thomas-like feelings and help me find a kind word to share. Amen.

Kay E. Huggins

APRIL 19

JOHN 20:26–29

Seeing and Believing

Jesus said to him, "Have you believed because you have seen me? Blessed are those who have not seen and yet have come to believe."

John 20:29

Did seeing Jesus on Easter morning give the disciples an advantage? Was Jesus' appearance a splash of glory to confirm divine status?

According to John's account, Jesus' disciples were to continue his mission until reconciliation covered the world. To do so, they had to see differently. The resurrected Lord taught his disciples to see the world through the glory of his resurrection. Seeing through resurrection glory established a gospel belief in possibilities so strong his disciples continued his mission.

For all who follow the risen Lord, including the first disciples, the connection between seeing and believing is crucial. Faithful seeing, however, needs no Easter morning advantage. It can be learned! It is the practice of seeing the world from a resurrection perspective. Jesus blessed both those who saw and believed on Easter morning and "those who have not seen and yet have come to believe."

Savior Jesus, bless my eyes today to see possibilities for wholeness everywhere . . . then help me live by what I see. Amen.

Kay E. Huggins

APRIL 20

JOHN 20:30–31

Believing Brings Life

. . . and that through believing you may have life in his name.

John 20:31

Jesus' disciples did not immediately grasp the consequences of his resurrection for their daily living. Yet after overcoming the desire that Jesus remain with them always, the disciples began to understand the necessity of his departure and the blessing of their new life. After his ascension, "living resurrection" became a comprehensive practice for his followers. The new community was devoted to conquering fears, forgiving sins, bringing peace, caring for the needy, and expanding love—according to the way of Jesus.

The community discovered great joy in the practice of living this way and wanted to share the experience. Carefully, the followers put together a comprehensive remembrance of Jesus to explain the hope and the Spirit among them. All committed his story to heart; some practiced reciting the tale as sermon; and some recorded it in books and letters. These exercises had one purpose: that others would know the precious gift of life that flowed from Jesus.

Dear Jesus, bless the church this day with passion and persistence in living resurrection. May the church offer life to all. Amen.

Kay E. Huggins

APRIL 21

Acts 4:32–35

Believers with One Heart and Soul

Now the whole group of those who believed were of one heart and soul, and no one claimed private ownership of any possessions, but everything they owned was held in common.

Acts 4:32

The practice of living resurrection is beautifully recorded in Acts as the story of the Spirit's creation of a new community of love. Rather than an institution with rules and standards, this community grew together as one body, with one heart and one soul. Sharing was their comportment, and joy, their attitude. The description of the early church seems almost too good to be true. But as generosity and joy chase away fear and despair, many a believer gains insight into the community of those who follow Jesus.

During the Easter season, consider the ways the church has cared for others and for you. Name those who stood by your side when times were dangerous and those who invited you into new forms of service. Recollect the church's stands for justice and expressions of great compassion. Celebrate the Spirit's recreation of the church. Remember, love is the heart of living resurrection.

God of all, I thank you for the love and witness of the church. Refine the church this Easter season. May we love boldly and broadly. Amen.

Kay E. Huggins

APRIL 22

PSALM 133:1–3

Life Forevermore

For there the LORD ordained his blessing,
life forevermore.

Psalm 133:3

Psalm 133 focuses on the spiritual unity essential to a pilgrimage to Jerusalem, but let's consider another aspect of that psalm: life forevermore. This announcement was deeply rooted in covenant as God's intention to bless the whole creation through the biblical nation of Israel.

With the gift of Jesus, a child of that covenantal heritage, God established a new covenant. All were invited into life—into a living resurrection. No longer did hope dwell in a distant future; hope was present. No more did folks long for God's season of blessing; blessings abounded every day. In Jesus, and among his community of followers, God's realm was present and yet to come. This new covenant was a life overflowing with love.

After Easter, Psalm 133 sings a new reality: in Jesus, God ordained life forevermore. As you prepare for the second Sunday of Easter, make that blessing your guide.

God of all ages, I thank you for the blessing of life forevermore. May I live this precious life today and always. Amen.

Kay E. Huggins

APRIL 23

ISAIAH 50:4–9A

Having Adversaries

Who are my adversaries?
Let them confront me.

Isaiah 50:8b

Do you have adversaries? Some people might say that if you don't, it means you haven't really stood for anything. But if you're anything like me, you are polite and well-behaved. You learned from a young age to be respectful and know your manners. You are *nice.*

One of the greatest threats to Christianity is our insistence on being nice. I know, this is hard to hear! We don't want to ruffle feathers. We want people to like us. But Jesus, who loved all people, certainly ruffled feathers. He made people angry because of the truths he shared. Jesus was not always well-behaved or polite.

Our reading from Isaiah reminds us that sometimes people will not agree with us and might even be angry with us. But if what we are doing and what we stand for is *of God*, God will see us through.

Loving God, help me stand for your love, justice, and mercy. Strengthen me and uphold me so that I might serve you. Amen.

Kate S. Forer

APRIL 24

Psalm 31:9–16

With Us

Be gracious to me, O Lord, for I am in distress.

Psalm 31:9

As a pastor, I often get asked the question, "Where was God?" For example: Where was God when I was suffering? Where was God when that shooting occurred? Where was God the day of the earthquake? Where was God during my cancer treatments?

The answer is always the same. God is with us *in* our suffering, *in* our distress, and *in* our struggle. God knows our pain and our distress. In the life, death, and resurrection of Jesus Christ, God intimately experienced the struggle and pain and distress of humanity, and God comes particularly close to us in our struggles even now. Where was God? God was, and always is, with us.

Mysterious God, thank you for being with me in my distress, in my pain, and in my suffering. Help me to know that when you feel far away you are as close to me as my breath. Amen.

Kate S. Forer

APRIL 25

PSALM 31:9–16

At Our Worst

For my life is spent with sorrow,

. . . .

and my bones waste away.

Psalm 31:10

The psalmist is at a very low point, in a dire moment of sorrow and sighing. Have you ever felt that? I know there have been times in my life when I've experienced deep grief. At those times, I was not able to eat and felt as if I was wasting away. Many of the grief psalms eventually turn into psalms of thanksgiving. Even so, it's important to stay in grief for a while and not rush beyond verse 10.

Tomorrow, we can get to the hopeful stuff. But for now, let's remember that we worship a God who loves us at our absolute worst, a God who knows us when we have hit rock bottom, and a God who still loves us when we are at the lowest of the low. God invites us to feel the dark and dreary parts of human existence and to come through them to the other side.

Holy God, thank you for holding me while I cry. Amen.

Kate S. Forer

APRIL 26

PSALM 31:9–16

Trust

But I trust in you, O LORD;
I say, "You are my God."

Psalm 31:14

In the ancient world, the gods were immortal beings of honor and glory. They did not suffer and die. Only humans did that. But then the God of Abraham entered, the God of Jesus. Now this was a different kind of God. This God, the one and only God, is the One in whom we trust—not to make us victorious but to show us gentle compassion, hopeful love, and unending mercy. It is this God whom we claim to belong to and whom we know intimately through Jesus Christ.

We trust in a God who knows suffering. Our God, through the incarnation, knows the rumbling of an empty stomach, a crick in the neck, a cry of grief.

Everlasting God, I trust in your presence in me and around me. Amen.

Kate S. Forer

APRIL 27

JOHN 20:19–31

Offering Peace

Jesus came and stood among them and said, "Peace be with you."

John 20:19b

Every Sunday morning in our church we pass the peace. "Peace be with you," we say. We don't share the peace merely to catch up or be social. We share the peace as a practice of reconciliation. There are times when I have had a conflict with people in my congregation. Being able to go up to them after confession, look them in the eye, and shake their hand means a lot. It means that we are trying to leave that conflict behind us and that we wish each other God's peace.

When Jesus appeared to his disciples in the upper room after his death, I think he was doing something similar. His disciples had just denied him and left him to die alone. They pretended they didn't even know him. When Jesus wished them peace, it must have been to leave the past behind and embrace the new Easter world together.

Holy One, thank you for always offering us forgiveness and second (or third, or fourth . . .) chances. Amen.

Kate S. Forer

APRIL 28

1 PETER 1:3–9

New Birth

Blessed be the God and Father of our Lord Jesus Christ! By his great mercy he has given us a new birth into a living hope through the resurrection of Jesus Christ from the dead.

1 Peter 1:3

Every time the sun rises, God offers us a new day and fresh hope. Every time we remember the new birth Jesus Christ provided for us through his death and resurrection, God offers us a "living hope."

The words "living hope" imply that Jesus' message will go on living far into the future. Because the Gospel is living, we continually find God's word in new places, even in dark and scary places like the grave. We have been born into this new and living hope through the mercy of God. While we once may have felt dead inside, we have been offered a new life of living hope!

Merciful God, we give you unending thanks for the mystery of our faith and the love that you show us. Amen.

Kate S. Forer

APRIL 29

PSALM 16

Seeing God

You show me the path of life.
In your presence there is fullness of joy;
in your right hand are pleasures forevermore.

Psalm 16:11

As Christians, we believe that Jesus is God. When we wonder what God is like, we can simply look to Jesus to get a glimpse of God's identity. Sure, there's a lot about God that will always remain a mystery or be beyond our own understanding. But Jesus is as close as we can get. In following Jesus, we are following the way of God.

In our psalm for today, the psalmist writes, "You show me the path of life." That's a pretty good way to describe the Christian life. Jesus led us on a path of love, service, humility, hospitality, justice, and freedom. Walking this path leads us into such joy, such fullness of life. It is, quite simply, the best way to live.

Courageous Christ, help me to walk in your ways and to offer my hands in service and love. Amen.

Kate S. Forer

APRIL 30

PSALM 80:1–2, 8–19

The One at Your Right Hand

But let your hand be upon the one at your right
hand,
the one whom you made strong for yourself.
Then we will never turn back from you;
give us life, and we will call on your name.

Psalm 80:17–18

The New Testament speaks often of the risen Lord Jesus seated at the right hand of God (Luke 22:69; Acts 7:55; Rom. 8:34). The Apostles' Creed—one of the earliest confessions of the church—proclaims that Jesus ascended into heaven and is seated at God's right hand.

What difference do these words make to us? The psalmist suggests that we can take comfort from the fact that God holds Jesus closely and firmly. Just as God holds fast to Christ, we know that Christ, in turn, holds fast to us.

There are times when all of us will feel weak or frightened, ashamed or sad. But at *all* times, God is with us in Christ—and the love of God through Christ will never let us go.

Eternal God, help us remember that we are not alone. Amen.

Christine Chakoian

MAY 1

HEBREWS 11:29–12:2

Not Alone

Therefore, since we are surrounded by so great a cloud of witnesses, let us also lay aside every weight and the sin that clings so closely, and let us run with perseverance the race that is set before us.

Hebrews 12:1

Somctimes life brings extraordinary challenges, such as grave illness, financial trials, or broken relationships. Political unrest, economic upheaval, or natural disasters can also upend everything familiar in our lives.

When we go through unsettling times, it helps to remember that we are accompanied in prayer by brothers and sisters in faith, and we are surrounded by the faithful who have gone before us. When they faced immense challenges, they did not give up, nor did they try to overcome their distress alone. Instead, they turned to faith to see them through, trusting that God was with them all along. Jesus himself endured the cross by persevering in faith—knowing that suffering and shame were never the last word.

Lord, help us to feel your presence and the presence of those who have gone before us. Amen.

Christine Chakoian

MAY 2

PSALM 80:1–2, 8–19

Imploring God

Turn again, O God of hosts;
look down from heaven, and see;
have regard for this vine,
the stock that your right hand planted.

Psalm 80:14–15

My grandmother was the first to teach me not to be shy in asking for God's help. When my father had a terrible health scare, I had the privilege of praying with Grandma. I began my prayer using carefully chosen words and lofty phrases. As soon as I said "Amen," Grandma burst out with her own prayer. She begged God to intervene, recalled the many ways God had shown grace in the past, and recapped our own family's faithfulness. Grandma even reminded God of the promises God had made in Scripture. Even if my father had not survived his crisis, I have no doubt that Grandma would have trusted that God heard every word she said.

This psalm is a wonderful example of passionate and fearless intercessory prayer. Precisely when we are at our wit's end, when we have no certainty of the outcome of our loved ones' fate, Scripture urges us to implore God boldly.

O God, you have been with us all along. Bring life again to us now. Amen.

Christine Chakoian

MAY 3

ISAIAH 5:1–7

God's Housecleaning

He expected justice,
but saw bloodshed;
righteousness,
but heard a cry!

Isaiah 5:7b

In difficult times, we can be dumbfounded about how we got into this situation. Sometimes, there is no one at fault; an unpreventable illness emerges, or a storm crashes onto our home. At other times, we can point fingers at others whose corruption, selfishness, or deceit caused calamity and hurt.

But sometimes, we come face-to-face with our own role in disasters, large or small. We discover the ways in which we have failed God. God leads us to see the ways we have neglected justice and have been complicit in suffering. God leads us to hear the voices of those who cry from neglect, despair, and hunger, pushed away from hope by our own unrighteousness. When these painful truths emerge about the impact of our choices, it can be tempting to turn away from God in shame. Even in our failure, God's love does not abandon us. God longs for us to reach out with love in Christ, whose name we bear.

Loving God, open our eyes to the ways our choices harm others. Amen.

Christine Chakoian

MAY 4

LUKE 12:49–56

Painful Divisions

Do you think that I have come to bring peace to the earth? No, I tell you, but rather division!

Luke 12:51

I hate conflict. I cringe whenever people hurt each other's feelings, even unintentionally. But sometimes, fights are unavoidable and can be inspired by faith.

Jesus warns us that following him can sow seeds of division, even in families. Today, just as in biblical times, Jesus' ways do not always conform to our social or religious norms. For example, those who embrace compassion for the bankrupt or drug addicted can be rejected by others who want eye-for-an-eye justice. Those who welcome refugees and immigrants can be rejected by those who want to protect our land at any cost.

Not all battles are worth fighting. In our fraught political environment, it is sometimes wise to set down our differences and seek peace. Yet Christ warns us that there are times when we must pray for discernment and find courage to speak the truth in love (Eph. 4:15).

Dear God, guide us on how to speak the truth in love. Amen.

Christine Chakoian

MAY 5

PSALM 80:1–2, 8–19

God's Welcome Arms

Restore us, O LORD God of hosts;
let your face shine, that we may be saved.

Psalm 80:19

When the news around us feels relentlessly grim and our feelings grow gloomy, everything we do begins to feel pointless.

Precisely at times like these, the psalmist invites us back into prayerful relationship with God. Whatever our feelings, they are welcome at the throne of grace. Whatever our circumstances, they are not invisible to God. Whatever our fears, they are already known in God's heart. We are urged to return home to God's welcome arms.

As we turn to God again, we discover once more that we may have forgotten how God's light "shines in the darkness, and the darkness did not overcome it" (John 1:5). God's face still shines with love. And that resilient love, which planted life in us in the first place, has the power to restore us to life once more.

God of light, when we are wilting in the darkness,
restore us to your life once more. Amen.

Christine Chakoian

MAY 6

HEBREWS 11:29–12:2

A Legacy of Faith

Yet all these, though they were commended for their faith, did not receive what was promised, since God had provided something better so that they would not, apart from us, be made perfect.

Hebrews 11:39–40

We are not the first to face challenges; the "cloud of witnesses" that came before us endured untold hardships (12:1). Their witness continues to encourage us: as they persevered through their own difficulties with faith, so can we. Indeed, they surround us still and urge us on with courage.

Yet it is not only sympathy that they provide us; for it is the very legacy of their faith that we carry, and the fruits of their labor are in our hands now. As the writer of Hebrews testifies, "they would not, apart from us, be made *perfect*"—or better translated, "complete." The saints' efforts cannot be fulfilled without our own, and we, in turn, will pass along the work in progress of God's reign until Christ comes again. Until then, the messy, sacred work of faith is ours to do. Thank God that we do not do this work alone and that its completion rests in Christ's strong hands.

Gracious God, strengthen us to carry on with courage, for the sake of all your saints. Amen.

Christine Chakoian

MAY 7

JEREMIAH 1:4–10

You Are Not Your Labels

Then I said, "Ah, Lord GOD! Truly I do not know how to speak, for I am only a boy." But the LORD said to me,
"Do not say, 'I am only a boy.'"

Jeremiah 1:6–7a

When our son was born, we painted his walls blue. When our daughter was born, we painted her walls pink and purple. Should we be surprised that our boy likes blue and our girl likes purple? Labels like "girls" and "boys" are laden with expectations. Sometimes we embrace these expectations and conclude that they define us.

The word *only* can become yet another label. Jeremiah believed he didn't qualify for prophet work because he was "*only* a boy." Perhaps Jeremiah had been trained to believe that children shouldn't talk during worship or ask questions about faith, so he bought into the "only" talk.

I have a lot of "I am only" phrases policing my dreams and curiosity. But God negates these negative inner voices, as he did with Jeremiah.

How about you? How do you fill in this blank?: "I am only a______." What might God have to say about your self-imposed label?

Lord, empower us to be the disciples you call us to be. Amen.

Samuel Son

MAY 8

JEREMIAH 1:4–10

More than Our Citizenship

See, today I appoint you over nations and over kingdoms,
to pluck up and to pull down,
to destroy and to overthrow,
to build and to plant."

Jeremiah 1:10

Our need to belong is so great that we often choose conformity over the truth. Even a self-proclaimed individualist can succumb to the ideas of a mindless mob, as was seen in the German intellectuals who joined Nazism.

When Jeremiah's prophetic words against Judah's fleecing of the poor were deemed unpatriotic, he was pushed down a well. As the son of a priest, Jeremiah had his familial identity intertwined with his state identity. So where did Jeremiah get the courage and perspective to speak against his country?

God uprooted Jeremiah's identity from the soil of family and statehood and re-rooted his identity in God's action and God's calling. A Christian is one who is appointed "over nations and over kingdoms."

I began this devotion by noting how much we love to belong. A Christian *belongs* to God, so a Christian can speak God's truth, no matter the cost.

Lord, help me to remember that I am, first and always, your child and servant. Amen.

Samuel Son

MAY 9

PSALM 71:1–6

Trusting God

For you, O Lord, are my hope,
my trust, O LORD, from my youth.
Upon you I have leaned from my birth;
it was you who took me from my mother's womb.

Psalm 71:5–6

Trust is not learned; it is instinctual. We survive our infancy because of our instinct to trust. For example, a baby trusts its mother to provide life-giving milk. You might say that we are born with our hearts and mouths wide open.

Sometimes we trust too much. A study out of England showed that seven out of nine children, though diligently taught not to trust strangers, followed an unknown adult out of the playground.* Kids default to trust.

Our ability to trust is instinctual, but the object of our trust can sometimes be misplaced. In today's reading, the psalmist speaks of re-centering trust in the Lord. We can make no mistake in trusting God, who rescued us after we trusted the wrong things. The psalmist declares God's righteousness, that is, God's inclination to make things right.

Lord, today I trust you above all else. Amen.

Samuel Son

*Adam Withnall, "Stranger Danger: Chilling TV Experiment Shows 7 of 9 Children Leave with Adult They Don't Know," *The Independent*, September 4, 2013, US edition.

MAY 10

Psalm 71:1–6

Praising God to Know God

Upon you I have leaned from my birth;
it was you who took me from my mother's womb.
My praise is continually of you.

Psalm 71:6

Scripture frequently underscores the power of words to shape our worlds, such as God creating with words in Genesis 1, Adam naming the animals paraded before him, and the Word becoming flesh in John 1.

The psalmist knows that the only way he could lean into the reality of God's faithfulness is to speak words of praise. Just as we experience love by declaring love, the psalmist also understands God's trustworthiness by praising God's faithfulness. Understanding requires this kind of commitment and intimacy.

St. Augustine said, "I believe in order to understand."* He spoke these words, and many others, to express his faith in Christ crucified. God's Word, the psalmist's words, and St. Augustine's words all inspire our word and witness to the God we love.

Lord, I praise you for your great love today. Amen.

Samuel Son

*Saint Augustine of Hippo, *De Trinitate* (Venice: Paganinus de Paganinis, 1489), VIII, 10; X, 24.

MAY 11

HEBREWS 12:18–29

Sacrifice Speaks God's Word

. . . and to God the judge of all, and to the spirits of the righteous made perfect, and to Jesus, the mediator of a new covenant, and to the sprinkled blood that speaks a better word than the blood of Abel.

Hebrews 12:23b–24

The final seconds of Abel's life must have been horrifying. Death on its own is harrowing enough. But imagine that the last face you see is that of your brother, whom you loved and trusted, as he murders you.

Jesus was also murdered. He was sold for silver coins, deserted by friends, and betrayed by his people to the cruelest Roman execution. The death of Jesus is as tragic as Abel's. But, as this Scripture states, Jesus' shed blood spoke a better word. Death couldn't silence the Word of God, and Jesus' sacrificial death declared a new covenant. Jesus' death issued an invitation into a kingdom that no earthly fiefdoms could defeat.

To say Jesus' blood speaks a better word is also to say that Abel's death had a word, as do the deaths of everyone killed by unjust violence. God hears the words and cries of his people and speaks for them. Likewise, God notices the small daily sacrifices we make in God's name.

Lord, speak for those whose lives were cut short by violence. Amen.

Samuel Son

MAY 12

LUKE 13:10–17

Removing the Blinders of Prejudice

And just then there appeared a woman with a spirit that had crippled her for eighteen years. She was bent over and was quite unable to stand up straight. When Jesus saw her, he called her over and said, "Woman, you are set free from your ailment."

Luke 13:11–12

When my wife got pregnant with our third child, we decided to finally buy a minivan. As soon as we got our minivan, we began to notice other minivans wherever we went. I thought, "When did everyone start buying minivans!" The truth is that our brains can't interpret all the images entering our eyes, so they do some filtering. We see only what we deem important. In my case—minivans!

Jesus saw the woman whom no one else saw because she was important to him. Most people didn't see this woman because she wasn't a person who could put any shine on their reputation. The leaders even blamed her, which is a telltale sign of prejudice.

Evidently, not only does what we see reveal what's in our brains, but also what we see reveals what's in our hearts. I wonder how many people we don't see because of our prejudices and, subsequently, how many healings we miss.

Lord, help me to see today those whom I did not see yesterday. Amen.

Samuel Son

MAY 13

LUKE 13:10–17

Courageously Choosing Compassion

When he said this, all his opponents were put to shame; and the entire crowd was rejoicing at all the wonderful things that he was doing.

Luke 13:17

Today we read the story of Jesus healing a "crippled woman" on the Sabbath. The religious leaders, already suspicious of Jesus' power, try to nail him on a technicality. He performed this healing on the wrong day of the week. Jesus pushes back, pointing out that suffering must be attended to whenever it occurs. His words shame the leaders.

The crowd whooped joyously when Jesus laid a major put-down on his opponents. At first, it seems as if the crowd is displaying *schadenfreude*, which means deriving pleasure from another's humiliation. But read the passage again. The people rejoice not at his put-downs but at "the wonderful things" Jesus was doing.

Jesus' courageous act liberated both a woman in need and the crowd who witnessed the event. They rejoiced in God's glory.

Merciful God, may I focus on your love rather than on another's sin. Amen.

Samuel Son

MAY 14

EZEKIEL 37:1–14

The Church That Came Alive

"I will put my spirit within you, and you shall live, and I will place you on your own soil; then you shall know that I, the LORD, have spoken and will act," says the LORD.

Ezekiel 37:14

"It's a dying church," the committee told me. "Your job is to help them close gracefully." What I found in that church, however, was not a discouraged but a determined Holy Spirit that declared, "Not yet!" But how could that Spirit, so apparent in this small congregation, be expressed?

"Let's invite our presbytery of 110 churches to hold their quarterly meeting here and show them hospitality like they've never experienced before!" somebody said. So that's what we did. There were moments of panic as the date for our presbytery meeting drew closer. More than two hundred people would be coming, although the sanctuary seated only one hundred. Those who trust our Lord, however, discover that our Lord provides, in our case via folding chairs. Everyone packed our sanctuary that day, and the meeting was a big success. Dry bones came to life. The church has not been the same since.

Lord, may we never underestimate your enlivening Spirit. Amen.

Bill Heck

MAY 15

Acts 2:5–18

Prayers of Laughter

"Indeed, these are not drunk, as you suppose, for it is only nine o'clock in the morning."

Acts 2:15

Our support group for those dealing with mental illness met on the first Monday of every month. We often started with a *lectio divina* approach to a Scripture passage. Each person listened for a particular word or phrase in the passage that stood out for them. We'd all had some painful experiences in life and were always looking for a word of hope. Often we found it in Scripture. After we listened to the passage read three times, we each explained how we thought the Spirit was speaking to us that evening.

We had some fascinating discussions and shared some very personal stories. What was surprising, however, was that rather than burdening our group with sorrow and worry, the personal sharing often lead to freedom and laughter. I sometimes wondered if anyone who happened to pass by our meeting place and heard our laughter would question, like those witnesses to the day of Pentecost, "Are they drunk?" No one ever stuck their head in to ask what exactly we were up to. But if they did, thanks to St. Peter, I had a ready reply, "No! We're not drunk. We are just rejoicing in the Spirit of God."

Lord, we offer you today our prayers of laughter. Amen.

Bill Heck

MAY 16

ROMANS 8:22–27

Joyful Groaning

We know that the whole creation has been groaning in labor pains until now. . . . We ourselves, who have the first fruits of the Spirit, groan inwardly while we wait for adoption, the redemption of our bodies.

Romans 8:22–23

It may seem silly to groan over a tomato seed. Yet that is what I find myself doing every spring. I plant those tomato seeds in small pots of soil, add water, and set them in a sunny place on my patio. Every day I inspect them, as though that might speed up their birth process. Then, when they finally begin poking out of the soil, gently bent and ready to uncurl, I catch myself groaning, joyfully groaning, in anticipation. At last, new life is emerging!

I do not know if Paul ever grew tomatoes. But I understand his anticipation and every soul's anticipation for the new life, joy, and freedom of Christ's Spirit as it emerges in our lives. This new life in Christ cannot just be intellectually grasped; it has to be experienced. There may be no better way of expressing this emergence than to see this Spirit being born in us each day. Are you looking for the evidence of Christ's Spirit emerging in your life today? Are you groaning in anticipation?

Lord, hear our prayers of anticipation and satisfy our longing for new life. Amen.

Bill Heck

MAY 17

EZEKIEL 37:1–14

Bag of Bones

He said to me, "Mortal, can these bones live?" I answered, "O Lord GOD, you know."

Ezekiel 37:3

She was just a bag of bones lying there on my front porch. The only sign of life was her tail thumping against the wooden floor. Such a pathetic brown dog with sores covering her skin, yet she had such a kind face. She won my heart. First came a good meal and then a bath. For a whole month, I fattened her up and treated her sores until nothing showed on her coat except small, smooth scars. We became good friends.

Living alone at that time in a rural setting, I was glad to have a protector who barked when strangers approached the yard. I was grateful to have a friend who chased the critters out of my garden. Whenever we took a walk, she became so excited chasing a squirrel up a tree or flushing birds out of the tall grass. I never ceased to marvel about how what was once a bag of bones, like the field Ezekiel saw, could become so full of vibrant life. Praise be to God, who breathes new life into us all.

What will you reveal today, Lord, that we might witness your Spirit of life? Amen.

Bill Heck

MAY 18

JOHN 15:26–27

Spirit of Truth

"When the Advocate comes, whom I will send to you from the Father, the Spirit of truth who comes from the Father, he will testify on my behalf."

John 15:26

Times when I have been taken by surprise, embarrassed in my unpreparedness, and stammering in my response to unexpected situations are sometimes the moments when I have been most truthful. How can that be?

As Jesus prepares to leave his disciples and wants to entrust them with his ministry, he tells them not to worry when they find themselves in a difficult situation and are at a loss for words. Jesus explains that there will be a Spirit of Truth, his own spirit, that they can trust to speak through them. I have always tried to be prepared, but life has taught me how difficult, if not impossible, this can be sometimes. There are always surprises, no matter how thoroughly I prepare. So I am hoping I might learn to be more relaxed. I hope I might learn to put more trust in the One who works within and around me. I trust Christ's Spirit will help me find the right words to say and the courage to do what I must do whenever life surprises me.

Lord, help me, help us all, to trust you, our Spirit of Truth. Amen.

Bill Heck

MAY 19

ACTS 2:5–13

One Language

All of them were filled with the Holy Spirit and began to speak in other languages, as the Spirit gave them ability. . . . And at this sound the crowd gathered and was bewildered, because each one heard them speaking in the native language of each.

Acts 2:4, 6

I expected it to be a struggle when I went to worship as an English-speaking Presbyterian in a Spanish-speaking Pentecostal church. So I was relieved to hear the pastor say that the service would be testimony in song. Each member stood before the congregation and sang beautifully. I sat enthralled until I heard the pastor call my name.

I panicked and politely declined. But the good pastor was not easily dissuaded. "This is how we give glory to our Lord, Brother Bill. Just give us *one* song?" I could not refuse. I'd never felt more desperate. I searched my anxious mind for anything appropriate, and after a long pause, I decided on "Just a Closer Walk." I made it through one verse and started the chorus when I sensed a stirring in the congregation. They were singing with me. I sang in English, they in Spanish, but we were all speaking one language: the language of faith. It was truly a pentecostal moment.

Free us, Lord, to speak the language that all your children understand. Amen.

Bill Heck

MAY 20

JOHN 3:1–10

Beyond Our Control

Nicodemus said to him, "How can anyone be born after having grown old? Can one enter a second time into the mother's womb and be born?"

John 3:4

Whatever you may think of Nicodemus, you have to admire his persistence. He struggles to understand this *strange*, uncontrollable Spirit who Jesus describes. It must have been extremely challenging for Nicodemus, a well-educated, highly respected, deeply religious man. I believe he wants to make this Spirit fit into his life but can't. Yet he never gives up on Jesus. Nicodemus's soul seems to long for what his mind cannot quite grasp. I hope we might show this same persistence in faith as we follow the impulse of our own souls. It is tempting to shy away when challenging new scriptural truths appear in a passage we thought we understood. Yet how can we? If we really trust this Spirit who is intent on constantly surprising us and offering us rebirth, don't we have to trust Christ's Spirit in Scripture more than our own interpretation? Don't we have to live with discomfort sometimes as we await whatever new thing God is creating in our lives?

Lord, grant us persistence and the willingness to be reborn. Amen.

Bill Heck

MAY 21

MATTHEW 13:3–4

Listen!

"Listen! A sower went out to sow."

Matthew 13:3b

How often do we fail to just listen? A child clamors for our attention, but we are on our smartphone, addicted to the glowing screen. A relative wants to talk, but we are too busy to stay very long. A neighbor has information to share, but we walk away. Listening with attentiveness is a rarity these days. And yet, Jesus calls us first to listen if we are to really hear, understand, and then integrate his Word.

We live in a culture of constant distraction that interferes with our ability to hear. If we do not hear, we cannot listen, and if we do not listen, we cannot live in new ways. I find that parables such as this one, which are so familiar, oftentimes get glossed over and fail to receive our deep attention. So this week, let us go deep into this one parable as a way of meeting Jesus again. As you listen attentively to this parable, how can you tune in in new ways? How can you open not just your ears but your soul, your mind, and your heart to the Spirit?

Help me to hear your voice, O God who is always speaking. Amen.

Shannan Vance-Ocampo

MAY 22

MATTHEW 13:5–7

Unsustainable

"Other seeds fell among thorns, and the thorns grew up and choked them."

Matthew 13:7

The parable of the Sower is told in agrarian language and metaphor to speak to the listeners in the time of Jesus. Today, most of us are not farmers, and we are cut off from land and soil, the daily rhythms of growing food from the ground. The portion of the parable to focus on for today tells of two places the seeds are unsustainable. There is rocky, poor soil that leads to lanky, shallow-rooted plants that die when the sun first hits them. And there are thorns that choke the plants before they can make their way above the soil line.

There is a reason plants create so many seeds: nature knows that not every seed will make it. Last season, I decided to save seeds from some of the plants I grew in my garden, and I was amazed to find out just how many seeds come from the head of one flower. The abundance shocked and surprised me. I am planning to grow them this year, and I wonder how many will make it. Will my soil and preparations be enough?

Help me to believe in your goodness, O God who is always providing abundance. Amen.

Shannan Vance-Ocampo

MAY 23

MATTHEW 13:8

Fertile

". . . some a hundredfold, some sixty, some thirty."

Matthew 13:8b

How do you get good soil for growing? Last year I went to a farming conference that spent a lot of time focused on soil preparation. The premise is that the earth, our soil, is sick from pollution, pesticides, and general neglect. If the soil is rebuilt, not only will plants prosper, grow, and produce, but also the earth will be healed. I oftentimes wonder to myself, "What does it mean that we have willingly harmed the earth, the creation?"

Jesus talks about good soil; God provides the good creation. Shouldn't our primary focus be making sure soil remains "good" so that people will be fed, abundance will be shared, and the creation can live into its purpose of stunning diversity and beauty? How can good soil remind us of the intricate bounty that God offers everyone and everything? What is the quality of the soil around you? Is it healthy? Is it fertile? Is it ready for seeds? How can you find the answers to these questions?

Help me, O Creating God, to care for the earth and its precious soil. Amen.

Shannan Vance-Ocampo

MAY 24

MATTHEW 13:9, 18

Hear!

"Let anyone with ears listen!"

Matthew 13:9

If we read through Matthew 13 without skipping verses 10–17, which is what the lectionary this week would have us do, we would hear Jesus explain why he uses parables to explain God's Word: it is so that the listeners pay closer attention! Jesus notices that most people do not listen fully or see completely. A parable is told to create an environment of both listening and seeing. It isn't meant to be easy; it's meant to be challenging so that listeners have to pay more attention. A parable is about holy imagination that allows us to tune into what the Spirit would have us know. As you go through your day today, how can you encounter your experiences like a parable—how can you both listen and see? How can deeper and even repetitious attentiveness change what you see and what you hear? Do you encounter something new? Does something routine gain greater significance? At the end of the day, what did you notice? Where did the Spirit show up?

Guide me, O God, to listen and to see with new ears and new eyes. Amen.

Shannan Vance-Ocampo

MAY 25

MATTHEW 13:19–21

Taken

"Yet such a person has no root . . ."

Matthew 13:21a

I have a book that I consult for my backyard gardening that has a page in it with illustrations of different sorts of root systems. Some are shallow and interconnected, creating their own sort of strength. Others are deep, searching for nutrients and water at all depths of the soils. Root systems for annual and perennial plants are different. There are old trees in my yard that have impressive root systems. When I encounter them, they always cause me to rethink where I am about to plant something. Some plants grow underground for a season or two before anything is evident above ground. Roots are not one-size-fits-all.

This makes me wonder about this parable as it relates to the spiritual roots of people. Oftentimes we get caught up by thinking we have to "root" ourselves spiritually in the same way those around us do. Maybe each of us has different spiritual roots, of different sizes, qualities, and needs. Perhaps we need different systems of roots for different seasons of life. No matter what, we need roots. Because without a root system, we are starved and unfed.

O Lord, help me to grow strong roots that reach out for you. Amen.

Shannan Vance-Ocampo

MAY 26

MATTHEW 13:20–22

Empty

". . . it yields nothing."

Matthew 13:22c

Sometimes, nothing grows. Sometimes, nothing prospers. This is hard for us to hear in the North American cultural context in which growth at all costs is prized. As a pastor, I oftentimes hear stories of emptiness. The marriage that doesn't make it. The pregnancy that ends in unspeakable loss. The diagnosis that cannot be fixed. The relationship that harms rather than heals. Not all lack of growth is explainable. Some things just are.

I don't have good answers for these situations; I am not sure anyone does. Platitudes are not helpful. The only thing that can heal in these moments is presence and care. But what about the times when growth of one kind leads to death and destruction of another? I am sitting with grief these days about how the harm being done to God's creation is willful and intentional, done in the name of economic growth. How are we meant to live as people of God when this sort of willful death is around us? As we encounter this ecological parable this week, what are we called to? What sort of faithful and healing "sowing" are we called to pursue?

Living Lord, grow in me a new beginning. Amen.

Shannan Vance-Ocampo

MAY 27

MATTHEW 13:23

Ready

". . . in one case a hundredfold, in another sixty, and in another thirty."

Matthew 13:23b

An abundant harvest is a beautiful thing. But it does not happen on its own. It is the result of countless weeks of hard work, preparation, and, oftentimes, prayer. As the month draws to an end, what new ways of hearing this parable have come to you? Has the spiritual preparation been different or new? Did something strike you differently? In the past year, my personal spiritual practice has been to get outside more. Like most people in our culture today, I am too often trapped inside. I am reminded, as I listen to this parable, that Jesus told it while outside. If we are disconnected from the land, how much are we disconnected from being able to hear and understand the parables of Jesus? The more time I spend outside, the more I find that my devotional reading of the Word has changed. The harvest of spiritual growth takes time, attention, and sometimes a change in scenery. What do you need to do at the end of this month so that the harvest is new?

God of abundance, help me to change so that I can see and hear anew. Amen.

Shannan Vance-Ocampo

MAY 28

ISAIAH 43:1–7

I've Found Where I Belong

Bring my sons from far away
and my daughters from the end of the earth.

Isaiah 43:6b

A large group of us from the church gathered at the airport to welcome our new refugee family from Sierra Leone. They thought only one person would be there to greet them, but when they saw all of us with balloons, gifts, and signs of greeting, they felt they had finally found refuge from the storm. We drove them directly to our church's fellowship hall for their first meal. Then the mother, Phebian, said words that made me cry: "Now, [for the first time in three years], I no longer feel like a refugee; I've found where I belong."

Three days later was Mother's Day. "This is a new beginning for our church," I said. "In the Mende language, the word for home is *payla*. Let us all now turn toward this beloved family and say to them, 'Payla!'" And as we did so, our church home became a more holy home, with arms as wide as Christ.

May our faith be enriched by the stories of your deliverance, as told by the people you bring us. Amen.

Hope Harle-Mould

MAY 29

MARK 1:35–39

Holy Interruptions

And Simon and his companions hunted for him [Jesus]. When they found him, they said to him, "Everyone is searching for you."

Mark 1:36–37

A mentor once told me, "Pay attention to the interruptions." They are the cracks in our daily routine through which God can pry open fresh thoughts, connect us face-to-face with new people, or revitalize us.

One day a woman stopped by the church and asked how I was doing. I told her how pressured and busy I was at this particular time of year, with many projects and tasks to keep in motion. Her immediate response was to begin telling me a story.

"Mother Teresa and a few sisters from her order were once traveling by train. It was a frustrating trip because the trains were running behind schedule. As they were switching to their final train, one of the sisters came and reported, 'Mother, they've just announced that our train will be delayed for four hours!' Without hesitation, Mother Teresa brought out a book from within her robe and calmly said, 'We are blessed that God has seen fit to give us the gift of these four hours.'"

God, give us eyes to recognize your divine redirections in our lives. Amen.

Hope Harle-Mould

MAY 30

PSALM 23

If God Wanted Me to Have an Animal . . .

I shall not want.

Psalm 23:1b

One of the members in my church lost her husband just three years before I became pastor there. While the woman was grieving, her daughter suggested, "Why don't you get a cat or dog to keep you company?" The mother replied, "Look, if the Lord wanted me to have an animal, the Lord would provide an animal!"

When summer came, the congregation held Sunday worship outside under a large tent, as was their custom. The pastor warned that a stray cat had been recently noticed hanging around the church. Sure enough, during the service, the cat appeared, walking up the aisle. During the sermon, the cat came right up to the woman who lost her husband and leaped onto her lap. The woman looked at the cat. The cat looked at her. When the benediction came, the woman took the cat home and named it Pumpkin.

We receive more than we ask for from God, who gives us more than we can imagine. God can even herd cats!

Thank you for answering our prayers with your unpredicted providence of more! Amen.

Hope Harle-Mould

MAY 31

MARK 10:35–45

No Self-Service

"But whoever wishes to become great among you must be your servant, and whoever wishes to be first among you must be slave of all."

Mark 10:43b–44

Each one serves one. I learned this from my father, who was also a pastor. After the words of institution, Dad gave the plates of bread to the elders to distribute to the people. When they returned, Dad would serve each of the elders.

When I became a minister, I made each-one-serve-one a tradition of mine as well.

But on one particular Sunday in my former church, one of the six servers made a mistake. After returning from serving the congregation, he helped himself to a piece of bread before giving his plate to me to put on the Communion table. He had failed to notice that with the final plate, I always serve the other servers.

I whispered to the server, "There's no self-service in Christ's church." Smiling, I invited him to receive a *new* piece of bread, one made sacramental by how it was given and how it was received, from one servant of all to another servant of all, each one serving one.

Help us put your parables of servanthood into practice. Amen.

Hope Harle-Mould

JUNE 1

JOHN 13:31–35

See How They Love One Another

"By this everyone will know that you are my disciples, if you have love for one another."

John 13:35

I was watching a recording of one of our church's worship services. After enjoying the anthem and children' message, I started to fast forward to the sermon. But before doing so, I paused and watched more intently. Something astonishing caught my eye—the passing of the peace.

At first the scene just resembled scattered chaos—shaking of hands, chitchatting. But then people just couldn't stay in their pews. The aisle filled up with friendliness and micro-miracles unfolded.

One parishioner walked way up to the front to greet someone in a wheelchair. Another crossed over to an elderly person, and they laughed together. On the far aisle, a child was lifted up and actually passed around! Yet another member sought out someone who I knew had been newly diagnosed with a serious illness. The two spoke intently and then embraced.

It was said of the early church by outsiders, "See how they love one another!" At our church, we simply call it the passing of the peace.

Teach us how to love each other, and fill us with the joy divine. Amen.

Hope Harle-Mould

JUNE 2

Mark 12:41–44

The Widow's Pledge

A poor widow came and put in two small copper coins, which are worth a penny.

Mark 12:42

When I was growing up, my Presbyterian minister father never revealed to us how much money anyone in the congregation gave to the church. Except once.

Ruth Spencer was an active member of our church. I could tell from visiting their home that Ruth's husband didn't make a lot of money at his job. But he and Ruth were active in the life of our church.

One day out of the blue, Mr. Spencer died and Ruth was left with two young sons to raise. In the fall of that year, the church began its annual stewardship drive. My father assured Ruth that she needn't feel any pressure to keep her pledge at the same level. When the pledges came in, Ruth Spencer had *increased* her pledge, despite—or perhaps because of—all she had been through.

Of all the people in that church who could have easily afforded to give more, it was this woman who lifted her devotion to Christ to a new level.

She has lifted my devotion to Christ ever since.

May your faithful widows among us stir us to give with joyful abandon. Amen.

Hope Harle-Mould

JUNE 3

LUKE 14:7–14

Spaghetti Dinner

But when you give a banquet, invite the poor, the crippled, the lame, and the blind. And you will be blessed, because they cannot repay you."

Luke 14:13–14a

Sharon decided *not* to go to our church's spaghetti dinner. How could she? Her cousin's son had just died by suicide. But then she changed her mind: *I did sign up to help in the kitchen, but most of all, Sue's counting on me, and I won't let her down.* (Six weeks earlier, Sue had had a heart bypass.)

Sharon showed up to help but told no one the sorrow in her heart. The kitchen volunteers were efficient, happy-go-lucky, and friendly. Half the evening was gone before Sharon realized she was having fun. For the first time in a long time, she had been able *not* to think about her cousin's heartbreaking situation.

That Sunday I told the congregation: "We thought we were putting on a fundraiser for our church. We didn't realize that we were *being* the church, serving up heaps of hope and healing—along with a lot of pasta."

Dear God, bless this food to our health and us to thy service. Amen.

Hope Harle-Mould

JUNE 4

GENESIS 1:1–2:4A

Sabbath: The Gift of God

And on the seventh day God finished the work that he had done, and he rested on the seventh day from all the work that he had done.

Genesis 2:2

For those of us who live in the northern hemisphere, June is the beginning of summer, a long-awaited season of warmth after a long winter. June also marks the approach of summer vacations, which offer a break from regular work and busy lives. When we take vacations, we practice Sabbath, a pause from regular work. In Canada, summer often finds us playing in the wilderness.

After creating the world, God rested. God took a Sabbath. God's creatures did their reproductive and generative work, bearing fruit and multiplying, and resting too.

We need rest so that we can do our work as stewards of God's creation. The meaning of *dominion* (1:28) is not the same as *dominate*. It means taking responsibility over all creatures: tending to them, caring for them, being stewards in the midst of serious issues like climate change. Let us rekindle our God-given vocation of being stewards of all creation.

God, help us become faithful stewards. Amen.

HyeRan Kim-Cragg

JUNE 5

PSALM 8

The Majestic Wonder of God's Creation

O LORD, our Sovereign,
how majestic is your name in all the earth!

Psalm 8:9

One of the joys of listening to or singing old hymns is the precious memories they evoke. This is particularly true of hymns we learned in our childhood. Such hymns are formative for our theology and faith in ways that can last a lifetime.

"How Great Thou Art" is one such hymn I learned when I was young. This hymn is based on Psalm 8. I do not actually remember how young I was when I heard the hymn for the first time. I do not think I memorized the lyrics right away. I certainly did not analyze the theology behind it. What I do remember, however, is the majestic feeling I had as I heard the tune and hummed along. It made me shiver with awe. The music of this hymn captured the awesomeness of God and the beauty of God's creation. This hymn still gives me shivers.

Let us sing this hymn as we celebrate God's presence and our place in the world. Hallelujah!

HyeRan Kim-Cragg

JUNE 6

2 Corinthians 13:11–13

Holy Kiss

Greet one another with a holy kiss. All the saints greet you.

2 Corinthians 13:12

Have you ever greeted one another with a holy kiss? For those of us from socially conservative cultures, the apostle Paul's advice is puzzling. Even for those of us living in a liberal Western culture, it is not easy to imagine a holy kiss between strangers in a church.

Hugging is one thing, but a holy kiss? No way!

Paul's advice about a holy kiss was dispensed to a conflict-filled church in Corinth. People quarreled, and the community suffered from divisions. No wonder Paul advocated for a sign of reconciliation. Knowing this, we begin to appreciate the truth that faith is not an abstract, disembodied idea but a living, breathing conviction that requires a vulnerable yet bold physical action. After all, we are Christians who believe in God through Jesus, the Word made flesh. Through the voice of Paul, God also asks us to enact signs of peace.

Incarnate God, empower us to live in peace. Amen.

HyeRan Kim-Cragg

JUNE 7

2 Corinthians 13:11–13

God Is Three in One

The grace of the Lord Jesus Christ, the love of God, and the communion of the Holy Spirit be with all of you.

2 Corinthians 13:13

Can you find the Trinity in the Bible? The first answer is yes, because the Trinitarian formula is found in 2 Corinthians 13:13, the farewell of Paul: "The grace of the Lord Jesus Christ, the love of God, and the communion of the Holy Spirit be with all of you." Such a formula is also found as a part of Jesus' last commandment: Baptizing "in the name of the Father and of the Son and of the Holy Spirit" (Matt. 28:19).

The second answer is no, because the exact word never appears in the Bible. The doctrine of the Trinity emerged hundreds of years after the Bible was written by our ancestors in the Christian faith. Due to the Trinity's enigmatic nature, our neighbors in other religions ask, "Do you believe in one God or three?" The answer may be both yes and no again. In the logic of faith, God is three in one and God is one in three. On a mathematical level, it does not make sense, but as a meaningful paradox, it does!

God of mystery, we celebrate trinitarian, interdependent relationships. Amen.

HyeRan Kim-Cragg

JUNE 8

MATTHEW 28:16–20

Goodbye and New Beginning

When they saw him, they worshiped him; but some doubted.

Matthew 28:17

Have you ever traveled to a mountaintop where heaven and earth seem to meet? Jesus' disciples (minus Judas) have. Eleven disciples were invited to the mountaintop so that they could witness Jesus' authority coming both from heaven and from earth. This was probably necessary because some still doubted (v. 17).

We know that they ran away when their teacher Jesus was arrested and killed. We know that they failed to accompany Jesus to the end. Indeed, they were scared and fearful of the brutal violence that Jesus and many others experienced when they challenged Roman imperial authority. They were not certain that they could accept a vocation that might cost them their lives.

We understand their feelings and anxieties, yet we also know that these fearful disciples were given a second chance. Jesus asks them to take up the cross and carry the commandment of Jesus with the blessed assurance: "Remember, I am with you always, to the end of the age" (v. 20b).

Dear God, we thank you for your promise to be with us to the end of the age. Amen.

HyeRan Kim-Cragg

JUNE 9

MATTHEW 28:16–20

The Great Commission

Go therefore and make disciples of all nations, baptizing them in the name of the Father and of the Son and of the Holy Spirit.

Matthew 28:19

The "go therefore and make disciples of all nations" commandment propelled many Christians from Europe and North America to go to other parts of the world and proselytize. This last word of Jesus in the Gospel of Matthew fueled the zeal of many Christians to undertake a so-called civilizing mission in the nineteenth century. Unfortunately, some of these missionary acts were done with an imperialistic view that others were "heathens" who were lost in darkness with little, if anything, to offer the world.

Within this type of missionary thinking, discarding one's own religious and cultural practices was prerequisite to become Christian. Some modern missionaries have adopted a cross-cultural approach that has a better understanding of the value inherent in all cultures. Many Christians today live in religiously pluralistic cultures and wrestle with how to respect other religions without losing sight of how to live out their calling as Christians. As we celebrate Trinity Sunday, let us remind ourselves of God in relationships.

God, help us build up respectful relationships with those who are different from us. Amen.

HyeRan Kim-Cragg

JUNE 10

PSALM 1

Trees

They are like trees
planted by streams of water,
which yield their fruit in its season,
and their leaves do not wither.
In all that they do, they prosper.

Psalm 1:3

The most amazing things happen when we take time to rest under trees. Try it! Feel the rough bark against your back; listen to the wind moving through the leaves; and notice the dappled sunlight through the branches. Psalm 1 reminds us that those who meditate on the law of God, including the command to rest, shall be like trees. It is only when we get to know trees that we understand what the psalm means.

This past year, Ethiopians planted 350 million trees in twelve days, smashing a world record. They took this step to mitigate climate change and rejuvenate the soil of their land. There is healing in trees. Let us find a tree, lean on it, feel its strength, and revel in its stillness.

May we bear fruit as your disciples, dear Jesus. Amen.

HyeRan Kim-Cragg

JUNE 11

JOSHUA 3:7–17

Feet First

When the soles of the feet of the priests who bear the ark of the LORD, the Lord of all the earth, rest in the waters of the Jordan, the waters of the Jordan flowing from above shall be cut off.

Joshua 3:13

God's instructions in this passage are very specific: God is ordering the priests who are carrying theark of the covenant to step into the Jordan River so that the soles of their feet are submerged. I love this! I love how there is no gray area here. God left no room for anyone to say, "Well, I'll stick one toe in. That will count." No, God is specific in instructing these priests: put both soles of both feet in the water, *and then* I will do what I will do. Both feet have to commit before God will move.

Scripture teaches us repeatedly that we need to commit, that lukewarm faith is a waste of time. Why is it still so hard, then? We live mired in the mud of the human condition, on the banks of the river we long to step into. Praise be to God that, with God's help, we can take the step we need to take! We can plunk both feet into the Jordan River and do our part in the ongoing, holy work of God.

O God, give me the courage to step on in. Thank you! Amen.

Lindy Thompson

JUNE 12

PSALM 107:1–7

We Are It

Then they cried to the LORD in their trouble,
and he delivered them from their distress;
he led them by a straight way,
until they reached an inhabited town.

Psalm 107:6–7

People come to Christianity by many ways and means. I have been a Christian my whole life, and that presents challenges of which I have to be aware. For example, if I think generically of God delivering someone from distress, if I'm not careful I might think like a child, meaning I might picture a big wind moving a person literally from a dangerous place to a safe one, or a bolt of lightning destroying an enemy—something resembling a fairy story more than the movement of God. But look at the passage. How does God save these people from distress? By sending them to—wait for it—*other people!* To an inhabited town! In this Scripture, God delivers by delivering people to each other.

We really are the hands and feet of God, friends. God trusts us that much. With God's help, we can ease one another's distress.

God, I want to be your hands and feet in this world. Show me today how you want me to help your people. Amen.

Lindy Thompson

JUNE 13

PSALM 107:33–37

The Promise of Transformation

He turns a desert into pools of water,
a parched land into springs of water.

Psalm 107:35

The writer of this psalm is making a big statement here. This individual is claiming that God will turn a desert (picture rolling sand dunes and cacti) into pools of water (picture an oasis with trees, ponds, and animals drinking) and a parched land (picture your unwatered yard in the dead of August) into springs of water (picture the same yard with springs of water bubbling out of the ground and children squealing as they splash in the puddles).

These are huge changes. One thing is becoming something entirely different; one reality is giving way to a new, completely transformed reality.

This is how God works. This is what God does. This is God's specialty: transforming, changing, drawing out the good, leading on to the new. God facilitates the emergence of something never before seen, bringing out and bringing forth.

This is the grace of God in our daily lives, in our relationships, in our communities, and in our world. Thanks be to God for this gift of grace!

O God, fulfill your promise of transformation in your world and in me. Amen.

Lindy Thompson

JUNE 14

PSALM 43

Choose Hope

Why are you cast down, O my soul,
and why are you disquieted within me?
Hope in God; for I shall again praise him,
my help and my God.

Psalm 43:5

Do you talk to yourself in your head too? For me, the running commentary never stops, and it's not always helpful. The tone of my inner monologue depends on what I have been reading or listening to lately. If I have been reading Scripture and listening to good teaching, I am more likely to be kind to myself or to give myself at least a helpful instructive word. But if I am in a phase of being short on time and long on stress, there is no telling what negative phrases will bounce around in there. I almost have to rescue myself from myself sometimes and purposefully fill my mind with the goodness of God instead of whatever happens to be replaying at the moment.

The psalmist is speaking to his own soul, seeking to discover the root of his unhappiness, and he reminds himself of the appropriate response—to once again place his hope in God. This was the solution for the psalmist, and it is the solution for us too.

God, when I struggle, remind me that my hope is in you. Amen.

Lindy Thompson

JUNE 15

MATTHEW 23:1–12

Returning to Humility

They do all their deeds to be seen by others. . . . They love to have the place of honor at banquets and the best seats in the synagogues, and to be greeted with respect in the marketplaces, and to have people call them rabbi.

Matthew 23:5–7

These verses hit many of us where we live, and they certainly speak to society at large. We receive so many messages communicating that the most important thing is to look good. Social media feeds right into this aspect of our humanity. We want the best parts of our lives to be seen by others so that they will think well of us.

Wanting to put our best foot forward and to make a good impression is not a bad thing in and of itself, but it can be a slippery slope. When we get too caught up in gaining the affirmation of others, we can lose the substance of our original goal. Jesus says, "All who exalt themselves will be humbled, and all who humble themselves will be exalted" (v. 12). Through the life of Jesus, God teaches us the value of serving others. If we want to be disciples, we will imitate Jesus and practice humility—no matter how many times we mess up and have to humbly begin again.

God, help me to focus on what you have said is important—serving others with humility. Amen.

Lindy Thompson

JUNE 16

PSALM 34:1–8

Sing Anyway

I will bless the LORD at all times;
his praise shall continually be in my mouth.
My soul makes its boast in the LORD;
let the humble hear and be glad.
O magnify the LORD with me,
and let us exalt his name together.

Psalm 34:1–3

How can I bless the Lord at all times? I already mentioned how I struggle with a constant inner monologue—how can I manage to praise God continually instead? God has provided an answer—music! Song! By singing, we can truly "bless the LORD at all times."

This is where people begin to balk and bring up their subpar singing voices—but friends, this is not a performance. This is communication with God, who made and loves us. Singing is one of the best and quickest ways to get something into your head and keep it there, and hymns are wonderful vehicles for glorifying God. Any type of music will work—whatever speaks to you and is easy to remember. There is always "Jesus Loves Me"—because he does.

God's gift to us of music and singing provides us with the perfect way to "exalt [God's] name together."

God, thank you for music. Please help me to sing a song of praise in my heart today. Amen.

Lindy Thompson

JUNE 17

1 JOHN 3:1–3

God's Child

See what love the Father has given us, that we should be called children of God; and that is what we are.

1 John 3:1

Throughout our lives, we are given names and titles and labels and identification numbers that are meant to tell us who and what we are. However, the most important aspect of our identity is stated plainly in this verse: we are children of God.

If we believe this, it is a life-changing statement. We no longer have to search for where we belong. We belong to God. We are God's children. God is our loving parent. God is where each of us started, and God is where we will end. We have our answer. We know to whom we belong.

There is nothing more important than this, and now that we know it, we are commissioned to go tell everybody. No one should live their lives not knowing to whom they belong.

The love of God encompasses all. May we, in every aspect of our living, share this love freely.

God, I am your child. Thank you for loving me. I love you too. Help me to share your love with everyone, all my life long. Amen.

Lindy Thompson

JUNE 18

Isaiah 49:1–7

God's Vision

The Lord called me before I was born,
while I was in my mother's womb he named me.

Isaiah 49:1b

George Alexander Louis is a big name for a little boy. But this little boy also has an even bigger title: His Royal Highness Prince George of Cambridge. When William and Kate, Duke and Duchess of Cambridge, welcomed their firstborn son into the world on July 22, 2013, he had a special destiny. Because of the unique family into which he was born, young George's future was ordained while he was still in his mother's womb. He would be king one day.

For most of us, life's path is laid out with a good deal less certainty. But that doesn't mean there's no plan for our lives. Isaiah reminds us that God has known us since before we were born. We spend our lives living into God's vision for us.

Lord, help me to trust your call in my life. Amen.

Carlos E. Wilton

JUNE 19

Psalm 40:1–11

God's Inclination

I waited patiently for the Lord;
he inclined to me and heard my cry.

Psalm 40:1

Long ago in elementary school science class, we learned about simple machines, such as wheel and axles, inclined planes, and pulleys. Little did we know that these simple machines could make life easier for people all over the world.

For example, anyone who navigates the world in a wheelchair understands the value not only of wheels but also of an inclined plane—a ramp—in getting around. A simple inclined plane transforms an impassable curb into a way forward.

Psalm 40 highlights the power of an incline. God inclines to us, leaning forward so that we can reach God. Such is the image used by the psalmist to depict God's accommodation to us. God listens and opens the way before us!

O God, thank you for inclining to us and hearing our cries. Amen.

Carlos E. Wilton

JUNE 20

Luke 17:11–19

Release the Joy!

Then he said to him, "Get up and go on your way; your faith has made you well."

Luke 17:19

In this story from Luke, Jesus heals ten people who have suffered from leprosy. He tells them to go show themselves to the priests to prove that they are cleansed and no longer need to be shunned by society.

After doing so, they face a question . . . what to do with the joy of their healing? Nine of those healed simply go back to living. One returns to Jesus to share the joy.

Joy is meant to be shared, especially the joy that wells up from the deep springs of our faith in those moments when we truly recognize God's goodness to us.

We can never be certain how welcome our faith sharing will be. But joy makes it easier. Who doesn't welcome the opportunity to hear of a friend's deep joy?

Holy God, may we share the joy of knowing you with someone today. Amen.

Carlos E. Wilton

JUNE 21

1 CORINTHIANS 1:1–9

In God's Good Graces

I give thanks to my God always for you because of the grace of God that has been given you in Christ Jesus.

1 Corinthians 1:4

The Greek word *charis* forms the root of our English word *charisma*. We often apply this word to politicians and movie stars who have a magnetic personality.

But back in Paul's day, folks had a different understanding for *charis*. In classical Greek, *charis* meant something like "delightful grace." In Greek mythology, Zeus has three lovely daughters, the three graces: Splendor, Mirth, and Good Cheer. A grace was a delight to the eye and to the spirit.

There was also a political definition for the word *charis*. It meant kindness or favor shown by an all-powerful king to his subjects. If you were in the king's "good graces," you made out all right.

Paul celebrates the promise at the heart of our faith: that in Christ, we are found to be in God's good graces.

Thank you for your grace, O God. Amen.

Carlos E. Wilton

JUNE 22

1 Corinthians 1:1–9

Paid in Full

. . . so that you are not lacking in any spiritual gift as you wait for the revealing of our Lord Jesus Christ.

1 Corinthians 1:7

"I'd like to return this," said the woman to the store clerk, gift box in hand.

"I'm sorry, ma'am, but that gift is not returnable."

"Can I exchange the gift for something of equal value?"

"I'm sorry, but there's nothing else of equal value."

"Could you at least credit my account?"

"I'm afraid I can't do that either. You see, the purchase price has already been credited to your account in full. And you get to keep the item."

"I don't understand," the woman replied, shaking her head. "Somebody must have paid an awful lot for this."

"You can't imagine how much," the clerk answered quietly.

Paul built his entire ministry on Christ's gift of grace. There is no gift more undeserved, nor more completely paid for.

God of grace, we thank you for the gift of your salvation. Amen.

Carlos E. Wilton

JUNE 23

JOHN 1:29–42

Knowing Our Place

"This is he of whom I said, 'After me comes a man who ranks ahead of me because he was before me.'"

John 1:30

For centuries the words, "You should know your place" have been used to oppress people. The saying has been a potent tool for enforcing systems of discrimination based on race, gender, class, and age. Therefore, we may feel unnerved when we hear these words from John the Baptist, because they indicate that he knows himself to be inferior.

But this situation is different. John goes on to name his place as the one who steps aside for Jesus. This episode represents much more than human hierarchy, because Jesus—while fully human—is no ordinary man.

The exhortation to "know our place" in the world can be unjust and painful. But our place with Jesus offers justice and healing. Once we discover that place and claim it, all our other relationships are seen in a new light.

Healer God, help me to claim my own place at your feet. Amen.

Carlos E. Wilton

JUNE 24

JOHN 1:29–42

All Religion Is Local

They said to him, "Rabbi . . . where are you staying?"

John 1:38b

All politics is local, or so they say. An electorate cares the most about whether the snow is plowed and the potholes are repaired.

When two disciples of John the Baptist ask the Lord where he is staying, Jesus invited them to "come and see" (v. 39). The two seekers, Andrew and Simon, follow Jesus home that day and find out that he is staying close by. Later they will discover that Jesus lives even closer still; Jesus comes to abide in their hearts.

When God chose to become incarnate in the birth of Jesus to Mary and Joseph, God went local and lived among us. Discipleship continues to center on naming and proclaiming God's presence within our hearts, churches, and communities.

Jesus, we are awed that you chose to live among us. Amen.

Carlos E. Wilton

JUNE 25

PSALM 16:1–11

Dependence and Deliverance

For you do not give me up to Sheol,
or let your faithful one see the Pit.
You show me the path of life.
In your presence there is fullness of joy.

Psalm 16:10–11a

There was a period when a new crisis rocked my world every few months. You name it, and I faced it: miscarriage, death of a marriage, death of a beloved family member. It was a dark time. And yet, there was much for which I was grateful. My work was fulfilling. My sons were healthy and thriving in school, Scouts, and youth group. Choral music provided me opportunities to give voice to God's promises of hope and comfort. Worship provided weekly reminders that I could rest secure in God's steadfast love, even as I moved through the valley of the shadows.

I won't kid you. During this time, I did see glimpses of the pit, but I did not go down into it. This psalm was one of those to which I turned, to lament and praise, to remember the counsel of the Lord. May it be so for you, whatever your circumstance today.

Life-saving God, you accompany us along the path of life. Let us rest secure in our goodly heritage and take comfort when glimpses of the pit might otherwise overwhelm us. Amen.

Sarah F. Erickson

JUNE 26

GALATIANS 5:1, 13–25

Spirit-Led Living

For if we live by the Spirit, let us also be guided by the Spirit.

Galatians 5:25

The first twenty-odd years of my working life were spent with the American Red Cross Blood Services. The Red Cross believes that meeting blood needs is a community responsibility, requiring healthy people to donate blood to help others. A caring community can do far more than one that pits competing needs against one another, hoarding resources instead of sharing generously. I've always thought of blood donors as living out the greatest commandment: "You shall love your neighbor as yourself."

The closing verses of this week's passage in Galatians focus on the individuals in community manifesting the fruit of the Spirit (vv. 22–23). Guided by the Spirit, the community together demonstrates care for one another sufficient to overcome the self-indulgent, divisive action of others.

In a politicized, polarized society, let the Spirit guide your way of life to consider the common good and to demonstrate your commitment to supporting your community responsibly.

Spirit of truth, lead us to show our love to our neighbors in ways that bear good fruit. Amen.

Sarah F. Erickson

JUNE 27

LUKE 9:51–62

Focus on the Future

When the days drew near for him to be taken up, he set his face to go to Jerusalem. And he sent messengers ahead of him. On their way they entered a village of the Samaritans to make ready for him; but they did not receive him, because his face was set toward Jerusalem.

Luke 9:51–53

When I am focused on a deadline, I can think about little else. This singularity of purpose has its risks. It can discourage others from supporting me along the way if my demeanor communicates, "If you can't keep up, don't bother."

I wonder if that's what it was like to follow Jesus. So intent was he on fulfilling his mission to restore Israel, his laserlike focus did not seem to acknowledge the alternative views he encountered. Preexisting commitments took a back seat when the invitation to follow as a disciple was extended.

Discipleship in the way of Jesus is focused on the kin-dom of God, not our personal wants and desires. This may entail sorting out competing claims before we can fully commit to following Jesus, who is so focused on his mission that it seems as if we will never be able to keep up.

Jesus, you invite us to join you on the way to Jerusalem. Help us focus on proclaiming the kin-dom of God even as we sort out our priorities. Amen.

Sarah F. Erickson

JUNE 28

2 Kings 5:1–14

Keep It Simple

"Father, if the prophet had commanded you to do something difficult, would you not have done it? How much more, when all he said to you was, 'Wash, and be clean'?"

2 Kings 5:13b

On my better days, I try to operate by the KISS principle: keep it short and simple. The less-complicated way can lead to the same solution as a complex one. Why overthink or over function when you can go on to the next thing, right?

This passage is a vivid caution about the perils of making things more complicated than necessary. Like Naaman, we can make assumptions based on our own experience and presume a solution will fall short. Like the King of Israel, we might overreact and presume the worst.

It is better to follow Elisha's example. The instructions were simple enough. And when Naaman heeded wise advice and accepted Elisha's prescription, he got what he hoped for, just not in the manner he expected to.

What answers to your prayers for healing might you be missing because you imagine more is better? Listen for the simple response and prepare to be surprised.

God of simple surprises, help us look for the simple amid the complex, knowing that you work in ways both complex and straightforward. Amen.

Sarah F. Erickson

JUNE 29

GALATIANS 6:1–16

Follow This Rule

So then, whenever we have an opportunity, let us work for the good of all, and especially for those of the family of faith.

Galatians 6:10

One of my mantras is "Do the best you can with what you have to work with, every chance you get." This doesn't mean be the GOAT (greatest of all time) every day. It means that while each day differs, I can still do the best I can under the circumstances. It reminds me to keep plugging away, whatever I'm facing.

I take heart in this reminder of Paul's, that while I carry my own load, I am called to share and bear burdens with others. In community, I take heart in being a plugger, trying to do what I understand is the next right thing, knowing I am not alone.

When considering that the family of faith includes the whole world that God so loves, I am encouraged to work for the good of all, not my own self-interests. I take heart in Paul's promise of the new creation that comes through Christ and of the peace and mercy that are part of that promise.

Jesus, help me have the grace to bear the burdens of others while sharing my own as I seek to live among neighbors in ways that work for the good of all. Amen.

Sarah F. Erickson

JUNE 30

Psalm 66:1–9

Make a Joyful Noise!

Make a joyful noise to God, all the earth;

. . . .

Bless our God, O peoples,
let the sound of [God's] praise be heard.

Psalm 66:1, 8

I am an early riser, waking with the sun for morning rituals of coffee, quiet time, and daily walks. At this time of year, however, quiet is a bit of a misnomer. Through open windows come the morning's chorus of bird song, punctuated by a rooster's crowing. Breathtaking sunrises illuminate the skies with ribbons of bronze and gold, rose and dusty blue. The neighborhood hums to life amid these glorious sights and sounds. As I go about my walk, snippets of favorite hymns and psalms punctuate my consciousness and set my pace. "How majestic is your name!" (8:1b) or "The heavens declare the glory of God!" (19:1, NIV) have been known to escape my lips before I know it.

As I begin each day with thanksgiving for a fresh start, it's good to be reminded of the Lord's deliverance that has brought me this far, by faith and hard work and tender care.

God of all creation, we give you thanks and praise for bringing us to this day. Guide our steps so that we may be faithful servants and stewards. Amen.

Sarah F. Erickson

JULY 1

GALATIANS 5:1, 13–25

Freedom through Love

For you were called to freedom . . . only do not use your freedom as an opportunity for self-indulgence, but through love become enslaved to one another.

Galatians 5:13

This week the United States will celebrate July 4. The day is set aside to celebrate American independence from Great Britain in 1776. We know that, then as now, nations are not independent but interdependent on one another if we are to survive and thrive. Conflicts arise when governments are unwilling to look beyond their own self-interests.

Self-indulgent behavior labeled as personal freedom runs smack up against a roadblock in this passage. Paul's exhortation to become enslaved to one another in love is yet another reminder of how the freedom of love binds us to one another and the common good. Free will is subject to the will of God, as lived in Christ and inspired by the Spirit.

Christ set us free for love of neighbor. Doing what I want is not always best for my community. This passage is a timely reminder to consider carefully what freedom means.

Jesus, in you we can find freedom: freedom for love of neighbor and the common good. Let us set aside selfishly indulgent acts, caring lovingly for others as we care for ourselves. Amen.

Sarah F. Erickson

JULY 2

PSALM 24

Gaining Perspective

Those who have clean hands and pure hearts . . .
will receive blessing from the LORD.

Psalm 24:4–5

It's good to be in the loop, to know you belong, to be accepted for who you are. We all seek validation and approval. All these things and more are poured out on us by the God who created and loves us beyond measure. But there's a problem.

Many of us were taught to read Scripture from the perspective of the "good guys." Because we know the end of the story, we read the psalmist's words as a people redeemed rather than as the perpetrators of injustice. So what's the issue? We subconsciously learn to overlook the fact that none of us have clean hands. None of us have pure hearts. Therefore none of us are worthy of God's blessing. Our hands are clean, and our hearts are made pure only by God's grace.

If God can look deep within me; see every nasty thought, impure motive, and evil desire; and still extend grace and make me clean, perhaps I can attempt to exercise even a fraction of that grace with my neighbor.

Release me from any feelings of entitlement, O God, and remind me daily of your mercy and grace, without which I am nothing. Amen.

Andy Blackwelder

JULY 3

2 SAMUEL 6:5

Bursting with Joy

David and all the house of Israel were dancing before the LORD with all their might.

2 Samuel 6:5a

I was eleven years old, and it was past my bedtime. My favorite team was playing in the championship game, which was in overtime. Curiosity overcame my brother and I, so we quietly turned on the TV in our shared bedroom and watched the muted screen. With 2.1 seconds remaining, down by one point, I didn't think there was much hope. But a full court pass and a turnaround jumper at the buzzer gave my team the win! I flung open the bedroom door and ran through the house shouting in joy. I had never worn the jersey, but I felt the victory.

David and the people of God were parading through the streets, transporting the ark of God, and they danced with all their might. Joy is contagious and can draw in even those watching from a distance. I'm trying to remember the last time I had a buzzer-beater, championship game-winning reaction to all that God is doing. Our God is worth celebrating, and there's enough joy to go around.

Overwhelm us with joy, we pray, and receive our elation—even dancing—as our offering of thanks. Amen.

Andy Blackwelder

JULY 4

EPHESIANS 1:3–8A

Recognizing Freedom

In him we have redemption through his blood, the forgiveness of our trespasses, according to the riches of his grace that he lavished on us.

Ephesians 1:7–8a

I've never lived in a place where purchasing and shooting fireworks was legal. So it has always been the epitome of irony to me that my neighbors celebrate their independence by lighting fireworks, effectively breaking the law. The very structures that afford us autonomy empower us to make choices that violate them. Most of us simultaneously value freedom and undermine it constantly.

God went to great lengths to liberate and release us from the burden of sin. In Christ we are free! What have we done to deserve this? Have we followed all the rules? Have we confirmed ourselves to be worthy? Often, we do just the opposite. Our efforts have proven only to offend. The harder we try, the farther we fall. In Christ we are free, and yet we still struggle, day in and day out. Fortunately for us, God's grace overflows. In Christ, every bad decision, misjudgment, mistake, and shortcoming is washed away again, and again, and again.

God, our redeemer, thank you for accepting us just as we are. Even flawed and imperfect, you love us still. Amen.

Andy Blackwelder

JULY 5

PSALM 85:8–13

Listening Intently

Let me hear what God the LORD will speak,
for he will speak peace to his people.

Psalm 85:8a

I've always wondered about receiving signs from God. When I hear people talk about signs they've received, I find myself thinking of all the other ways they could have interpreted the sign. A lot of times their story includes a sign that nudged them in the direction they were already hoping to go. Either God is extremely accommodating or some of us are misinterpreting signs. Or could it be that our hopes open us to participate in the message God has for us?

What the psalmist longs to hear is shalom—peace, contentment, completeness. Don't we all? What if God is speaking shalom to us today? How would we know it if we heard it? That's part of the journey, but the psalmist says with confidence: God *will* speak peace to his people. May we live with assurance that God's word for us is shalom. May we live with the hope that our ears may be tuned to hear God's voice.

Never stop speaking, Lord, and give us ears to hear. Amen.

Andy Blackwelder

JULY 6

AMOS 7:7–15

Shushing Influence

"O seer, go, flee away to the land of Judah, earn your bread there, and prophesy there."

Amos 7:12

As the nurse was leading me to an exam room, she stopped by the scale. I wondered what my weight might have to do with my sore throat, but I reluctantly climbed on. After the exam, the doctor wanted to talk about the number in my chart. I wanted to walk out. I wasn't here for a lecture on my diet and my exercise habits. But it was a conversation I needed to have, so I had to endure it.

Amos was given a word from God to deliver to Israel, and it wasn't good news. The priest Amaziah told Amos to keep on moving and stop all the negative talk. Amos assured him that the word was not his own but a warning from God.

I am more like Amaziah than I like to admit. I, too, want to hear from God only when it's an affirming and reassuring word. But if God's word never challenges us—if it never says anything we couldn't just say to ourselves—we have no use for it.

God, help us to hear your word, even when it is hard to accept. Amen.

Andy Blackwelder

JULY 7

MARK 6:17–29

Silencing Truth

For John had been telling Herod, "It is not lawful for you to have your brother's wife." And Herodias had a grudge against him, and wanted to kill him.

Mark 6:18–19a

I hope we all have trouble relating to this story in Scripture because it ends with John's head being presented to a woman who promptly gifts it to her mother. Not exactly a story we dwell on in children's Sunday school. This story, however, may be more familiar than we realize. John is silenced for speaking truth. In a disruption of King Herod's dramatic saga, John spoke out against the abuse of power he witnessed. While everyone else bit their tongue, John spoke. The truth John spoke ultimately led to an elaborate scheme to make sure his voice was never heard again.

We need voices of accountability in our lives. Unfortunately, most of us silence those voices by ignoring them, dismissing them, or burying them under other opinions we'd prefer to hear. Maybe we're not calling for anyone's head, but just because a voice makes us uncomfortable or inconvenienced doesn't mean the person speaking deserves to be silenced. Sometimes those messages that are hard to accept are the very words of God.

Brace us, Lord, to hear your voice even when your message unsettles us. Amen.

Andy Blackwelder

JULY 8

EPHESIANS 1:12–14

Receiving the Blessing

In him you also . . . were marked with the seal of the promised Holy Spirit.

Ephesians 1:13

I have not often participated in the Black Friday shopping frenzy on the day after Thanksgiving, but one particular year my wife and I arrived early to stand in line for a door-buster deal. The deal was too good to pass up, and we were convinced the hundreds of people in front of us would snatch up the store's supply. We began to convince ourselves that there was no way we'd be fortunate enough to leave that day with what we came for. Then the doors opened, and everyone pushed their way into the store and scattered throughout the aisles. We walked briskly, directly to the item. No one else was around. It occurred to us then that every person in the store thought every other person was after the specific thing they wanted. We all created competition where there was none.

It's hard for many of us to fathom that God's love does not follow the laws of supply and demand, but rest assured: there's enough to go around.

We know your love is not in limited supply. Help us not to create an atmosphere of competition where there is none. Amen.

Andy Blackwelder

JULY 9

PSALM 85:8–13

Fearing God?

Surely his salvation is at hand for those who fear him,
that his glory may dwell in our land.

Psalm 85:9

It's summertime and life claims to be free and easy (or at least freer and easier) in these weeks. Our Creator's seasonal handiwork includes wildflowers and warm winds, refreshing oceans and lakes. But our twenty-first-century sensibilities do not generally embrace a fearsome God. Some of us fear snakes and bees and even some of our Christian siblings more than we fear God. But when we recognize that God's immeasurably creative power is awesome to the point of being fearsome, it indeed makes us tremble a bit.

While we swiftly pass through these summer days, it's easy to forget how extraordinary our surroundings are. The psalmist notes that when God's glory dwells in our land, "righteousness and peace will kiss each other" (v. 10). This is splendidly fearsome indeed!

We come before you, God of all creation, with reverence and awe. Help us to recognize your holy power in our midst. Amen.

Jan Edmiston

JULY 10

AMOS 5:1–9

Easily Distracted

Seek me and live.

Amos 5:4

Some of us are more easily distracted than others. Maybe we follow every shiny object or maybe we simply lean toward random everyday idolatries. It is remarkably easy to make life about ourselves. Thousands of years after the prophet Amos bemoaned the fact that God's people were worshiping Ba'al even in spiritually significant places like Bethel, Gilgal, and Beersheba, Robert Robinson wrote, "Prone to wander, Lord, I feel it, prone to leave the God I love" in the hymn "Come, Thou Fount of Every Blessing."[1]

In every generation, God's people struggle with worshiping what is not God. Throughout these summer days, we are reminded to keep our focus on the One who gives us life here on earth and after our days on earth are over.

Holy God, we are indeed prone to wander away from your path. Remind us that the abundant life you promise comes from seeking you in a world teeming with distractions and temptations. Keep us focused on what gives us life today. We pray in Jesus' name. Amen.

Jan Edmiston

1. *Glory to God* (Louisville, KY: Westminster John Knox Press, 2013), #475.

JULY 11

AMOS 9:1–4

Judgment Is Not Pretty

I will command the sea-serpent, and it shall bite them.

Amos 9:3

God is not kidding. In Amos's fifth and final vision, God continues to condemn Israel and Judah for worshiping false gods. The city of Bethel—where Jacob once dreamed of a ladder to heaven—was now home to a lovely shrine. The problem was that the shrine honored Ba'al, and the Hebrew people occasionally worshiped there too. And so there would be blood and death and no escape. Even if God's people try to hide under the sea, God will send sea creatures to eat them.

This is not the God of gentle Jesus, meek and mild—but Jesus was not so meek and mild himself. God is serious about faithfulness. God is dead serious about the inevitable destruction that comes from idolatry.

God of all that is loving and pure and good, we confess our attraction to the idols of this world. The truth is that we love many things more than we love Jesus. Forgive us our idolatries and make us long for you alone. Amen.

Jan Edmiston

JULY 12

AMOS 9:11–15

Sweet Wine

They shall plant vineyards and drink their wine,
and they shall make gardens and eat their fruit.

Amos 9:14

Throughout this country, perhaps as you are reading this, fruit and vegetable pickers are harvesting food that is not theirs. They are picking tomatoes and grapes and lettuce for very low wages. They are living in substandard housing and—if they are immigrant farmers—their status could be tenuous.

The grapevines in Palestine were known for creating sweet wine, but for many years, as Amos prophesied, exile and captivity by their enemies meant that their harvests were taken. The joy of eating food from their own gardens had been taken away.

But God promises restoration. A day is returning when they will drink their own sweet wine again. This is the promise of the One who holds us accountable but also—by grace—offers restoration.

God of vineyards and olive trees, wheat fields and grasslands: we thank you for fresh opportunities to move out of destruction into the light. We praise you for your grace beyond measure. Move us into the light that we might enjoy the fruits of our labor. Amen.

Jan Edmiston

JULY 13

COLOSSIANS 1:15–23

Fluent in the Language of Praise

He is the image of the invisible God, the firstborn of all creation.

Colossians 1:15

If you've ever been rescued, the words, "Thank you, God" possibly fell from your lips with little thought. As a teenager, I was floating mindlessly in the ocean on an innertube when a wave knocked me off and left me floundering in water that was deeper and farther from the shore than I'd realized. I am not a strong swimmer. Despite knowing that I could drown, I made it to the shore gasping and exhausted. Words fell out of my mouth in between breaths. "Thank you, God. Thank you for saving me." It's all I could say.

Paul offers a hymn about the praise-worthy attributes of Christ to the Colossians that we would do well to learn by heart. Jesus is the living image of God and comes with all the divine power of God. This is an excellent day to praise God for every good thing we notice—and even those we don't.

Amazing God, make us fluent in the language of praise today. Amen.

Jan Edmiston

JULY 14

1 Chronicles 14:1–2

Everybody Needs a Hiram

King Hiram of Tyre sent messengers to David, along with cedar logs . . . to build a house for him.

1 Chronicles 14:1

We need each other, and not only when we are sick or troubled. We need each other if we ever hope to do what most of us pray each Sunday: that God's will be done "on earth as it is in heaven." Because the world is a mess, we need a variety of partners to bring about any semblance of God's realm. We need civic partners from schools and government. We need interfaith and ecumenical partners. Maybe our best partners are the very people we aim to serve: the homeless, the bullied.

Hiram was an unlikely partner for David. Both were successful kings and could have been staunch rivals. But—like a modern-day diplomat or community organizer—Hiram offered his best to David in hopes of building something more important than a palace. He was building a good kind of power that benefitted a broader part of the world.

God, grant us the gifts of organizing coalitions for good that we might indeed work toward your will on earth as it is in heaven. Amen.

Jan Edmiston

JULY 15

1 CHRONICLES 15:1–2; 16:4–13

Whose Job Is It?

He appointed certain of the Levites as ministers before the ark of the LORD, to invoke, to thank, and to praise the LORD, the God of Israel.

1 Chronicles 16:4

Most of us have jobs unique to summertime: weeding, mowing, grilling, cleaning that grill. I was always assigned the summer baking—thanks be to God.

In the time of King David, the Levites were assigned the task of invoking, thanking, and praising God. They "got to" carry the ark of the covenant. Asaph was the leader of this praise team, and his name is connected to twelve psalms.

Some congregations still call their worship leaders "the Praise Team," but this is one job that each of us can claim. No longer do the professionals get all the fun or assume all the obligation to "invoke, thank, and praise" God. No longer are pastors and music directors and Christian educations the ones who do these things on everybody else's behalf. We who claim to follow Jesus, by virtue of our baptism, *get* to do these things. And they make our lives richer and lighter. Every day we get to connect with God.

Thanks be to you, O Holy One, who delights in our prayers, who relishes our creativity, and who longs to be known. Amen.

Jan Edmiston

JULY 16

PSALM 23

Want

The LORD is my shepherd, I shall not want.

Psalm 23:1

Needs versus wants. Sometimes, our needs and wants converge with each other. I need and want more tranquility in my life. More often, however, our needs and wants seem to diverge to reflect different desires. I need to work on filing my taxes, which are due tomorrow, but I want to spend that time watching my favorite television shows. I need to save money to pay the taxes I owe, but I want to spend it on a weekend trip with the kids.

In this reality, I'm struck by the psalmist's radical confession that our Shepherd fulfills not only my needs but also my wants. When I trust and follow God, what I need and want are provided by God. God provides for me in such a way that I do not want anything else. Even when I do not know what it is I need or want, God's gracious and generous provisions cover me. I both need and want to trust and follow this Shepherd.

Help us to trust your guidance as our Good Shepherd, who meets all our needs and wants. Amen.

Yena K. Hwang

JULY 17

PSALM 23

Restore

[The shepherd] restores my soul.

Psalm 23:3

To restore means to return to a former, original state by mending. Our souls are weary with the burdens of living: the twenty-four-hour news cycle filled with nature-made and human-made terrors, unexpected diagnoses, expected but not desired consequences of choices made, along with the daily grind that accompanies life. Being "too busy," we can easily ignore that we are weary.

No questions asked, no blame assigned, God restores our worn-out souls by providing space and time for our rest. Notice that the psalmist says God "makes me lie down" (v. 2). Restoration begins with allowing God to take control of us. Restoration happens when we lie down and receive nourishment from the gifts of earth. Restoration occurs when there is an intentional step toward not only creating a sacred space but also claiming the sacred spaces in the ordinary places of life. What do you need to claim this time and space for the restoration of your soul this week?

Restore and rejuvenate our souls in your grace and mercy, for we are weary from what we have witnessed and experienced. Amen.

Yena K. Hwang

JULY 18

PSALM 23

Even Though and Even Through

Even though I walk through the darkest valley,
I fear no evil;
for you are with me.

Psalm 23:4

Fearless. I wish I could be fearless. Yet I am aware, fully, of all my fears. I fear high places and wind blowing against my face. I fear failure, not being good or smart enough, and drawing criticism. I fear that my weaknesses will override my strengths. I fear living out the end of my life alone, although I do not fear death or dying.

Unfortunately, God's promise is not to take away our fears with the waving of God's magical rod and staff; God's promise is to provide support and comfort even through the shadowed valleys of our life where we have to face our fears. While out and about on Halloween one year, my then-three-year-old son encountered a teenager dressed in a scary costume. He stopped in his tracks. He looked at what stood between him and a basket of candy, hesitating over his next move. Then he shouted, "It's just a guy!" and walked through his fear to receive his treat. Our fears may show up in various places, but God will be our constant support.

Thank you for accompanying us through those shadowed valleys of life. Amen.

Yena K. Hwang

JULY 19

PSALM 23

Comforting Presence

I fear no evil;
for you are with me;
your rod and your staff—
they comfort me.

Psalm 23:4

When my son started attending a child-care center, he would not leave the house without selecting one of his favorite *I Spy* books. The book served as his comfort object, something that reminded him of home and the time we spent playing "I Spy" together. His little mind wanted a tangible reminder of the home and family that he had to part with for six hours a day. His book was like the blanket the Linus character in the cartoon strip *Peanuts* carries—his rod and staff of comfort.

We are never too old to have comfort objects. Most days, a verbal reminder of God's presence alongside me is enough. However, occasionally I need a tangible reminder of God's presence. Sometimes, my friends and family serve as this tangible reminder; at other times, I use a small rock or a silver cross necklace around my neck. What everyday object can comfort you as you face a difficult task today?

Thank you for your rod and staff, in various forms, that provide comfort through all the circumstances we face each day. Amen.

Yena K. Hwang

JULY 20

Psalm 23

Table of Grace

You prepare a table before me
in the presence of my enemies.
Psalm 23:5

The table symbolizes a sacred space. In my home, the kitchen table is a place where we gather daily to nourish ourselves with food, where we receive guests with a cup of tea, where we marvel at how the child is now big enough to sit at the table to be nourished. The table is where we celebrate another year of life added and remember the life that has departed. At my church, the Communion table is where we remember and celebrate Christ's sacrifice, his ministry to the folks in marginal places of life. We offer ourselves, receive new members, and make commitments to serve the Lord, all at the table.

So to read "You prepare a table before me" followed by "in the presence of my enemies" is a little jarring. Why is my enemy present at the table? Because God's table is prepared for all, open to all—even those whom I see as enemies. To receive God's prepared table is to receive the challenges that come with it.

God, help us to receive the challenges present at your table, even the call to the ministry of reconciliation. Amen.

Yena K. Hwang

JULY 21

PSALM 23

Abundance

You anoint my head with oil;
my cup overflows.

Psalm 23:5

My grandparents lived through the devastating civil war in Korea. My father was born a year before the Korean War broke out and experienced living as a refugee, as his family was displaced from their home during the war. They experienced scarcity of food, water, and the basic necessities of life. As a result, when I was a child, even if I left just a few grains of rice in my bowl, my grandmother would get upset. When I would complain and refuse to finish what was in my bowl, my grandmother would eat it. For my grandmother, who lived through the war and the poverty that followed, frugality was a way of life. Nothing was ever wasted or taken for granted.

For my grandmother, who lived through scarcity, God's promise of abundant provisions was liberating news, one she held on to all her life. There is a sense of carefree abandonment in the way God anoints us and overfills our cups. God's love is abundant love, able to cover all and then some.

Thank you for your gift of abundant love. Help us to receive it with gratitude and share it in joy. Amen.

Yena K. Hwang

JULY 22

Psalm 23

Followed

Surely goodness and mercy shall follow me
all the days of my life.

Psalm 23:6

In this world of social media, new words are created and existing words take on an added meaning. *Selfie* is a new word in the era of social media. The concept of being "followed" has taken on a new meaning. You can "follow" someone to receive their updated postings on that person's social media sites like Facebook or Twitter. Conversely, when you are being "followed," it means that your follower receives updates of your postings. The number of followers you have on these social media sites can indicate your popularity. A large number of followers even creates celebrities. Pre-social media era, being "followed" had a creepy connotation. Changing times, changing meanings!

While the number of followers I have on my social media might make me feel like part of a community, the most important thing in my life is having God's goodness and mercy follow me. It is good to count on God's goodness and mercy to follow me all the days of my life. No matter what circumstance I may encounter, I am empowered by this knowledge.

Lord, I wish to follow in your footsteps of goodness and mercy as I serve you in this world. Amen.

Yena K. Hwang

JULY 23

1 Peter 1:17–23

A New Identity

You have been born anew . . . through the living and enduring word of God.

1 Peter 1:23

Being ordained as an elder; seeing my infant son and husband baptized at the same time; watching my confirmation mentee become a member of the church: It's in moments like these when I feel a deep, genuine love move through the church as we welcome and celebrate the Spirit's call on the lives of those whom God has chosen, and I am reminded of our communal identity as God's chosen people.

Often the idea of being "born anew" is seen as a solitary, discrete act between an individual and God. But in 1 Peter 1:17–23, we are reminded that our new life and new identity in Christ are not separate from our communal lives. In fact, it is our collective identity as followers of Christ that sets us apart, through our "genuine mutual love" for one another (v. 22). This communal love characterizes our new identity in Christ.

Almighty God, let our lives in our communities reflect the knowledge that we are your chosen people, seen in our deep, abiding love for one another. Amen.

Alexis Presseau Maloof

JULY 24

GENESIS 18:1–14

No Limits

"Is anything too wonderful for the LORD? At the set time I will return to you, in due season, and Sarah shall have a son."

Genesis 18:14

My toddler likes to ask me the same questions every night as I'm tucking him into bed. "Mommy, do you love me? How much do you love me? When do you love me?" It's become a routine, a choreographed expression of assurances he looks for before sleep, with him asking and me answering, always the same. Yes, I love you, more than anything, without limits. I love you all the time. I never stop.

Sarah needed assurances as well. When she overheard it said in verse 10 that she would have a son, she was incredulous. Then in verse 14, God says again, assuring her directly, that she will have a son. There are no limits on God's love: nothing is too wonderful, and you will have a son. Sarah needed to hear it more than once, and often, so do we. We are elected, God's chosen, beloved by the Almighty, whose love for us has no limits. Hear it as often as you need to.

Thank you, Lord, for it seems too wonderful to be true that you have chosen us as your people and given us your limitless love. Amen.

Alexis Presseau Maloof

JULY 25

1 Peter 2:1–3

On Being Fed

Like newborn infants, long for the pure, spiritual milk, so that by it you may grow into salvation.

1 Peter 2:2

I remember trying to choose what solid food I should introduce my baby to first. My husband and I debated the nutritional merits of bananas, avocados, and mushed peas. It felt like such an important decision; his growth and development would rely on my choices in solid food, so I was careful with each initial spoonful.

In the Epistle of 1 Peter, we have been reminded that we have been born anew in Christ. As spiritual beings, we are never too old to be nurtured and fed. In order to grow, we must have a balanced and well-rounded diet; we need community, love, trust, and abundance, and the understanding that our identity as God's people is constantly growing and being transformed. Being fed is an ongoing process. Even after my son grows up and can feed himself, I hope to have instilled in him the importance of being attentive to what we put into our bodies.

O God, guide us, your chosen people, toward the spiritual foods that will help us grow into our salvation. Amen.

Alexis Presseau Maloof

JULY 26

PSALM 134:1–3

Standing by Night

Come, bless the LORD, all you servants of the LORD,
who stand by night in the house of the LORD!

Psalm 134:1

Nighttime can be scary, as children will tell you. What seems innocuous in the day can become menacing in the night. But despite the malevolence we often associate with darkness, we know that God created both light and dark, day and night. What does this means for us as God's chosen people?

We aren't sure what group is being described as standing by night by the psalmist in verse 1 of Psalm 34, but it is followed by an exhortation to lift our hands high to God, the traditional position of prayer at the time. In times of uncertainty and fear, God's people can call on the Lord through prayer. The psalmist reminds us here of our identity as God's people, and we can be reassured that whatever the circumstance, the love and promise of God's love remain. Whether we are standing guard or taking watch in the night, we serve the God who created the darkness. We have nothing to fear.

God who created both day and night, we bless you and praise you as we lift our hands high. Amen.

Alexis Presseau Maloof

JULY 27

PSALM 119:49–56

Comfort for God's People

This is my comfort in my distress,
that your promise gives me life.
Psalm 119:50

When I was a child, my grandfather seemed larger than life to me. Large in stature, tall, and broad, he treasured his grandchildren. I remember waiting with anticipation to hear his booming voice shout that he had arrived home from work. My grandfather recently passed from this world into God's heavenly kingdom. When he died, I felt like that little girl again, yearning to hear his voice.

The truth is God makes no promises to God's people that we will not suffer, nor does God promise to relieve us of our suffering. What God does promise is that we will not go through suffering alone. In verse 52 (NIV) the psalmist says, "I remember, LORD, your ancient laws, and I find comfort in them." God's covenant is a wellspring of comfort and hope, reminding us that, whether in life or death, we are always God's promised people. The hope we have is that God will walk with us and suffer alongside us, as Christ did, and through Christ, we have never-ending life.

Thank you, God, for reminding us that, even in our lowest places of suffering and pain, your promises endure both in life and in death. Amen.

Alexis Presseau Maloof

JULY 28

EXODUS 3:16–22

Full Hands

I will bring this people into such favor with the Egyptians that, when you go, you will not go empty-handed.

Exodus 3:21

The gap between the haves and the have-nots is the largest it's ever been, and it keeps growing. We are constantly receiving the message that we need *more*, and under this is an anxiety that more is not enough. Often called the "ideology of scarcity," this way of thinking runs counter to the biblical understanding of God's abundance.

God promises the enslaved people of Egypt that they will leave enslavement with full hands. God calls on creation to multiply and promises a land of milk and honey; God operates from a mindset of abundance, which Walter Brueggemann describes as, "there will be enough to go around, so long as each of us takes only what we need."[1] As God's chosen people, this understanding changes the way we live in the world. God's generosity asks us to recognize our own abundance so that we may use our full hands to fill those of others.

God of abundance, help us live the theology of abundance and reject the worldly mindset of scarcity. Amen.

Alexis Presseau Maloof

1. Walter Brueggemann, "Enough Is Enough," *The Other Side* 37, no. 5 (November–December 2001).

JULY 29

EZEKIEL 34:1–16

A God Who Rescues

I will rescue them from all the places to which they have been scattered on a day of clouds and thick darkness.

Ezekiel 34:12

Days of clouds and thick darkness seem to be all too plentiful in our world. We are facing the largest refugee crisis of our time. Millions are displaced and without access to proper water or shelter due to devastating natural disasters. Overburdened communities are vilified, blamed, and ignored. Where are the shepherds?

In Ezekiel 34, God asks the prophet to preach against the kings of Israel, the empire of the day, whom God likens to shepherds who have abused their sheep. These leaders sought their own good before that of their people, feeding themselves first while the sheep starved and scattered. The imperial powers, both then and now, fail to fulfill their duty to bind up the injured and strengthen the weak, so God vows to search for his scattered sheep and to "bring them out from the peoples and gather them" (v. 13). The understanding of God as the rescuer of the chosen people is desperately relevant for the world today.

God of the oppressed, may you rescue your chosen people from the faraway places they have been scattered and feed them with justice. Amen.

Alexis Presseau Maloof

JULY 30

EXODUS 1:8–2:10

Resisting Oppression

But the midwives feared God; they did not do as the king of Egypt commanded them, but they let the boys live.

Exodus 1:17

Dietrich Bonhoeffer was a theologian in Nazi Germany known for his opposition to Hitler's systematic enslavement and destruction of Jewish people. When many members of the churches were silent in the face of genocide, as an act of faith, Bonhoeffer chose to speak out in resistance.

The midwives in the Exodus story faced their own faith dilemma. Should they systematically kill all the male Hebrew babies as commanded, or should they let them live? Oppression—the cruel and unjust use of power and authority—often targets people of different races, classes, and religions. How we respond to the oppression of God's people is a matter of faith.

Do we value the dignity of humans created in the image of God, or do we exploit those who are different at home and abroad for cheap clothing and food? Do we speak out against systematic racism that costs people their lives and freedom or remain conveniently, comfortably silent?

God of rescue, we thank you for those who speak and act on behalf of the oppressed. May I have the courage to be one of them. Amen.

Sue Washburn

JULY 31

EXODUS 1:8–2:10

From Compassion to Action

He was crying, and she took pity on him.

Exodus 2:6

One of my children was a colicky baby who cried for many heartbreaking hours at a time. She'd be passed from one set of arms to another as my partner and I tried to soothe her. We walked miles up and down the hallway of our home, singing and gently bouncing her in our arms. As exhausting and frustrating as it was, we didn't leave her alone with her newborn tears. Like Pharaoh's daughter, our first response to the sound of a child crying was compassion, followed by action.

Pharaoh's daughter and, later in the Gospels, Jesus allow pity or compassion to move them to action for people who are vulnerable or broken. Often though, compassion, literally *suffering with* someone, makes most of us feel awkward and uncomfortable. Instead of looking at and then reaching out to a crying addict or homeless woman, it's easier to look and walk away. What would our world be like if we allowed our compassion to inspire us to look and then respond instead of to look and then look away?

Jesus, we praise you for your ministry to those who are vulnerable and difficult. Help us to do the same. Amen.

Sue Washburn

AUGUST 1

PSALM 124

Escaping the Fear

We have escaped like a bird
from the snare of the fowlers;
the snare is broken,
and we have escaped.

Psalm 124:7

The night before I started chemotherapy, I panicked. I realized cancer had caught me in its net, and there was no easy way forward. Treatment promised months of misery, but skipping the treatment meant death. Like many people with a life-altering diagnosis, I looked for an escape. I prayed for instant healing. I searched alternatives online. I bought prayer beads and listened to James Earl Jones read the New Testament as I lay nauseous in the dark. I searched desperately for something that would allow me to break free. I wanted escape. But that was not to be.

Breaking the snare that had caught me was not about escaping the situation but being set free from the fear. Like the psalmist, I had to trust that the Lord was on my side. God's freedom for me wouldn't be an instant escape, but a slow miracle coming drip by drip from the chemo bag. God promises to be with me.

Lord, in times of trouble, we trust that you go with us and offer us a way to cope. Amen.

Sue Washburn

AUGUST 2

PSALM 124

What's in a Name?

Our help is in the name of the LORD,
who made heaven and earth.

Psalm 124:8

As a producer of an overnight talk show, I would screen calls from folks who couldn't sleep at night and wanted to talk. The host was a kind, gentle man—a healer more than a pontificator. My first question was, "What is your name?" because there were no anonymous callers allowed.

"Mrs. Thomas" or "Mrs. Wilson" many of the older women would reply.

"No," I'd say, "What is your *first* name?"

"Mrs. William Thomas," they'd reply, adding their husband's first name.

Names offer us identity and grounding—connection to a time, place, or culture. But like women only known by their spouse's identity, names can confine and trap us. The psalmist recognizes that there is one name that can free us—the name of the Lord. The name of the Lord can help us when we are overwhelmed or angry or even when we can't sleep. The Bible offers many names for God and compels us numerous times to "call on" the name of the Lord, a God we know and on whom we can depend.

Lord, we call on your name to help us face the challenges of our lives. Amen.

Sue Washburn

AUGUST 3

MATTHEW 16:13–20

One of Us and One with God

Now when Jesus came into the district of Caesarea Philippi, he asked his disciples, "Who do people say that the Son of Man is?"

Matthew 16:13

The meeting for vacation Bible school seemed to be going on forever. We had discussed the general theme and then started talking about who had registered. For the small, tightly knit community that meant looking at each child's information and remembering how they fit into our group.

"That's so-and-so's grandson," or "she's the friend that my nephew brought last year," or "her parents just bought the old farm on the hill." Each child had a connection in the history of the church community. When Jesus asks the disciples who he is, they are trying to connect Jesus to their history and their community, to connect him to what they already know. They link him to John the Baptist, Elijah, and Jeremiah.

But Jesus' identity goes beyond his heritage and community. He is the Messiah, Son of the Living God. He is both one of us and at one with God. He is the embodiment of God's hope and the friend we invite to participate in our lives. Jesus connects us to something bigger than ourselves.

Jesus, thank you for coming into our lives and connecting us to God. Amen.

Sue Washburn

AUGUST 4

MATTHEW 16:13–20

Do the Work (of Jesus)

"I will give you the keys of the kingdom of heaven, and whatever you bind on earth will be bound in heaven, and whatever you loose on earth will be loosed in heaven."

Matthew 16:19

"Don't feed the beast." That saying has become my shorthand for not escalating the negative emotions that surround me, whether it be angry children, unhappy church members, or political strife. We often hold the keys that allow us to "bind" and "loose" certain things into the world around us. We don't choose what happens in our lives, but we can choose how we respond.

We can let loose the metaphorical beast with a stream of negative thought, talk, and action when things get stressful. Or we can learn to bind and tame the beast so that it doesn't hurt us or others.

We can learn to manage our own fear and anger and pain so that we don't send it out to others. The life and teachings of Jesus give us keys we need to do the emotional and spiritual work needed to manage our responses to the world around us. The keys Jesus gives us include prayer, Scripture, companionship, shared meals, healthy touch, and forgiveness. What other keys has Jesus given you?

Jesus, we are grateful for the keys you have given us. Amen.

Sue Washburn

AUGUST 5

ROMANS 12:1–8

The Body Renews the Mind

Do not be conformed to this world, but be transformed by the renewing of your minds, so that you may discern what is the will of God—what is good and acceptable and perfect.

Romans 12:2

We each know how our body responds to fear—a pounding heart, weak knees, or sweaty palms. I've experienced this bodily fear when I've faced surgery, gone to "rough" neighborhoods to invite kids to vacation Bible school, and stepped into a pulpit. But these responses have also come with renewed insight into what God is doing in my life.

So often we think about "renewing the mind" through study or debate, with the brain leading the way. But neuroscience research is showing us that what happens with our bodies has an impact on our thoughts. What we see, hear, touch, and feel influence how and what we think. This was certainly true of the apostle Paul when he was struck blind on the way to Damascus and heard the risen Christ. His body and his beliefs together underwent a total transformation. We can renew our minds by leading with our bodies, literally stepping out in faith to encounter God in totally transformative ways.

Word become flesh, thank you for the gift of renewal that comes from our bodies and minds. Amen.

Sue Washburn

AUGUST 6

EXODUS 14:19–21

Taking the First Step

The LORD drove the sea back by a strong east wind all night.

Exodus 14:21b

The Hebrew slaves hurried from their homes only to find themselves smack up against the Red Sea with the Egyptian army in hot pursuit. The cloud that assured them of God's presence had left the front of the band of travelers and was now behind it.

What did this mean? The Hebrews weren't at all sure. They complained to Moses, asking whether he had brought them out of slavery to die and claiming that they were better off in Egypt. Moses tried to assure them with "Do not be afraid, stand firm . . . keep still" (vv. 13, 14). But now the Egyptians could be seen approaching and God seemed far away.

Then the strong east wind blew and blew, creating a dry pathway through the water for them to walk safely across. Who was brave or trusting enough to take that first step, to begin the long journey that was ahead of them, the exodus that would form them as God's people?

God of the universe, I pray for complete trust in you that pushes me to take the first step. Amen.

Carol A. Wehrheim

AUGUST 7

EXODUS 14:22–31

Hearing the Whole Story

Israel saw the great work that the LORD did against the Egyptians.

Exodus 14:31a

It was all over. The Israelites had safely crossed the Red Sea. But the parted waters came back together when the Egyptian army tried to cross. But before the narrator tells of the "great work that the LORD did," we learn that the Israelites saw all the Egyptians dead on the shore. Why include this sentence? Did God want them to see that their enemy had been destroyed and that they were safe? Or did God want them to see the consequences of their freedom, that God had rescued them at the cost of the loss of many lives?

As we read this passage, we might ask ourselves how we include the story of the other, the enemy, or the losers when we remember the past. Without the inclusion of those stories, our formation as God's people is not complete.

God, open our eyes, ears, and hearts to the stories that have been ignored or hidden by conquerors throughout history. Amen.

Carol A. Wehrheim

AUGUST 8

MATTHEW 18:21–22

Seventy-Seven Times

"Lord, if another member of the church sins against me, how often should I forgive?"

Matthew 18:21

At the beginning of Matthew 18, Jesus instructs his followers about life together and about caring for the little ones, the most vulnerable in the community. But he also sets these vulnerable ones forth as an example of faithfulness.

Now Peter wonders just how much forgiveness should be offered. One suspects that he has a situation in mind. The same question may be rolling around in yours. Is forgiving someone always the best move? Isn't there a limit to how often you can really forgive the same person? What happens when you can't forgive someone or someone won't forgive you?

In his initial answer, Jesus doesn't set any limits to how often. The number he gives is huge, whether the Greek is translated as seventy-seven times or seventy times seven. Forgiveness, while not unique to the Christian faith, is critical to the life of the church and to our lives as families and communities outside the church. How do we look on forgiveness based on Jesus' answer?

God of love, lead me to an understanding of forgiveness that seeks the best for the one I am forgiving and for me. Amen.

Carol A. Wehrheim

AUGUST 9

MATTHEW 18:23–32

The Wideness of God's Mercy

When his fellow slaves saw what had happened, they were greatly distressed.

Matthew 18:31a

The parable Jesus told to explain his answer about forgiveness is an exaggeration. No slave could possibly pay back what the first slave owed his master. Clearly Jesus used this huge number to extend his answer to Peter. Still the master forgave the debt, totally, choosing not to sell everything the slave had, including his family. When other slaves saw that same slave refuse forgiveness for a much smaller sum, they could not hold back. This unwillingness to forgive as he was forgiven had broken the community. The trust necessary to bind a group together can no longer include the first slave.

The exaggerated debt the first slave owed reminds us of the mercy of God, which should be overwhelming to us, as overwhelming as the sum forgiven by the master. Once we recognize the extent of God's mercy, we can only attempt to show some portion of that mercy to others. How then do we understand forgiveness in our own lives? What supports the forgiveness we offer to others?

God of overwhelming mercy and forgiveness, open our hearts to offer that forgiveness to others. Amen.

Carol A. Wehrheim

AUGUST 10

ROMANS 14:1–12

Welcome Everyone

Welcome those who are weak in faith, but not for the purpose of quarreling over opinions.

Romans 14:1

Paul has not been to Rome, but he has heard about problems in the Christian community there. He talks about the factions as weak or strong, not right or wrong. The weak are those who believe these restrictions are necessary for them to be faithful to God; the strong do not. Reading this passage carefully, you discover that Paul doesn't take sides, but he urges all the people to be tolerant of what the other side finds necessary to be faithful. Only in this way will the church, the community of faith, be a united rather than a fractured body of Christ.

In verse 10, Paul asks his readers, "Why do you pass judgment on your brother or sister?" The quarreling in Rome and in many congregations today is about how we live as God's people from day to day. We would do well to heed Paul's words that end this passage: "So then, each of us will be accountable to God" (v. 12).

God of mercy and love, remind us, hourly if necessary, that your love and mercy cover everyone. Amen.

Carol A. Wehrheim

AUGUST 11

PSALM 114

Memories Make the Community

When Israel went out from Egypt . . .

Psalm 114:1a

An important part of being God's people, a community of faith, is the communal memories, going all the way back to the foundational stories of our faith. Psalm 114 provided that remembering, an opportunity to recall how God formed this people as they journeyed through the exodus and settled in a new land. In that story, we also paused to consider how the story sounds to those who lost the battle, particularly the Egyptians. We cannot ignore God's concern for all people.

Psalm 114 is the second of the Hallel Psalms (113–118) that were sung at the joyful festivals and at Passover. Verses 1 and 2 acknowledge God's role in bringing God's people out of slavery and forming them as a people of God. The tone is exuberant and almost has you marching as you read it. What a pleasant way to prepare to gather with God's people to worship the Lord on the Sabbath! What faith memories do you bring?

God of the exodus, we praise your holy name and give thanks for all that you have done and continue to do for your people and your creation. Amen.

Carol A. Wehrheim

AUGUST 12

PSALM 114

Trembling Together

Tremble, O earth, at the presence of the LORD . . .
who turns the rock into a pool of water.

Psalm 114:7a, 8a

Psalm 114 describes the earth itself responding to God's redemptive action, with seas fleeing and mountains skipping. The song praises God as so powerful and tremendous that no part of creation can escape noticing and reacting. If even geographic features are in awe of God, how much more should we be! This image invites us to see ourselves as part of God's created order, to share in the trembling of all the earth at the presence of God.

Nearly every translation uses the word *tremble*. Trembling can indicate fear, but it can also suggest excitement or great joy. The book of Psalms includes so many experiences and expressions of human interaction with God, from lament to celebration and from very personal to broadly communal, and—as we see in Psalm 114—even beyond humankind. Take a moment to reflect on the emotions and sensations present in relationship to God as an individual, as a part of your community or congregation, and as a small piece in God's vast creation.

God of mercy, I pray that my heart and soul will be open and responsive to your work in the world. Amen.

Carol A. Wehrheim

AUGUST 13

ISAIAH 56:1

Maintain Justice

Thus says the LORD:

Maintain justice, and do what is right,
for soon my salvation will come,
and my deliverance be revealed.

Isaiah 56:1

The theme of this chapter of Isaiah is covenant. Isaiah is talking to the community of Israel in exile about the meaning of their deeply held religious beliefs. I cannot help but imagine, as Isaiah delivered these words to the people of ancient Israel, that they responded much like many of us might respond today: "Easier said than done!" We live in a world of stratification, dominated by injustice and inequality. As diverse people of faith, we might have a firsthand understanding of oppression and marginalization, or we might have lived life without ever encountering hardship.

Regardless of our particular status, God is clear that our connection to the Holy One is intimately connected to how we treat one another. Our righteousness comes from maintaining justice, whether it is interacting personally with those facing poverty or homelessness or advocating in our communities and world for life-giving policies that offer health care or seek equity for all God's children.

Holy and gracious God, give me the strength to do justice, love mercy, and walk humbly with you. Amen.

Kerri N. Allen

AUGUST 14

1 SAMUEL 7:3

No Other Gods

"Put away the foreign gods and the Astartes from among you."

1 Samuel 7:3

Of the Ten Commandments, the first commandment states clearly: "You shall have no other gods before me" (Exod. 20:3). For the people of ancient Israel, this admonition included foreign gods and false idols alike. In this chapter of 1 Samuel, the Scripture is connecting deliverance from the Philistines to a relationship with God. God offers freedom when the people choose God over idols.

As twenty-first-century Christians, we must wrestle with what idols we put before God. Where do we need deliverance in our lives? From pastors to political figures, money to prejudices, each of us holds onto symbols that harm ourselves, others, and, subsequently, our relationship with God.

Choosing relationship with God over idols is about living together in community. It's about how we care for the least, the lost, the lonely—the most marginalized in our midst. Having no other gods but the Holy One means drinking deeply from the love that God extends to us and sharing that love with the world around us.

God, help me to have a heart that beats only your name and love into the world. Amen.

Kerri N. Allen

AUGUST 15

PSALM 130:1–2

Hear My Cry

Out of the depths I cry to you, O LORD.
Lord, hear my voice!

Psalm 130:1

As a healthcare chaplain, I find the psalms are some of the best tools in ministry. They are raw accounts of direct human communication with God, and they reveal that the most devoted religious humans have always wrestled with questions about God. Here the psalmist is expressing painful emotion and demanding a response from God. Old Testament biblical scholar Walter Brueggemann describes it as a psalm of "disorientation."[1]

Some people are uncomfortable making demands in everyday life, let alone making demands of God. That is unheard of! Yet here it is, written in the Bible: God's people have cried out their deepest pains and insisted that God respond.

The psalmist is not crying out to just anyone, but to the Holy One with whom the people of Israel have covenanted, with whom the people have a long-established relationship. It is a relationship that is established over generations, with highs and lows, nurtured and strengthened by the honesty of sharing with God our deepest and darkest pains.

Gracious God, help me to share my pains and not try to hide them from you. Amen.

Kerri N. Allen

1. Walter Brueggemann, *The Message of the Psalms* (Minneapolis: Fortress Press, 1985).

AUGUST 16

MATTHEW 8:1–3

Radical Restoration

Jesus reached out his hand and touched the man. "I am willing," he said. "Be clean!"

Matthew 8:3 (NIV)

Sometimes I wonder if we get so caught up in the miracles of Jesus that we miss the radical message that is embedded in his actions. This is not solely a story about Jesus' supernatural ability to offer physical healing but a story about his power to bring justice to those who are on the margins. When I say justice, I am thinking of the Old Testament, where one of the definitions includes restoration of wholeness.

Leprosy was more than an awful skin disease; it was highly contagious, and the sufferer was often stigmatized and banished from society. Jesus' radical action was not in healing the man but in touching him. Jesus' touch restored the man not only to physical health but also to the community.

This story reminds me of Saint Teresa of Calcutta. Mother Teresa embodied Jesus' radical actions by touching the untouchables of India. Her work, like Jesus', was radical because she extended love and care to those whom no one else would acknowledge.

Lord Jesus, help me to embody and extend your radical love into the world. Amen.

Kerri N. Allen

AUGUST 17

PSALM 138:1–8

Song of Thanksgiving

I give you thanks, O LORD, with my whole heart;
before the gods I sing your praise.

Psalm 138:1

What I enjoy most about the Psalms is that they are poetry, detailing the most intimate of conversations between the psalmists and God. Their raw honesty and authenticity solidify their ability to communicate with us in contemporary times. The psalmists never attempt to hide any feelings, and in Psalm 138, this psalmist is rejoicing after coming through a difficult time. She is singing a song of thanksgiving! Her song of thanksgiving does much more than just thank God; the psalmist also makes a proclamation about God.

She understands that her experience says something important not about her personal deliverance but about God's character. And, as such, she proclaims the good news of God's steadfast love and faithfulness. Whatever darkness the psalmist walked through, she understood God to be a constant and faithful presence. And now she understands her thanksgiving must include proclaiming or testifying to God's devotion and love for God's people.

Holy One, thank you for all the wondrous and mighty ways that you work in my life. Amen.

Kerri N. Allen

AUGUST 18

2 CORINTHIANS 10:16–18

Humility in Christ

For it is not those who commend themselves that are approved, but those whom the Lord commends.

2 Corinthians 10:18

In 2 Corinthians 10, the author is writing to the Christian community gathered in Corinth and appealing to them to exhibit the gentleness of Christ. The letters to which we are privy in the Scriptures are one-way communications. We never get the full picture of what was going on in the community, but we might assume from the tone of 2 Corinthians that the community struggled with humility and relied on their human action rather than on God's.

They seem in direct contrast to the psalmist of Psalm 138. Instead of giving honor and thanksgiving to God, they are ready to take all the credit for themselves, relying on human action over divine grace. That doesn't sound much different from how far too many operate today. In today's world, it feels like we disregard the holy teachings of Jesus for false prophets and profits. This writer of 2 Corinthians both admonishes and urges the Christian community to find their strength and power in the humility and meekness of Christ.

Gracious God, when hubris overpowers, supply me with humility and grace. Amen.

Kerri N. Allen

AUGUST 19

GENESIS 50:17–20

Forgiveness

"Even though you intended to do harm to me, God intended it for good."

Genesis 50:20

This Scripture passage picks up just after Jacob died and was buried. Joseph's brothers were concerned that Joseph would seek revenge against them, for they knew that they had wronged Joseph many years before. This passage offers important insights into how we forgive as religious people.

As Christians, I think we sometimes suggest or demand forgiveness too quickly, not understanding it as a process. A couple of the main elements are present in this Genesis lesson. First, the brothers asked for forgiveness. It was not assumed that they would get it or that, because Joseph had a relationship with God, he would definitely offer it. Joseph's brothers understood that they had done something wrong and that they needed to seek forgiveness.

Another important element that we learn about forgiveness in this passage is that Joseph connects his ability to forgive to his relationship with God. Forgiveness has the powerful ability to heal wounds, but that healing begins with God. We do not do this on our own.

Holy and gracious God, enable me both to seek forgiveness and to forgive. Amen.

Kerri N. Allen

AUGUST 20

1 Thessalonians 3:12

Let Love Flow from You

And may the Lord make you increase and abound in love for one another and for all, just as we abound in love for you.

1 Thessalonians 3:12

Jesus named loving one another "the greatest commandment" and built his ministry on this cornerstone.

Out of his great love, Christ laid down his life for the world. Such love, when received, compels us to love. Yet too often when we try to love just as we are instructed to, we end up bitterly disappointed. Our love of neighbor sometimes goes unacknowledged by others, which in turn drives us into deep sadness. We feel unappreciated and even question the need to love our neighbors. If we are not careful, this sadness will eventually solidify our hearts and turn them into stone.

Truthfully, our love is selfish and seeks self-gratification. God's love, on the other hand, flows abundantly. We can truly love our neighbors when we understand that our love originates not from ourselves but from God.

God, you are the source of love. May it flow through me like living water. Amen.

William Cheung

AUGUST 21

COLOSSIANS 4:2

Let Prayer Instruct You

Devote yourselves to prayer, keeping alert in it with thanksgiving.

Colossians 4:2

As I was growing up, I was always told to say my prayers. My parents reminded me to "pray in your sleeping and in your waking." So I prayed before every meal and every exam. Each time I prayed, I felt a sense of fulfilling my duty as a Christian. But something was missing.

As I grew older, I began to realize that my prayers simply functioned as a wish fulfillment checklist. While it is important to lay out our needs before God, prayer must be much more than a one-way request.

Prayer must also be relational. Our moments of meditation offer us the opportunity to listen and deepen our encounter with God. God invited us to listen as well as speak, to learn God's language. In silence, we wait. In silence, we reflect. Let prayer instruct us about God's answers.

God, speak to us in our time of silence with you. Instruct us. Amen.

William Cheung

AUGUST 22

ROMANS 10:17

Let Faith Develop You

So faith comes from what is heard, and what is heard comes through the word of Christ.

Romans 10:17

When I talk to others about faith, I often say, "The way you live in this world will be defined by what you believe in." In fact, the more you believe in something, the more you will steer your life toward that belief. It's no surprise, then, that our faith will determine our footprints in this world.

Faith gives purpose and meaning to life. It is through faith in Christ that we begin to develop a sense of identity that connects us to God. Such faith cannot be developed by human hands but rather is a gift from God. By the power of the Holy Spirit, the faith that we receive is life-giving. Faith ushers in a new way of living in the world; we learn to place our trust in God and in God's promises. Let faith develop us.

God, as our faith journey continues to grow, may we walk with you. Amen.

William Cheung

AUGUST 23

PSALM 119:105

Let Scripture Enlighten You

Your word is a lamp to my feet
and a light to my path.

Psalm 119:105

What is the first thing you look for when a thunderstorm brews outside and the power inside your house suddenly goes out? My guess is that you look for a flashlight.

Power outages can bring a sense of unrest into our homes. The darkness can disorient even those most familiar with the layout of the house. But once a light has been lit, the entire house becomes visible again. What was once covered in darkness has now been uncovered by the light.

Our life journey includes pockets of darkness. The Scriptures act as the flashlight that guides us along the darkened path. Its wisdom and comfort shines through the darkness and brings back order to replace chaos. We all need the Word of God to be the light that brings us back into God's warm embrace. Let Scripture enlighten us.

God, let your Word be our light. Amen.

William Cheung

AUGUST 24

ROMANS 15:13

Let Hope Surround You

May the God of hope fill you with all joy and peace in believing, so that you may abound in hope by the power of the Holy Spirit.

Romans 15:13

Nine years ago, I said good-bye to my father for the last time. After my father was ravaged by cancer, our family knew that he was not long for this world. In the hospital, the doctors came by to check on my father's vitals, but they found no signs of improvement.

An overwhelming darkness engulfed me when my father died. I wallowed in despair as we prepared his funeral. During his service, however, something amazing started to happen. My tears of sorrow turned into tears of joy and peace. It was then that I realized that I had been placing my hope in the world. I should have been placing my hope in God. God's hope reminds us that death is not final. Eternal life awaits those who believe. Let hope surround us.

God, in times of despair may you fill our hearts with hope. Amen.

William Cheung

AUGUST 25

EPHESIANS 4:32

Let Forgiveness Restore You

Be kind to one another, tenderhearted, forgiving one another, as God in Christ has forgiven you.

Ephesians 4:32

Forgiving those who sinned against us can be extremely difficult. Whether the hurts were intentional or accidental, they can leave us with scars.

In spite of our natural desire to get back at those who hurt us, God offers another path. The path of forgiveness. Forgiveness doesn't mean taking offenses lightly. Rather, forgiveness reassures us that there is enough love from God to willingly restore the relationship.

Restoration also happens when we forgive ourselves. I can think of countless times when I was unable to forgive myself for mistakes I made. However, Scripture teaches us that the strength of forgiveness does not come from us but from God. Through God's forgiveness, we are restored as children of God. Let forgiveness restore us.

God, may we find healing in forgiveness. Amen.

William Cheung

AUGUST 26

PSALM 34:18

Let God Captivate You

The LORD is near to the brokenhearted,
and saves the crushed in spirit.

Psalm 34:18

With all the distractions of the world, it's easy to forget that God is the center of our lives. We tend to think about God when we are going through troubled times or when things are not going our way. But during normal days, God simply gets replaced by other gods. Money, fame, and worldly ambitions again take center stage in our lives.

We must remember that God is more than an afterthought. Our God is the creator of the universe who sent Jesus to die for our sins, the God whose love has captured the hearts and souls of many. In God's presence, we come to the realization that nothing in this world can compare to God. For this, we worship and glorify God, ever seeking God's presence to dwell among us. Let God captivate us.

God, you are our center. Captivate and draw us closer to you. Amen.

William Cheung

AUGUST 27

PSALM 139:1–6, 13–15

Creating

For it was you who formed my inward parts;
you knit me together in my mother's womb.

Psalm 139:13

There is an innate desire in all of us to be known and loved just as we are. Psalm 139 is a beautiful summation of what it means to be known and loved by our God. As I write this, I can feel the gentle nudges and movements of a growing child inside my own womb. Nurturing and sustaining a life within my own body has shown me not only how much love and awe is involved but also how much sacrifice and discomfort is involved in creating something new.

And yet, we, as humans, continue to create and try new things in spite of sacrifice, discomfort, and pain, because we also know that those go in tandem with the wholeness and joy of knowing that we have been participants of making something ourselves. Through that creative process, I believe that because we participated in it, we know it.

What will you create or what are you creating now that challenges you and helps you grow?

Holy Creator, grant us the creativity and endurance to bring about something new to this world for your glory. Amen.

Irene Pak Lee

AUGUST 28

PSALM 139:1–6, 13–15

Understanding

Even before a word is on my tongue,
O LORD, you know it completely.

Psalm 139:4

I grew up with parents who spoke English as their second language. There were several times in my youth when I would have to translate their English to folks who could not quite understand what they were saying or when my parents struggled to find the words in English to communicate what they were trying to say.

As I grew older and as email and texting became more prevalent, I realized that I had never really "heard" their mistakes until I could visually see them, because my mind continued to correctly autotranslate whatever they were trying to communicate. I could always understand what they were saying. The same thing happened as I began raising a child of my own. People would struggle to understand his toddler words, and yet I knew exactly what he was saying. Being known and taking the time to understand someone is a gift that is learned. May we make that effort today with someone whom we struggle to understand, whether it be across language, culture, or difference.

God, grant us the patience to understand as we seek to be understood. Amen.

Irene Pak Lee

AUGUST 29

1 Samuel 3:1–10

Up and Down

Then the LORD called, "Samuel! Samuel!" and he said, "Here I am!"and ran to Eli, and said, "Here I am, for you called me." But he said, "I did not call; lie down again." So he went and lay down.

1 Samuel 3:4–5

The first time I took my two-year-old out on a scooter, he was excited to try it out. I did a short demonstration, and he was ready. With a huge grin, he got on and did it for about five seconds. In that sixth second, he began to slowly lose his balance, and his little voice exclaimed "whoa!" as he fell down.

Without skipping a beat and with a smile on his face, he got back up and tried again. He fell and got back up three or four more times before a look of discouragement began to form on his face. After that, whenever we would try, I had to demonstrate again before he would do it, and now he's a pro.

I am reminded that we all need guidance and encouragement when we are up and when we are down. We need to find those voices who will tell us the truth and perceive what is happening around us. Who is that for you? Are you that voice for someone else?

Holy God, may we be the one to lift up someone today. Amen.

Irene Pak Lee

AUGUST 30

1 Samuel 3:11–20

Difficult Truths

As Samuel grew up, the Lord was with him and let none of his words fall to the ground.

1 Samuel 3:19

A gift and a curse that I had for a long time was trying to give people the benefit of the doubt when listening or speaking with someone with whom I disagreed. This was a gift because it's kind to give people the benefit of the doubt. It was a curse because I found myself hearing words or phrases that at times diminished my humanity or the humanity of others. I used to choose to "let it go" because of assumed ignorance around the statement the person made.

However, over the years, I've found myself empowered to speak difficult truths more boldly, especially if the humanity of those around me or myself are being diminished in any way, shape, or form. I've also learned that this difficult truth telling is met with a lot of defensiveness and sometimes anger. I realized that avoiding those reactions was not benefitting anyone, and it was keeping me from being fully who I am. No one should have to diminish himself or herself in order to lift someone else up.

Almighty God, teach us how to speak difficult truths in love. Amen.

Irene Pak Lee

AUGUST 31

JOHN 1:43–51

Seeing and Smelling the Roses

Nathanael asked him, "Where did you get to know me?" Jesus answered, "I saw you under the fig tree before Philip called you."

John 1:48

Throughout my life, it has usually been through the eyes of another that I have seen something that I had not noticed before. Sometimes it is as simple and delightful as my toddler stopping at every rose he sees to observe and smell it, thus allowing me to do the same. He also says hi to every ant he sees on the ground. Other times, throughout my faith journey, it has been someone recognizing a gift they see in me and then naming that gift to me. Usually I am surprised or taken aback at what they have noticed.

Nathanael was seen and known before he even knew Jesus, and when Jesus identifies him as already known, Nathanael is amazed and chooses to follow. Perhaps our challenge today is to start noticing and then naming those things around us that we normally wouldn't notice, whether that be roses along our walk, ants on the ground, or a gift in someone we see.

Help us to pay attention, O God, so that we might be seen and help others to see themselves more clearly. Amen.

Irene Pak Lee

SEPTEMBER 1

PSALM 139:13–18

Fearfully and Wonderfully Made

I praise you, for I am fearfully and wonderfully
made.
Wonderful are your works;
that I know very well.

Psalm 139:14

I grew up in a culturally Korean home in the United States. Navigating two cultures as a child was sometimes easy and sometimes confusing. For example, in Korean culture, if someone gives you a compliment, it is polite to reject that compliment several times rather than accept it. However, in U.S. culture, I learned that one is to simply say "thank you!" when receiving a compliment, and it is considered rude to reject it.

In general, though, I believe it's much easier to shower others with compliments and praise rather than noticing, honoring, and accepting the gifts we have within ourselves. I struggled with the balance of humility and false humility for a long time until I realized that the God who knows me loves me so thoroughly that there is nothing I can do or not do to deserve that love. Today, how can we give praise to God for all of the ways in which we are fearfully and wonderfully made?

Loving God, help us to remember the ways in which you see and know us. Amen.

Irene Pak Lee

SEPTEMBER 2

PSALM 139:13–18

Known in Song

I try to count them—they are more than the sand;
I come to the end—I am still with you.

Psalm 139:18

Years ago, several members of our church choir decided to form a separate "care choir" that visited shut-ins to sing hymns to them. It was a holy practice, and members loved it. I was scheduled to make a particular pastoral visit to a member in hospice care. She was someone whom I had noticed had all the hymns memorized and could sing them without holding her hymnal when she was at church. So I made some calls at the last minute to see if anyone could join me to sing a few songs to her, and almost everyone in the choir showed up.

We squeezed into her room, and we sang and prayed together. It was a gift to all of us as we saw her singing along with us, even as she was coming into her final days. Now, anytime I visit someone in hospice care, I will always sing a hymn to them, and sometimes I am startled and blessed again to hear their voice joining mine.

Loving One, remind us of the ways in which we are blessed to be a blessing to others. Amen.

Irene Pak Lee

SEPTEMBER 3

MATTHEW 25:34–40

Just Do It!

"Just as you did it to one of the least of these . . . you did it to me."

Matthew 25:40

Brandon was wearing his black chef uniform when we first met. He had been working at the Fredericton Community Kitchen for only one month. Previously Brandon had cooked in high-end restaurants, but all that changed when he saw the advertisement for his current position. When asked why he made the change, Brandon stated, as if it should be obvious to me, "Cooking for the homeless gives my life purpose. If I didn't cook, my guests would go hungry."

I do not know if Brandon believes in God. I did not ask. But as I watched the "least of these" stand in line to be fed, more than food was being served. As each person was greeted by name and welcomed to supper, they also received the gifts of dignity and respect. And as I stood to the side and watched, I felt the presence of the unseen guest at the table.

Stranger God, help us to see you and welcome you. Amen.

Kelly Higgins

SEPTEMBER 4

Psalm 139:1–6, 13–18

Watch Your Words

I praise you, for I am fearfully and wonderfully made.

Psalm 139:14a

Words have power. They can define how we feel about ourselves. And if we are told that we are "not good enough" on a regular basis, we may start to believe it and deny the beauty that lies within us. This happened to my friend Maeve (not her real name), who has beautiful green eyes that sparkle when she laughs.

From as far back as Maeve can remember, she was told that she was lazy and stupid. When her parents were drinking, the verbal abuse became worse. Maeve thought that if she tried to get help, no one would believe her. After all, her mother was a first grade teacher and her father was the Sunday school superintendent at their local church.

The psalmist's message that we are wonderfully made applies so aptly to friends like Maeve, who need us to remind them of their own worth and beauty. I know that I cannot take away the pain of Maeve's childhood, but I can be present to her when she needs me and can reassure her that she is enough. Why? Because she has been wonderfully made. Choose your words carefully. Others are listening.

God of words, thank you that we are fearfully and wonderfully made. Amen.

Kelly Higgins

SEPTEMBER 5

JEREMIAH 18:1–11

Strong Together

Just like the clay in the potter's hand, so are you in my hand, O house of Israel.

Jeremiah 18:6b

The Hebrew expression *s'i et ha-na'ar v'hahæziqi et yadek bow* means "Pick up the child and hold him by the hand." A more literal translation of these words reads: "Make your hand strong in his." Either translation brings comfort to me, for there is nothing like feeling the hand of someone who cares for you, especially when life is difficult.

And life can be filled with difficulties, such as a sick parent, a drug-addicted daughter, a clinically depressed teenager, or a lost loved one.

The prophet Jeremiah reminds us that there are actually hands to reach for when we feel overcome by life's burdens. God's hand is only a touch away, in the outstretched hands of the helpers who walk beside us.

God of outstretched hands, help me to accept the help you provide. Amen.

Kelly Higgins

SEPTEMBER 6

JOHN 11:30–36

Touched by Love

Jesus wept.

John 11:35 (NIV)

It has been two years since Steve (not his real name) took his own life. The pain and hopelessness Steve carried with him was just too much to bear. I still miss him. The day I learned that he had died, I sat on a bench in the park and cried. Even now there are times I think I see him in a crowd—a young man with a backward ball cap, boyish grin, and dark sunglasses. In that moment, time stands still.

Choosing to keep going is a daily struggle for many people. Depression, divorce, bankruptcy, and other serious issues, combined with the usual tasks of everyday living, can become overwhelming.

Knowing that Jesus wept when his good friend died has given me permission to feel my loss of Steve. I cannot change what happened to Steve, but I can continue to work with his family and advocate for better mental health services in my hometown.

God of tears, hold us close when we miss the ones we love. Amen.

Kelly Higgins

SEPTEMBER 7

Luke 14:25–33

Become My Disciple

"Whoever does not carry the cross and follow me cannot be my disciple."

Luke 14:27

What does it mean to follow in God's way? I ask myself that question quite often. Perhaps you do too. We can easily get caught up in the consumerism of North American culture and believe that our happiness is tied to how much "stuff" we have. But does "stuff" give our lives meaning?

Today's Scripture is an invitation to let go of our attachment to possessions as a first step in making way for a more meaningful life. Jesus invites us to make room for more sincere connections with others through acts of service, heartfelt conversations, and a deeper commitment to loving kindness.

Walking with God, do you need to carry all the stuff you have? Or can you let some of it go?

God who walks with us, prepare our hearts to understand what it means to follow you. Amen.

Kelly Higgins

SEPTEMBER 8

Psalm 139:1–6

A Letter to God

O Lord, you have searched me and known me.

Psalm 139:1

Dear God,

Thank you for the psalmist's words. I need reminding that you are present in my life. In fact, you will not let me go.

As I write to you, I grieve that others may not wish to be known by you. Life has made them afraid. When they tried to be who they truly are, the world rejected them and they were hurt. It will take them a long time, if ever, to trust the psalmist's proclamation that you know and love all your children.

Inspire me to be a positive role model for those who live in the shadows. May I speak gentle words of acceptance so that those who have been reticent can come forward and be who you created them to be.

We are as distinct as the many grains of sand in your creation. Help us to celebrate one another and offer encouragement and acceptance so that all may know your loving kindness and feel your abiding presence in their lives.

Servant God, inspire us to bring your acceptance and love to others. Amen.

Kelly Higgins

SEPTEMBER 9

PHILEMON 1:1–21

Transformed by Prayer

When I remember you in my prayers, I always thank my God.

Philemon 1:4

Do you take the time to talk with God? I know I am asking a very personal question, not one that is the stuff of conversations at neighborhood barbecues or community dances. And yet, I'm curious: Do you pray?

There are as many kinds of prayer as there are people praying them. Sometimes in the dark, we cry out to God hoping for an answer. Other times we speak with joy as we give thanks for a blessing. On still other occasions, our prayers are actions. We feed the hungry or sit at the bedside of someone who is dying.

For me, praying is as essential to my life as breathing. I pray to understand. I pray for guidance. I pray when I ask God to be present with those in difficulty, and I pray for our world leaders to be compassionate. But most of all, I pray to be transformed so that I will grow into the person God intended.

Praying helps us to know that within all of us, there is a light that is greater than the darkness of the world. I pray that we let our lights shine today.

God of the desert prayer, thank you for the prayers that change us. Amen.

Kelly Higgins

SEPTEMBER 10

1 SAMUEL 3:1–10

I'm Listening

Now Samuel did not yet know the LORD, and the word of the Lord has not yet been revealed to him.

1 Samuel 3:7

If only God would be so obvious when trying to tell me something. An e-mail, a phone call, or a face-to-face conversation would be so much easier than our usual conversations. Typically I listen hard, wondering if God is speaking through my thoughts (doubtful) or through others around me (frequently not). Discerning the voice of God is the subject of poetry and books, a topic for spiritual direction, something we discuss in our small group or Bible study conversations.

How do you hear God? I would, like Samuel, assume the guy in the room down the hall was calling me. I would never leap to the conclusion that God was saying my name. What a discerning priest is Eli, recognizing that this boy was hearing God's voice. And what courage Samuel must have had to respond to God, whose very presence was considered overwhelming.

God, help us and those around us listen for your call. Give us wisdom to discern your voice among all the clamor of this world. Amen.

Laura Mariko Cheifetz

SEPTEMBER 11

1 Samuel 3:11–20

It Isn't Always Easy

"See, I am about to do something in Israel that will make both ears of anyone who hears of it tingle."

1 Samuel 3:11

This is very awkward. God tells Samuel something pretty bad about his mentor's family. God plans to punish Eli's house. Between you and me, this is not what I would expect to hear from God, no matter how terrible Eli's sons were. I would imagine God and I might have delightful conversations, probably about me and my life, not about some other family. A conversation with God about me would be even more fun than taking one of those personality tests.

We don't always hear what we want to hear. This story is a reminder that most of the time, it's not about me. It's about something bigger than myself. And what faith for Eli to hear the message God gave to Samuel about his own house and to say, "It is the Lord; let him do what seems good to him" (v. 18). How very devastating and hard for a parent and priest to hear such news, after a lifetime of service. Eli's faith in God was bigger than the fate of his own family.

Dear God, give me the strength to hear the difficult things. May my faith continue to grow. Amen.

Laura Mariko Cheifetz

SEPTEMBER 12

PSALM 139:1–6

We Are God's

You search out my path and my lying down,
and are acquainted with all my ways.

Psalm 139:3

I find it disconcerting when my family or friends can see right through me. They tell me things I hadn't noticed or accurately guess what I'm thinking or feeling. This is also somewhat comforting, to be known so well. I do not need to put on a good face or spend much time explaining myself. I have friends whose reactions I can predict. I know their dietary preferences, their coffee order, and what will help them after a tough day.

This psalm proclaims how well God knows us. We do not have to explain ourselves to God; God knows the words we will say before they are even on our tongues. We are thoroughly known and loved. This is an immanent God, right here with us through it all, like our oldest, closest friend or the auntie who knows exactly what task to give us to do during difficult family visits to help us through. God knows all our ways. God loves us that much.

Holy One, you know me better than I know myself.
Thank you for loving me. Amen.

Laura Mariko Cheifetz

SEPTEMBER 13

PSALM 139:13–18

The Mind of God

I praise you, for I am fearfully and wonderfully made.

Psalm 139:14

Every time someone in my sphere has a baby, I marvel at all the things that had to go right for a baby to be born. We are physically complex creatures, and there are so many steps between living only in someone's imagination as a possibility and emerging as a whole human. The psalm tells us God knows us so well that God sees how we are all put together before anyone else sees it.

Then the psalm pivots to God's thoughts. At some point in my faith journey, I decided it seemed presumptuous to imagine we could know anything about God's thoughts. But if God knows us so well, what does that tell us about God's thoughts? The psalmist calls God's thoughts weighty and vast, "more than the sand" (v. 18).

This makes perfect sense. If God knit us together and understands who we are at our most elemental, then we have glimpsed how very complex and numerous God's thoughts must be.

God of mystery, I can only imagine what you know. Thank you for the gift of life. Thank you for knowing me and loving me. Amen.

Laura Mariko Cheifetz

SEPTEMBER 14

1 Corinthians 6:12–20

The Body as a Temple

Do you not know that your body is a temple of the Holy Spirit within you, which you have from God, and that you are not your own?

1 Corinthians 6:19

There's so much going on in this passage. If you read it out of context, it's like a splash of cold water on your face. A little judgmental, we might think.

The bigger story, of course, is not this checklist of behaviors. After all, any of us who hasn't fornicated or been with a prostitute or been dominated by food isn't automatically doing everything right. All of us are to consider what it means for our body to be a temple of the Holy Spirit within us.

I heard a pastor describe God's presence as our very breath within us. Our bodies are not just hosts for God, nor are they only ours to do with as we please. Our bodies are for glorifying God, even if they are growing older or if they aren't quite as mobile as they once were. God made these specific bodies, with all their assorted quirks, desires, and varying levels of usefulness, for God's work.

God, you came to be with us in the person of Jesus, who showed us how someone embodies your glory. Make me a temple. Amen.

Laura Mariko Cheifetz

SEPTEMBER 15

John 1:43–51

Known and Called

"Do you believe because I told you that I saw you under the fig tree? You will see greater things than these."

John 1:50

I have met people I do not know who say things like, "I know who you are." It's a terrible disadvantage, being caught flat-footed, in a moment where the other party knows you but you don't know them. Poor Nathanael. The first thing Nathanael says when he hears about Jesus is, "Can anything good come out of Nazareth?" (v. 46) and yet Jesus knows him so well already, as an Israelite of no deceit (v. 47).

Jesus seems to know about Nathanael, who becomes a disciple of Jesus. Those of us serving in leadership in our churches are called to be disciples. Some of us are deacons, or elders, or committee chairs, or youth advisers. People who see some potential in us think to call us, precisely because we are known.

I like to remember to identify a few faithful disciples, younger than I am, whom I can recommend for committees, as writers, or as speakers. Something good came out of Nazareth. Surely we can find something good around us.

God, help me to see the potential in others. Draw me out of myself to get to know others so that, together, we might better serve you. Amen.

Laura Mariko Cheifetz

SEPTEMBER 16

MARK 8:27–30

The Gospel Is Dangerous

He asked them, "But who do you say that I am?" Peter answered him, "You are the Messiah."

Mark 8:29

Peter declares Jesus to be the Messiah right after Jesus healed the blind man at Bethsaida, telling the man not to go into the village to display his renewed vision. Once it became clear to his disciples who Jesus was, such knowledge became a threat. In the Gospel of Mark, Jesus understood he was in danger. He knew what he was saying and doing in his ministry put him at risk. The Messiah was not a mighty and powerful king, with security forces to protect him. He wasn't particularly popular with those in power. The Messiah was shaking things up, disturbing people.

After ordering the disciples not to tell anyone, Jesus goes ahead and keeps on teaching and preaching. For someone worried about his safety, he sure took some risks.

I can be inconsistent. I can waver between cautious and bold. I can spend a week being judicious and then throw my worries into the wind and stand up to say whatever I am thinking. The gospel, after all, is bold. We follow a Messiah whose ministry put him at risk of the cross.

God, being a disciple is dangerous business. Give me courage, help me face the storm, and comfort me even as I disturb others with your healing, risky gospel. Amen.

Laura Mariko Cheifetz

SEPTEMBER 17

EPHESIANS 4:2

Courage Comes from God

With all humility and gentleness, with patience, bearing with one another in love.

Ephesians 4:2

There are so many times we need courage. A neighbor just discovered that she has lymphoma. I asked what she wanted me to pray for during our visit, and she said that what she needs most is courage.

Courage is the ability to step forward in a situation that seems risky or frightening. When facing treatment for a disease, we need the courage to step forward into the abyss to fight for our health. When taking a stand for what is right and just, courage pushes us out of our comfort zone.

The good news we receive from our faith is that we are never alone. When we have to say hard words or face a frightening disease, we can ask God to give us courage. Over the years, I have discovered that realizing God will provide what I need in the hard places—the right words, just enough power to move forward—gives me the courage I need to move forward.

Thank you, God, for giving me the courage to face the hard things today. Amen.

Jane Plantinga Pauw

SEPTEMBER 18

GALATIANS 6:9

Persistence Comes from God

So let us not grow weary in doing what is right, for we will reap at harvest time, if we do not give up.

Galatians 6:9

Rose was born in Burundi and at age twelve began a life of running, hiding, and searching for safety. Tribal genocide devastated her province, and she fled with her extended family beside her. Along the way, Rose married and had fourteen children. She describes years of starving while trying to protect her family.

Today, Rose and some of her family live in Seattle. They have housing and food. The children and grandchildren all go to school. Even though Rose and her husband never learned to read and write in their own language, she fights hard for each of her children to do well in school and to stay out of trouble.

Rose persisted, despite overwhelming difficulties. And almost every Sunday in church, she stands and, in her few words of English, raises her arms and face to the heavens and says, "Jesus! Thank you, Jesus!" The only thing that kept Rose going, when it would have been easier to give up, is the persistence she got as a gift each day.

Thank you, God, for helping me to keep going when it was the hardest. Be with those fleeing persecution and violence. May they be comforted by your presence. Amen.

Jane Plantinga Pauw

SEPTEMBER 19

JOHN 14:27

Peace Comes from God

Peace I leave with you; my peace I give to you. I do not give to you as the world gives. Do not let your hearts be troubled, and do not let them be afraid.

John 14:27

The Bible talks a lot about peace. The Old Testament calls it *shalom*, and it connotes a state where all is well: relationships are healthy, our hearts are at peace, all people flourish, and the earth thrives. The whole creation groans for shalom, and we long for that time when by God's grace the new heaven and a new earth display the fullness of shalom.

In the meantime, as we work and long for shalom, we are sometimes given a gift: the "peace that passes understanding." It seems too good to be true, but in the midst of broken and chaotic lives, God can show up with a peace that gives our hearts respite.

A woman is fighting a brain tumor, the most aggressive type you can get. Tears are just below the surface: both tears of grief and tears of joy. For her and others, the miraculous gift of "peace that passes understanding" brings feelings that all is well, even when life circumstances are bleak.

Healing God, I pray for those who are ill. Bring us peace even in difficult circumstances. Amen.

Jane Plantinga Pauw

SEPTEMBER 20

HOSEA 11:4

Kindness Comes from God

I led them with cords of human kindness,
with bands of love.
I was to them like those
who lift infants to their cheeks.
I bent down to them and fed them.

Hosea 11:4

Years ago I accompanied one of my parishioners to court. He had to face a judge for a ruling that could come with a huge fine and even jail time. As we walked, a poster on the wall caught my attention. It read, "Be kind to others. Everyone you meet is carrying a heavy burden." Just imagine the burdens being carried in that courthouse that day.

Kindness is like a balm to our hearts when we are troubled. In one of the most exquisite passages in the Bible, the prophet Hosea describes God as reaching out to the wayward people with "bands of love," gently bending down to them to feed them.

When we are suffering, words and acts of kindness are God's very arms reaching to us tenderly, like a mother brushing her baby's cheek. Our arms and words can bring God close to others when we remember that everyone we meet is carrying a burden.

God, remind me to be kind to others, mindful of their burdens. Be with me as I bear my own. Amen.

Jane Plantinga Pauw

SEPTEMBER 21

DEUTERONOMY 9:7

Really? Anger Comes from God?

Remember and do not forget how you provoked the LORD your God to wrath in the wilderness; you have been rebellious against the LORD from the day you came out of the land of Egypt until you came to this place.

Deuteronomy 9:7

Jamal was in line at the grocery store behind a woman who spoke very little English. The cashier grew impatient when the woman didn't understand his instructions. "No! It goes this way!" he snapped as she tried again and again to insert her card. The woman was flustered and close to tears.

As Jamal watched, his blood began to boil. How could this man humiliate this woman, who was just trying her best? Turning away from the cashier toward the woman, he told her that it was okay, that she was doing fine, and that he would stand with her as she inserted her card.

Jamal was feeling God's feelings along with God: anger at one person humiliating another. His surge of anger pressed him toward offering the balm of kindness and help to someone in need. When this happens, anger is from God.

Just and righteous God, your anger boils when your children are bullied and oppressed. Fill us with the anger you feel, that we may be instruments of justice. Amen.

Jane Plantinga Pauw

SEPTEMBER 22

PSALM 40:3

Wonder Comes from God

He put a new song in my mouth,
a song of praise to our God.

Psalm 40:3

I found myself lying on the grass, eyes just inches from the soil and the grass. As I looked, a tiny insect darted between the blades. My eyes refocused and rested on tiny specks of green between the blades of grass—moss, maybe? Then, once again, a miniscule creature circled the green looking for a hiding place. I found myself drawn into a mesmerizing eco-system so tiny that it had eluded me for the past forty-three years. I wondered how many microscopic creatures dotted the landscape beyond my sight.

When we wonder, we find ourselves in a universe swirling with detail beyond even the best human minds. How could you have thought of all these stunning details, God? I wonder what lies below the surface of this rock? I wonder how that hours-old baby knows how to nurse for the first time, or how the flowers know when to bloom.

At its deepest, wonder leads to God, whose mind holds such infinite imagination and wisdom that it boggles our minds.

How infinite are your thoughts, O God! I am in awe of you. Thank you for the wondrous universe you created. Amen.

Jane Plantinga Pauw

SEPTEMBER 23

GENESIS 18:4

Rest Comes from God

"Let a little water be brought, and wash your feet, and rest yourselves under the tree."

Genesis 18:4

During a recent trip to Israel, we found ourselves stuck on Shabbat with no food and no stores or restaurants open. The entire town had shut down—not a car on the road, not a light on in the shops. Families were dressed in their best and held freshly baked challah as they walked down the block to celebrate Shabbat with friends and extended family. As we watched, we felt a longing for a way of life peculiar to our family. Childhood memories of pot roast dinner at Grandma's after church on Sundays returned with warm nostalgia.

Many of us suffer for lack of rest—the kind of rest that simply sits and exults, with family or friends, in the goodness of life. When we rest, we give up any notions that we make the world turn. We turn it over to the One who really does make the world turn. We notice, see, revel in, and enjoy the simple gifts of God poured out on this particular day. When we rest, we see and know God.

Fill us with your beauty, O God, as we rest in you. Amen.

Jane Plantinga Pauw

SEPTEMBER 24

Psalm 97

A World Built on Justice

Righteousness and justice are the foundation of his throne.

Psalm 97:2b

I once spent a day observing traffic court. One case was particularly memorable. The offender lived and worked two hours away. His violation warranted time in our county jail, so the judge asked about his work schedule. Could he report to the jail by seven o'clock on Friday evenings? "Yes, sir!" The judge then sentenced the offender to serve time over the next several weekends.

I was surprised that a jail sentence could be completed this way. Later I had an opportunity to ask the judge about it. He said a sentence should not cause the offender to lose his job and further compound his problems. By serving time on weekends, the offender could pay a debt to society, learn from his mistake, and stay employed.

What comes to mind when you think of justice? The God we worship judges the world, and our actions have consequences. But justice is not the same as revenge. A traffic judge showed me how justice and mercy go hand in hand.

O Judge of all, I give thanks that you are both merciful and just. Amen.

Barrie Miller Kirby

SEPTEMBER 25

PSALM 97

World Created, Re-created

His lightnings light up the world;
the earth sees and trembles.

Psalm 97:4

As I write, yet another hurricane spins toward my home state of North Carolina. Coastal residents are boarding up the windows of their homes and businesses before evacuating. Farther inland, where I live, we are stocking up on bottled water, bread, and peanut butter. We are filling our cars with gasoline.

Like other people, I have prepared by making the necessary purchases and moving loose items from my patio into the garage. But I did something most people don't do while waiting for a hurricane. I transplanted some liriope in my front yard. I separated overgrown pieces and replanted them around a cedar tree.

Extreme weather reminds us of God's power. But the God who creates a hurricane also fashions the delicate purple liriope blooms. The storm will undoubtedly leave devastation in her wake. My transplanted liriope serves as a reminder: out of chaos, God brings life.

O God, as I face the storms of life, remind me that your creative power also re-creates. Amen.

Barrie Miller Kirby

SEPTEMBER 26

John 17:20–26

For the Sake of the World

As you, Father, are in me and I am in you, may they also be in us, so that the world may believe that you have sent me.

John 17:21

Were you ever in a play? Then you know that actors, dancers, singers, director, and others must work together so that the show can go on.

Chapter 17 of John's Gospel contains what is considered Jesus' high priestly prayer. Verses 20–26 are his prayer for the church. Jesus prays that future believers may be united in love with him, the Father, and one another. Jesus doesn't ask this for the sake of the church. He asks this for the sake of the world. Jesus wants others to see his followers' love and believe that God the Father has sent him.

Sometimes we forget that the church exists not for its own sake but so that the world may come to believe in Jesus. When we lose sight of that purpose, we are like a theatre troop stuck in endless rehearsal, never performing for a live audience. Let's remember our goal and work together, each doing our part so that the world may believe the gospel.

O God, help me remember my goal of sharing your gospel with the world. Amen.

Barrie Miller Kirby

SEPTEMBER 27

Acts 16:16–34

Who in the World?

While she followed Paul and us, she would cry out, "These men are slaves of the Most High God, who proclaim to you a way of salvation."

Acts 16:17

When Paul and his fellow travelers visited the Roman city of Philippi to share the good news of Jesus Christ, they encountered an enslaved girl. We know little about her. She was certainly not someone Paul and his companions expected to recognize them, their God, or the salvation they proclaimed. Yet there she was.

We can read stories throughout the Bible of unexpected people who proclaim the truth of God. Rahab, a prostitute of Jericho, says that the Lord the God of the Israelites is God in heaven and on earth. King Cyrus of Persia proclaims to the Judean exiles that the Lord, the God of heaven, charged him to build a house of worship. Eastern astrologers follow a star, seeking to honor the infant Jewish king. Paul, a Jewish persecutor of the church, becomes the primary apostle to the gentiles.

Sometimes truth is spoken by those we least expect to proclaim it. Who in the world would you never expect to speak the truth of God?

O God of all, open my ears and heart to hear and receive your truth. Amen.

Barrie Miller Kirby

SEPTEMBER 28

ACTS 16:16–34

A World on the Move

But when her owners saw that their hope of making money was gone, they seized Paul and Silas and dragged them into the marketplace before the authorities.

Acts 16:19

Here we see Roman resistance to those who proclaim the gospel. Businessmen seize Paul and Silas because the apostles' activity cuts into their livelihood. They fabricate charges, claiming that Paul and Silas are disturbing their city and promoting customs that are not Roman.

This episode, like many others, demonstrates that the Bible is a story of migration. From Abram leaving Ur to Paul arriving in Rome, God's people are on the move. Even Joseph and Mary with the infant Jesus seek refuge in Egypt, where their ancestors were once enslaved.

As the people of Israel wandered through the wilderness, the Lord told them to love the foreigners among them. God reminded them that their people were foreigners in Egypt (Deut. 10:17–19; Lev. 19:33–34). Yet in many countries, foreign immigrants still face resistance, just as Paul and Silas did.

Where are your ancestors from? What obstacle did they face in their new country? Who welcomed them?

I give thanks, O God, for those who left home to share the news of Jesus Christ. Amen.

Barrie Miller Kirby

SEPTEMBER 29

ACTS 16:16–34

The World Is Watching

About midnight Paul and Silas were praying and singing hymns to God, and the prisoners were listening to them.

Acts 16:25

An elder at one of my churches often reminded me that someone is always observing our actions. That was certainly the case with Paul and Silas. They were not directly sharing the good news with other prisoners. Yet their prayer and praises to God were overheard and resulted in many people becoming believers.

Behavior matters. A young man shopping at a Family Dollar store stepped into the checkout line behind a mother and toddler. The woman had a basket of merchandise. The young man didn't know her, but he asked, "Ma'am, would you let me pay for that?" The mother gratefully agreed. An older woman in line observed the exchange. When the young mother left, the older woman thanked the man for his kindness. She was so impressed by his example that she shared the story of his kind gesture at our church.

For many people, our actions are the only "gospel" they will ever read. The world is watching

Guide me, O God, so I remember that others are watching for your love. Amen.

Barrie Miller Kirby

SEPTEMBER 30

REVELATION 22:12–14, 16–17, 20–21

All the World Is Welcome

The Spirit and the bride say, "Come."
And let everyone who hears say, "Come."
And let everyone who is thirsty come.
Let anyone who wishes take the water of life as a gift.

Revelation 22:17

What an invitation! It extends not just to some. All who receive it pass it on. Everyone who thirsts is welcome. Anyone who wishes may drink. People from around the world come to the Holy City through gates that never shut. Yet some obvious sinners remain outside.

What gives? How can the image of a God who is both merciful and just fit with this scene? Such exclusion contradicts the picture of the father who runs to embrace his self-indulgent son trudging home. It clashes with Jesus, who prayed as he died that God would forgive his executioners.

Maybe it's not particular people who are excluded, but certain attitudes and actions. Maybe before entering the New Jerusalem, some things will have to be checked, such as hurtful viewpoints and behaviors.

Will everyone who wishes drink from the water of life? Let's hope so. But let's also examine ourselves. What will we need to check at the gate?

Gracious God, help me set aside whatever does not reflect your will. Amen.

Barrie Miller Kirby

OCTOBER 1

AMOS 8:1–7

The Good Fruit of Compassion and Honesty

This is what the Lord GOD showed me—a basket of summer fruit.

Amos 8:1

Several of the prophets use the metaphor of fruit to refer to the good deeds that come from faith. It's a great metaphor. Who doesn't like a sweet, juicy piece of fruit?

Jesus develops the metaphor further in John 15. Fruit comes from trees that are carefully tended, with roots that soak up the rains. Water, soil, and air combine to create delicious fruit. In the same way, faith in God, nurtured by worship and prayer, bears good fruit.

In today's reading, Amos describes bad fruit as selfishness, cheating, and disregard for the needs of the poor. He notes that God will not forget this kind of behavior.

Good fruit, according to Amos, must involve generosity to people in need and scrupulous honesty in the marketplace. Most of all, good fruit involves understanding that our everyday behavior—everything we do—matters to God.

Loving God, let our love for you bring the fruit of love, generosity, and honesty. Amen.

Lynne M. Baab

OCTOBER 2

AMOS 8:9–12

A Famine for God's Word

They shall wander from sea to sea,
and from north to east;
they shall run to and fro, seeking
the word of the LORD,
but they shall not find it.

Amos 8:12

Have you ever felt like nothing in the church prayers, sermon, or music relates to you? Have you ever read the Bible and had no words come alive? Amos refers to just such a famine of spirit, "not a famine of bread, or a thirst for water, but of hearing the words of the LORD" (v. 11b). This famine is one aspect of God's judgment on the people of Israel for cruelty to the poor and dishonesty in the marketplace.

Sometimes we feel distant from God because of our sin, and we need to confess and receive forgiveness. At other times, we've done nothing to cause those difficulties. If we blame ourselves for every hard thing in our lives and every moment when we feel distant from God, we will become paranoid and anxious people.

When we experience a famine of God's presence, we can ask God for wisdom to live in ways that enable us to hear and respond to God's voice.

Loving God, open our hearts so that we can hear your voice and bear fruit. Amen.

Lynne M. Baab

OCTOBER 3

PSALM 52:1–9

Trusting in God's Steadfast Love

But I am like a green olive tree
in the house of God.

Psalm 52:8a

It sounds so simple: Trust in God instead of riches. Love good and not evil. Yet wise Christians in every age remind us that we will spend our entire lives learning to do this.

Believing in God's goodness is a key component of trust. God's "steadfast love" is huge, but we can trust this love only if we take the time to notice all the ways God shows up in everyday life.

Psalm 52 gives a few hints about how to notice and trust. The psalmist refers to thanking God. I've been practicing daily thankfulness for more than twenty years, and it has helped me perceive God's steadfast love.

When we trust in God's love, we become like a vibrant tree thriving in God's house. We receive enough water to have healthy leaves and abundant fruit.

God of steadfast love, help me to practice daily gratitude. Amen.

Lynne M. Baab

OCTOBER 4

COLOSSIANS 1:15–20

A Hymn to Jesus the Creator and Sustainer

He himself is before all things, and in him all things hold together.

Colossians 1:17

I majored in biology in college, and some of my most intense "worship" experiences took place in the biology lab. I loved looking at algae and bacteria under the microscope. The intricate shapes spoke to me of God's amazing creativity. I also worked part-time for an astronomy professor, learning about the stunning size of the universe and the beauty of the stars.

I love the verses in Colossians 1 about Jesus' role in creation. Not only were all things created *through* Christ, they were created *for* Christ. In Christ, all things hold together. All those bacteria and stars show the careful handiwork of Christ as a member of the triune God.

Christ's role in creation is even greater than I imagined as a student in biology lab!

Creator God, help us to bring forth the good fruit of caring for your creation. Amen.

Lynne M. Baab

OCTOBER 5

COLOSSIANS 1:24–28

Good Fruit from Suffering

. . . which is Christ in you, the hope of glory.

Colossians 1:27b

Suffering as a source of growth is mentioned throughout the New Testament, especially by the apostle Paul. In Colossians 1, he says he rejoices in his suffering because somehow he is completing the sufferings of Jesus on behalf of the church.

For the first two (maybe three!) decades of my life as a follower of Jesus, I hated the idea that God could use suffering to bring good fruit. During those decades of trying to ignore biblical passages about suffering, I experienced many years of depression.

I've been free of depression for more than twenty years. My husband often tells me how he sees me as more compassionate and responsive to the needs of others.

I am so grateful for the mellowing of my spirit that he now sees. Truly, in some mysterious way, Christ has been formed in me, partly because of suffering.

Please use the hard moments of my life to produce good fruit in me. Amen.

Lynne M. Baab

OCTOBER 6

LUKE 10:38–42

Focusing on the Better Part

There is need of only one thing.

Luke 10:42a

I have always loved the title of a book by Danish theologian Soren Kierkegaard, *Purity of Heart Is to Will One Thing* (New York, 1847; repr., Wilder Publications, 2008). I have often pondered what is the one thing that matters most in life. What is the one secret that will help me have a meaningful career, enjoy my family, stay physically fit, and bear good fruit in my life?

Mary sits at Jesus' feet and listens to his words, ignoring the need to prepare food, and Jesus commends her for choosing the "one thing . . . the better part" (v. 42). But Mary's done three things: sitting, listening, and ignoring. Which is the one?

This story, like so many in the Bible, points to drawing near to Jesus as the one thing. That's it! The one thing is our relationship with a living God.

Jesus, help me to draw near to you as Mary did. Amen.

Lynne M. Baab

OCTOBER 7

LUKE 10:38–42

Drawing Near to Jesus

She had a sister named Mary, who sat at the Lord's feet and listened to what he was saying.

Luke 10:39

As a young adult, all the Christians around me insisted that we each practice a daily morning quiet time that consisted of reading the Bible and then praying.

But I found it easiest to read the Bible at bedtime, and I prayed best while walking! It took me many years to understand that Jesus is with us everywhere, and I could spend time "sitting and listening" in many settings in my life.

Throughout the history of the church, a wide variety of ways of drawing near to Jesus have been accepted and honored. What matters is making space to pay attention to the presence of Jesus with us, the One who teaches and guides us. Jesus is the One who brings good fruit when we obey and trust.

Jesus, thank you for accompanying us into every setting of our lives. Amen.

Lynne M. Baab

OCTOBER 8

2 Samuel 18:5–9, 15, 31–33

Caught

And he was left hanging between heaven and earth.

2 Samuel 18:9

In the thick of battle against David's fierce army, the mule on which Absalom was riding took a wrong turn, catching Absalom's hair in the branches of a great oak. He was caught, unable to move—hanging between heaven and earth, vulnerable to his enemies, unable to free himself from the complicated circumstances that brought him to this place. He waits for either the hand of violence or the touch of compassion to resolve his dilemma.

Who in your life is caught between heaven and earth? Perhaps not as dramatically as Absalom, but nonetheless bound by life's complexity? Where might you have the power to release another from being suspended between isolation and community, fear and grace, judgment and understanding? Where might a merciful word, gracious act of welcome, a hand extended in invitation, make all the difference for another? Is God directing your gaze to see the perplexity of another person's "caught" place?

Holy One, free me to recognize the pain and perplexity of another, to ask what love requires to ease the silent suffering of another caught between heaven and earth. Amen.

Melanie Oommen

OCTOBER 9

2 SAMUEL 18:5–9, 15, 31–33

Broken Hearts

"Is it well with the young man Absalom?"

2 Samuel 18:32

Violence begets violence. We need read only the morning newspaper to see the pileup of hatred upon revenge upon betrayal upon viciousness, layer upon layer. Of course it wasn't well with Absalom: when the question was posed, he was already dead by the hands of his father's soldiers. David and Absalom's story began and ended with violence.

We don't have to look far in the world around us to see the same fierce story playing out again and again, in international news and in the drama playing out down the street. Maybe it is even in our own home.

By faith, we allow our hearts to be broken open by this ancient and modern story. By faith, we pray that Jesus' witness of love will form our thoughts, our actions, our words. By faith, we can boldly enquire, "is it well with my sister?" "is it well with my brother?" and then work with love and diligence to make sure it is.

Peacebuilding God, grant us your courage to seek
the welfare of our neighbors, our enemies, ourselves,
committing again to live your life of peace. Amen.

Melanie Oommen

OCTOBER 10

Psalm 130

Expectant

I wait for the L*ORD*, *my soul waits . . .*

Psalm 130:5

What does it mean to live with expectancy for that which we most desire? Parents waiting for a new baby don't simply wait: they shop, read, start a college fund, prepare their home, reimagine what the future will be. A church family readies for service by finding out who their forsaken neighbors are, figuring out what they need, and asking what structures have brought them to the outskirts of justice.

Expectant waiting nudges us to prepare for that for which we long. Waiting is active. Waiting is a witness of love. Where do you yearn for the Holy to enter into your soul? The lives of your loved ones? The fabric of your community? The world?

It isn't our job to do all the work of preparation, but it is our gift and responsibility to do our part: to pray, to be vulnerable, to reach out, to dream, and to listen with love. We should expect that, by God's grace, we should help form the world in a more generous shape.

O Longing of our hearts, we wait for you and your ways. Show us how to live with expectancy. Amen.

Melanie Oommen

OCTOBER 11

EPHESIANS 4:25–5:2

God Can Work with It

Let all of us speak the truth to our neighbors. . . . Be angry but do not sin; do not let the sun go down on your anger.

Ephesians 4:25–26

Did you double-check your Bible to make sure the text really says "be angry"? Honestly, that's news to me. Somewhere I heard that Christians were supposed to be patient and kind, bearing all things, etc. But there is a place for anger, the kind that isn't left to fester and doesn't lead to worse offense. It is the anger that finds expression. I tell my neighbor (my spouse, my boss, my child) that I'm angry and why, as an act of faith.

How could that be an act of faith? Perhaps because truth is more important than comfort, because anger can be born of conscience. God planted within us compasses of conscience that move us further from our desire and closer to God's will for the world. Perhaps the first authentic thing we can do when anger wells up in us is to recognize it and name it for what it is. And then we can bless it as a gift and let it be shaped by love, choosing words and expressions that fulfill true righteousness and not the self-righteous sort.

Spirit of love, transform my anger into energy and passion to do your will of love. Amen.

Melanie Oommen

OCTOBER 12

EPHESIANS 4:25–5:2

Perfect Practice

Therefore be imitators of God, as beloved children, and live in love, as Christ loved us.

Ephesians 5:1–2

When my children were small and preliterate, they would listen carefully to the words I spoke when reading them picture books, studying the pictures that went with the words that I read aloud. Then, when they thought I wasn't paying attention, they would "read" on their own, carefully turning each page and repeating the appropriate words exactly as I had spoken them. It made me ever more careful of the books that I chose, knowing how carefully they imitated.

Could we be so attentive to God's actions? How have you known love—yesterday, last week, in your childhood? What did love feel like, look like, sound like? Is God's love the kind that you know when you see it, or do you have to practice to be awake to it? Can we be like a young child, reciting by heart words first spoken by the loving parent? Observing so carefully each consonant and diphthong of love? Christ is all around, in each generous act of compassion and courage. Might we have the will to imitate?

Christ Jesus, help us to practice to perfection how to live in love. Amen.

Melanie Oommen

OCTOBER 13

JOHN 6:35, 41–51

Blessed Hunger

Jesus said to them, "I am the bread of life."

John 6:35

Most of us get three meals a day, and then some. When we skip a meal, hunger hurts. I can't imagine living without my morning coffee, a bowl of steaming soup, or chicken curry. Our days are framed and our social calendars are punctuated by meals. Our need to be fed is constant. Yet Jesus says that the true bread is not rye or sourdough, but him, as elemental to our existence as a bowl of oatmeal in the morning. On his life and leading we can feast and be filled.

When life has worn us down, no other sustenance can revive us. That's how elemental the life of faith is. Jesus' life infused with mercy is the only thing that will truly satisfy our yearning for a purposeful, sacrificial life of love. And when we fall out of relationship and live on the surface of life, that hunger gnaws at us until we return to the holy feast of love. What would it look like if we tended our relationship with Jesus as consistently as we respond to our bellies?

Bread of Life, I am so grateful that my hunger keeps leading me back to you. Amen.

Melanie Oommen

OCTOBER 14

JOHN 6:35, 41–51

Ordinary

"Is not this Jesus, the son of Joseph, whose father and mother we know?"

John 6:42

A few years after graduating from high school in the boring hometown in which I was raised, I heard that a former classmate of mine had a starring role in a musical on Broadway. We had been the leads in our high school musical, and now he was a star? The guy who struggled to learn his lines, messed up his blocking, and failed repeatedly to hit the high note? I was glad for his success but also puzzled by it. How could I have been that close to brilliance and not known it?

Jesus claimed to be the bread from heaven, and his neighbors and friends wondered, where does this regular guy get these big ideas? But ordinary is what God knows best—like the mud that God shaped into Adam, God loves to work with our common bodies, our regular selves. Jesus offered his ordinary human life to a dream of salvation for all creation. May we follow such an example of faith, hope, and love.

Creator of all, take the ordinary mud of my life and use it for your extraordinary purposes. Amen.

Melanie Oommen

OCTOBER 15

PSALM 138

Practicing Gratitude

I give you thanks, O LORD, with my whole heart;
before the gods I sing your praise.

Psalm 138:1

One of the central practices of a wholehearted life, as author and professor Brené Brown describes it, is gratitude. She was surprised to discover in her research that joy follows gratitude.* People aren't grateful because they have joyful lives. Rather, because they cultivate a practice of gratitude, joy wells up in them.

The psalmist understands that gratitude requires intention and practice. We can start by declaring our intention to give thanks with our whole heart and to sing God's praise in specific ways. It helps me to find cues to lift up thanksgiving prayers throughout the day. Waking prompts me to recite a verse like the one above before even getting out of bed. Sitting down at the table signals giving thanks for food plus one other blessing. Washing hands invites gratitude for my baptism. Bedtime means naming the day's gifts by writing gratitude notes in a journal. Praise be that the more we practice giving thanks to God, the more our heart is given over to joy.

I will give thanks to you, O God, with my whole heart. Help me to sing your praise today. Amen.

Julie Coffman Hester

* Brené Brown, "Brené Brown on Joy and Gratitude," Global Leadership Network, November 21, 2018, https://globalleadership.org/article/brene-brown-on-joy-and-gratitude/.

OCTOBER 16

PSALM 138

Naming Prayers of Thanks

I bow down toward your holy temple
and give thanks to your name for your
steadfast love and your faithfulness;
for you have exalted your name and your word
above everything.

Psalm 138:2

In one church I had the joy of leading weekly preschool chapel. Arriving children would share prayer concerns, and teachers would give me these prayers with names. They were mostly prayers of thanks: for parents, siblings, pets, toys, butterflies, grilled cheese, Jesus, and the whole wide world.

After our Bible story and between enthusiastic songs, we'd pray. I'd share several prayers aloud, naming the child. I'd often see little heads pop up with delight when they heard their name and particular prayer shared aloud.

Our individual prayers are personal and specific. As we call God by name, we proclaim our own thanks and praises and affirm that God knows us by name. In prayer, we claim God's steadfast love and presence, and we affirm God's attention to us individually as a beloved child.

Our chapel prayers always ended with a group thanksgiving: "We'd *all* like to tell you thanks, God!" Indeed.

God, you know us by name and hear our prayers.
Thanks. Amen.

Julie Coffman Hester

OCTOBER 17

PSALM 138

Praying in the Past, Present, and Future

On the day I called, you answered me,
you increased my strength of soul.

Psalm 138:3

Prayer crosses boundaries of time. Even while praying in the present, we look back and forward. The God to whom we pray is the God we know because of all that has come before. We know God who is present in Scripture's stories of patriarchs and matriarchs, in its stories of Jesus and his disciples. We pray to God who has been there in our own past too.

With the psalmist, we look back and remember past prayers in which we called on God. We recall past prayers for healing, comfort, and direction. Sometimes we were strengthened as we prayed. Sometimes, perhaps, it took a long time before we knew God heard us. Some of us may still be waiting, in hope and faith. Because of what God has done in the past, we can pray in the present, even as we entrust the future to God. In this way, past, present, and even possible future times of doubt or pain become defined not by the trouble in them but by the way God is always present during them.

Ever-present God, you hold the past, present, and future. Help me to always trust in you. Amen.

Julie Coffman Hester

OCTOBER 18

LUKE 11:1–13

Learning to Pray

He was praying in a certain place, and after he had finished, one of his disciples said to him, "Lord, teach us to pray, as John taught his disciples."

Luke 11:1

How did you learn to pray? As a child at the dinner table, I learned to give thanks for daily bread. In worship, I learned to pray for forgiveness, for the community of faith, and for the world. In hospitals as a patient, family member, and pastor, I learned to pray for healing and strength. At gravesides, I learned to pray for peace and comfort. In workshops, I learned to pray in color, in labyrinths, with poetry, and alongside the news.

I suppose I should say I *began* to learn in those places and times. Each new day offers up a fresh opportunity to grow in prayer, doesn't it? Every new illness, grief, or joy teaches us something about prayer. God keeps speaking and showing up in new ways. Learning to open our ears to hear, eyes to see, and hearts to respond is an ongoing practice.

This year I'm learning to pray as I write. Even as I write these words, I am learning to pray with and for you. How are you learning to pray in these days?

Lord, teach us to pray. Amen.

Julie Coffman Hester

OCTOBER 19

LUKE 11:1–13

How Are We to Pray?

He said to them, "When you pray, say:
Father, hallowed be your name.
Your kingdom come."

Luke 11:2

The disciples want to know how to pray. They saw Jesus praying regularly. Perhaps they wondered: What are the right words, posture, place, and time? How do we get prayer right? But Jesus begins the lesson for them and for us by illuminating a relationship. It's not so much the *how*, but the *who*. Prayer is a conversation with God as a close, loving family member. Whatever word of address we use—Father, Mother, Lord, God, or something else—we speak and listen to One who knows us as a beloved child.

Then, in the next breath, Jesus reminds us that the One to whom we can speak so directly is, at the same time, hallowed—holy and set apart. Our prayers are to the One who reigns. With Jesus, we pray that God's kingdom will come in all its justice and joy.

How are we to pray? We pray as beloved children in relationship with the transcendent God, whose reign is sure. Thanks be to God.

Holy One, thank you for hearing my prayers as your own child. May your kingdom come. Amen.

Julie Coffman Hester

OCTOBER 20

LUKE 11:1–13

Praying for Daily Bread

"Give us each day our daily bread."

Luke 11:3

"It's not fair," the fifth grader said. We were in the middle of a hunger simulation. Our group was divided up something like the world's population. The majority had a communal pot of rice. A middle group had rice, beans, and water to drink. A tiny group had a full chicken dinner and dessert. There was grumbling by all except the table with cake.

"We don't have enough, and it's not fair," she said, eyeing the overloaded table. "No, it's not," I agreed. "What can you do? The rules say begging or stealing aren't allowed."

"We can pray . . . loudly," she said. Then she rallied her group to stand and pray the Lord's Prayer. "Thy kingdom come," they prayed, with escalating volume. "Thy will be done, on earth, as it is in heaven. Give us this day our daily bread. . . ." Eventually there was sharing by some from the cake table.

When we pray for daily bread, either alone or as a group, our plea is not personal but communal: give *us our* daily bread. God's kingdom vision is a radical one where no one goes hungry.

Give us all daily bread. Amen.

Julie Coffman Hester

OCTOBER 21

LUKE 11:1–13

Praying for Forgiveness

"And forgive us our sins,
for we ourselves forgive everyone indebted to us.
And do not bring us to the time of trial."

Luke 11:4

As a young adult, I took lifeguard training so that I could help keep swimmers safe at my summer camp. It's possible I'm remembering this wrong, but I recall one question that asked, essentially, "How will you react if you see someone drowning?" Despite all my other training, the correct answer was, "I don't know." We don't actually know what we will do under pressure. Still, we practice so that we will be ready, and we pray.

Forgiveness is a bit like lifeguarding. We can value it, practice it, and pray for our ability to offer it. When it comes right down to it, though, we don't know if we can actually forgive others until faced with the terrible need. Jesus teaches us to pray regularly for the strength to forgive, as we also ask God to forgive us. Even as we trust that God continues to dive in and rescue us, forgiving us over and over again, we pray that we can do the same for one another.

Lord, please forgive me, and help me to forgive others. Thank you for rescuing us all. Amen.

Julie Coffman Hester

OCTOBER 22

ISAIAH 7:10–16

Responding to God in Faith

But Ahaz said, I will not ask, and I will not put the LORD to the test.

Isaiah 7:12

When God told Ahaz to ask God for any sign he wanted, Ahaz refused to make the request, claiming he would not "put the LORD to the test." Elsewhere in the Bible, explicit instructions are given that we are not to test God, so in this way, Ahaz seemed obedient. Except, in this moment, God *told* Ahaz to test God and ask for a sign! God grew weary of Ahaz's refusal. Why did Ahaz refuse?

At times, I find myself afraid to ask God for things as well. Sometimes it is because I am afraid God will *not* answer. Other times, it is because I am afraid that God *will* answer. Just like Ahaz, once I have seen what God has to show me and once I have heard God's answer, it is then my turn to be faithful and follow as God leads. This can be scary. Yet, as Isaiah tried to tell Ahaz that God is always faithful, we, too, will see signs of God with us as we live into the challenge of being faithful to God.

God, help me to trust you, to recognize your signs in my life, and to follow where you lead. Amen.

Layton E. Williams

OCTOBER 23

ISAIAH 7:10–16

Accepting the Answers God Offers

Therefore the Lord himself will give you a sign. Look, the young woman is with child and shall bear a son, and shall name him Immanuel.

Isaiah 7:14

In previous verses, God instructed Ahaz to ask for any sign as "deep as Sheol or high as heaven" (v. 11b), but Ahaz refuses. So Isaiah revealed that God would offer a sign of God's own choosing—a child called Immanuel or "God with us." I have to imagine that, of all the signs Ahaz might have asked for God to give him, he would probably not have chosen a baby. And yet, that was the sign that God chose to demonstrate God's faithfulness and care.

How often do we find ourselves praying for God to show up in our lives in particular ways? As the hoped-for answer to a desperate prayer or the ideal outcome for an uncertain situation? How often do circumstances go differently than we expect or hope, leaving us questioning God's faithfulness, only to find God fully present with us in unexpected way? In Jesus, God delivered a promise that God is always with us in ways we may never expect or predict or even ask for, but which God knows we need.

Help me to see you, God, in the unexpected ways you are present with me. Amen.

Layton E. Williams

OCTOBER 24

Psalm 80:1–7, 17–19

Recognizing God in Charge

Restore us, O God;
let your face shine, that we may be saved.

Psalm 80:3

I am a natural problem solver. In any given moment, I scan a situation for potential risks or issues and identify ways to avoid them or fix them if needed. If I am not careful, I can fall into the trap of assuming that I always know the best way for things to be done and then easily become frustrated when others are not doing things in that way. My problem-solving skills can be helpful in a pinch, but they can also fool me into thinking that I know more than I do.

Psalm 80 reminds us that what saves us is not our own smart thinking or our inflated opinions of our problem-solving capabilities. Rather, what saves us is when the glory of God's presence is allowed to shine in the world, when God's love for us and for all creation is fully reflected in the ways we treat one another and the earth. It is not all on us, thank goodness!

God, help me to know that you are in charge and your loving presence is what saves the world. Amen.

Layton E. Williams

OCTOBER 25

Psalm 80:1–7, 17–19

Giving and Receiving Trust with God

Then we will never turn back from you;
give us life, and we will call on your name.

Psalm 80:18

As I imagine is true for many, the hallmark of my closest friendships is a deep trust between us. This trust has not only been established through shared values and experiences but also hard won through difficult seasons we weathered together. There have been times when we let one another down or hurt one another, but we managed to heal and rebuild our relationships. Such trust, I have found, is rare but beautiful.

Psalm 80 is about a people who shared this kind of deep trust with God, and it invites us to share that kind of deep trust with God as well. These people faced hard, scary times. At various points, they doubted God or turned away from the way God called them to live. And yet, they turned back, over and over, and again placed their trust in God to restore them. God knew they would fail again, and yet, God still chose to love and trust them unwaveringly. How incredible to know that this is also how God loves and trusts each of us.

God, thank you for being there and for loving and trusting me always. Amen.

Layton E. Williams

OCTOBER 26

ROMANS 1:1–7

God with Us as Human and Divine

The gospel concerning [God's] Son, who was descended from David according to the flesh and was declared to be Son of God with power according to the spirit of holiness by resurrection from the dead, Jesus Christ our Lord.

Romans 1:3–4

In his Letter to the Romans, Paul emphasizes Jesus' significance both "according to the flesh" and "according to the spirit." One of the key elements of traditional Trinitarian theology is the belief that Jesus was both fully divine and fully human. This is easy enough to say but a bit harder to wrap our minds around. Why does it matter that, in Jesus, God chooses to be with us as fully human and fully divine?

It means that God's desire to be with us was not satisfied by mere proximity. God chooses to be with us by experiencing humanness in all its beauty and pain and wonder and mundanity. In Jesus, we have the promise that there is nothing any of us can experience in which God is not present with us. There is no moment of our lives in which we are alone or abandoned. God is with us, right in the mucky humanness of it all, so that to be with God, we don't have to be anything more than what we are.

God, thank you for being with me no matter what. Amen.

Layton E. Williams

OCTOBER 27

PSALM 96

Jesus' Paradigm Shift

O sing to the LORD *a new song;*
sing to the LORD, *all the earth.*

Psalm 96:1

I remember the moment I found out I was going to be an aunt for the first time. I was twenty-one years old, and suddenly, there was this tiny baby I loved and wanted to protect at all costs. My whole perspective on life and the world shifted, and it never could go back to how it had been before.

Psalm 96 proposes that we are called to sing to God a new song, and as Christians, that new song is introduced to us with the birth of Jesus. Jesus offers us a whole new perspective on God's love and how we are called to love one another. Our responsibility is to embrace this new song, to sing it with joy to God. In order to do that, we have to let go of the old songs that we have carried around. How is the song of Jesus different for you than the songs of this world? How does this new song shift your perspective and the way you live?

Jesus, help me to sing your song with gusto. Help me to release my old worldly perspective and live as you teach. Amen.

Layton E. Williams

OCTOBER 28

TITUS 2:11–14

A Zealous Faith

He it is who gave himself for us that he might redeem us from all iniquity and purify for himself a people of his own who are zealous for good deeds.

Titus 2:14

Growing up in the southeastern United States, I learned early on that college football is more than just a game. In childhood, I spent fall Saturdays in Auburn, Alabama, tailgating with family and a few hundred thousand of my fellow fans. Later, I attended the University of Georgia and shifted allegiances, but my commitment to the sport remains the same. It is hard to explain the level of passion—zealotry, even—I feel about college football to people who do not get it.

I admit that I have not generally felt the same level of zeal for following the way of Jesus or doing good deeds. But what if these *were* the kind of things we were zealous about? What if we were as committed and excited about serving others as many are about sports? Might our children learn to share our passion from a young age, and might our commitment to doing good be a source of both joyful memory and ongoing consistency in our lives? This is the journey Jesus invites us to join him on. What a gift!

Help me, O God, to do good and follow Jesus with zeal. Amen.

Layton E. Williams

OCTOBER 29

MARK 10:46–52

What Do We Get When We Get What We Want?

Then Jesus said to him, "What do you want me to do for you?"

Mark 10:51a

"What do you want me to do for you?" These are welcome words for any of us to hear in response to our loud and repeated calls for help. And, like any of us with long-standing needs or desires, blind Bartimaeus had his answer ready: "My teacher, let me see again" (v. 51b).

A follow-up question might be: What do we do when we get what we want? Bartimaeus reached out to Jesus as both healer and teacher. He believed he would see again, and he had the courage to see his place in the world differently. Bartimaeus was eager and willing to continue to learn from Jesus by following him "on the way" (v. 52).

We are thankful, God, that Jesus the healer and teacher offers us a new way of seeing and a new way of living. Like Bartimaeus, may we also willingly respond to Jesus' offer. May we find the courage to continue to learn and grow as companions with him on the road of life. Amen.

Gordon Timbers

OCTOBER 30

PSALM 146

Together on the Road of Life

The LORD will reign forever,
. . . for all generations.
Praise the LORD!

Psalm 146:10

The best travel guides not only provide information about a chosen destination but also give helpful tips for travel along the way and interactions with fellow travelers.

In ten short verses, the writer of Psalm 146 speaks eloquently about the fullness and variety of conditions of those who share the human journey. Princes are mentioned, along with prisoners, strangers, the blind, the crippled, the oppressed and the hungry, orphans and widows, the wicked and the righteous—those who are happy in their relationships with God and others with whom they walk the road of life.

The reality of having to deal with difficult situations and difficult people is not denied, but there is a clear message of guidance and hope for mortals in all times and places. Happiness comes from trusting that "all generations" are held in God's loving care.

In our experiences of comfort and joy, we sing our praise and thanksgiving. In our times of difficulty and sorrow, we sing our trust and assurance. May the love of God work in us and through us. Amen.

Gordon Timbers

OCTOBER 31

RUTH 1:1–14

Discovering and Remembering

So she set out from the place where she had been living, she and her two daughters-in-law.

Ruth 1:7

Researching family history has become very popular. Those interested can pay fees and provide DNA swabs to learn more about their family background and cultural heritage. Ads for these services show customers happily discovering people who have a place in their family tree and whose words and actions have continuing significance.

The first chapter in the book of Ruth gives us the story of Naomi, who married Elimelech, and whose sons Mahlon and Chilion were married to Orpah and Ruth. In a time of great personal loss and difficulty, Naomi was comforted by expressions of love and concern from her daughters-in-law.

On this All Hallows' Eve, the day before All Saints' Day, we continue the tradition of remembering the dead, including both the well known and the unsung, people from whom we can learn lessons about faithful living and generous discipleship.

God, we are thankful for all those who came before us and made a positive difference to the people and world around them. May they teach us to become models for Christ-motivated ministry and mission. Amen.

Gordon Timbers

NOVEMBER 1

MARK 12:28–34

Continue the Story

"You are not far from the kingdom of God."
Mark 12:34b

The popular animated movie *The Book of Life* begins with the character Mary Beth taking a group of children on a secret museum tour. The children are introduced to the book of life, a wonderful volume that holds every story in the world. Using wooden figures, Mary Beth tells a story that begins on the Day of the Dead celebration in a small Mexican town.

Many amazing adventures ensue for the characters in this story as they travel through the Land of the Remembered and the Land of the Living. The movie ends with the audience being shown the *Book of Life* and being encouraged to write their own story.

Today's observance of All Saints' Day gives us an invitation to learn from the witness of those before us who have lived a life of faith and a challenge to make our own life and ministry meaningful.

God, we are thankful for those whose witness encourages us to be faithful in our own day and time. Help us to live as lights for those who will come after us. Amen.

Gordon Timbers

NOVEMBER 2

Mark 12:28–34

The Golden Rule

There is no other commandment greater.

Mark 12:31b

The idiom "familiarity breeds contempt" can ironically apply even to the well-known and well-loved words that have come to be recognized as the Golden Rule, a universally applicable guide for how to live a good and helpful life.

The best way to respect these well-known words, rather than take them for granted, is to make them operative within us. There is a poster titled "The Golden Rule" that shows the teaching as expressed by thirteen world religions. In addition to the rights and privileges of belonging to our particular groups, races, cultures, religions, and nations, we have the responsibility to live together in peace with everyone living on this earth in what can be described as a global village. Jesus empowers us with the needed reminder that we can best love others when we know ourselves to be loved by God—fully and unconditionally.

Though we are different from one another in many ways, we are one in our need to experience love and care. We are near to you, God, as we love and care for one another. Amen.

Gordon Timbers

NOVEMBER 3

RUTH 1:16–17

Companions on the Journey

"Where you go, I will go;
where you lodge, I will lodge;
your people shall be my people,
and your God my God."

Ruth 1:16b

There is something utterly heart-wrenching about the story of Naomi. She and her husband and two sons had to flee famine in their homeland and travel far to make a new home in a different country. This was a difficult experience then, as it is for many refugees even today. While there, her husband died, as did her two sons. Naomi and her two daughters-in-law were left widows, a very precarious position for women in the society of that time.

We can easily understand Naomi's cry of despair: "The hand of the LORD has turned against me"(v. 13b). But in the actions and declaration of her daughter-in-law, Ruth, she was given new strength and courage. Naomi's situation and perspective on life changed when she claimed Ruth's promise of a never-ending connection and kinship, a reflection of God's faithful love and care.

How good it is, God, when we experience the loving actions of those who stand with us in our times of need. May we who have been blessed be agents of blessing to others. Amen.

Gordon Timbers

NOVEMBER 4

MARK 12:28–34

So Close

"You are not far from the kingdom of God."

Mark 12:34b

On the way through life, we sometimes want to go back and revisit a place. This is because we later discover that we missed seeing something or someone of significance. Our attention was previously deflected by things that, in hindsight, seem unimportant.

In Mark 12:28–34, Jesus commends the legal expert for his understanding about the commandment to love God, self, and others. This way of living and loving is more important than the temple's rules and regulations about burnt offerings and sacrifices.

This leaves us wondering if the scribe who had this conversation with Jesus might have later come to the realization that he had indeed been "not far" from the One who embodied and personified the kingdom of God.

Help us, God, to recognize and appreciate the blessing of Jesus always with us. As we travel on the way, Jesus is as close to us as the next breath we take. Amen.

Gordon Timbers

NOVEMBER 5

HEBREWS 11:1–3

From Things That Are Not Visible

What is seen was made from things that are not visible.

Hebrews 11:3

They are invisible, but only to our eyes.

Their influence has left an indelible mark on our lives and the manner in which we live.

There are many included in our great cloud of witnesses whose faces we have never seen, voices we have never heard, and names we may have never learned. They are nonetheless a part of the cloud that surrounds us.

The assurance of things hoped for is the inheritance we have received from their faithful devotion and real-life examples. Our very lives give testimony to their legacy and the steadfast God in whom they placed their faith. The generations that have gone before help build in us a conviction of things not seen.

They are invisible, but only to our eyes.

What are the names included in your cloud of witnesses?

God of ages past, we give you thanks for those who have gone before us who have set an example of how to live a life of faith in the midst of the passage of life. Names known and unknown, we lift to you an offering of praise. Amen.

Brian Shivers

NOVEMBER 6

HEBREWS 11:4–7

Into Your Hands, O Merciful Savior

He died, but through his faith he still speaks.

Hebrews 11:4

There is a mystery at the end of all things. No one has come back bringing testimony of that which awaits us. No one, that is, except the One who was also there at the beginning of all things. But as for us, we wait in the mystery and grieve the loss while clinging to the promise that death does not have the final word.

None of us have to think very hard to recall a time we suffered a loss that shook us to our core, seemingly tearing our hearts from our body. We walk through our days discombobulated. There, in those liminal moments, we wait, wondering what might have been. There, the memory of the promise breaks forth.

Even when our loved ones die, through their faith, they still speak. These saints of light surround us even in their absence. We have seen that not even death can separate them from us, from Christ. Therefore, even at the grave, we make our song: Alleluia, alleluia.*

God of the living, God of those who have entered their eternal rest, into your hands we commend your servants.[1] May we ever hear their voices. Amen.

Brian Shivers

* Adapted from *Book of Common Worship, Pastoral Edition* (Louisville, KY: Westminster/John Knox Press, 1993), 916.

NOVEMBER 7

HEBREWS 11:7–9

Sometimes

Sometimes the plans go differently than imagined.
Sometimes they don't seem like plans at all.
Sometimes the directions are written in crayon on the back of a used napkin.
Sometimes it feels more like wandering lost in a distant land.
Sometimes the mistakes far outweigh the victories.
Sometimes fear leads to actions that are less than desirable.
Sometimes the promise looks more like a curse.
Sometimes looking forward leads to nothing more than a crick in the neck.
Sometimes hope finds itself draped in wrinkles, capped with gray hair, and moving on wobbly knees.
Sometimes "in spite of circumstance" becomes the narrative through which hope is born.
Sometimes faith is about walking through, about sometimes finding purpose, joy, love within the journey.
Sometimes is the land of Abraham.
Sometimes is our land too.
Sometimes is the place where God promises to meet us, heirs of the same promise.

God of promise, of always, of sometimes, meet us when we don't know where we are going. Keep our eyes on those who have moved through this strange land before. It is there we find hope for the journey. Amen.

Brian Shivers

NOVEMBER 8

HEBREWS 11:23

Beauty of a Child

Because they saw that the child was beautiful.

Hebrews 11:23

Every night, I have the privilege of praying with my daughter before she goes to bed. I love it when her voice rings out, cutting through the quiet house and inviting us to come join her for our nighttime ritual. It is actually more than a ritual; it is sacred. The ground on which we stand in her light yellow bedroom is holy.

When she was four, she spoke a prayer that changed my faith journey. She prayed, "God, thank you for mommy and daddy, grandmas and grandpas, and for . . ." then she said her own name. In that thin place where heaven and earth collide, she prayed for herself, by name. I don't know if someone taught her to do that, but I wasn't going to tell her to stop. I have often wondered if I possess the faith necessary to pray for myself, by name.

Sometimes the saints in our midst are under the age of ten and have sticky fingers and unkempt hair. We keep them close to our hearts, for they are beautiful.

God of names and saints of all ages, give us the courage to pray . . . for ourselves, by name. Amen.

Brian Shivers

NOVEMBER 9

HEBREWS 11:19–31

Say Her Name

By faith Rahab the prostitute did not perish.

Hebrews 11:31

Her name is Rahab, but they call her a harlot, a prostitute,
as if she can do that alone or by choice.
They mock her behind her back,
all in an attempt to strip her
of her humanity, narrative, dignity, identity, story, life.
Yet there she stands in power,
in the pages of history, an important person,
a transformative influence, a woman, a mother of hope—Rahab.
There she stands in a world that would rather silence her
than hear her voice and speak her witness,
that would rather call her names
than acknowledge her strength to write her own story.
She has a name, the one given her by her mother.
It's not the one you call her.
Her name is Rahab.

In your story, who are the people who the world would rather not name?

God of the nameless, the voiceless, may our lives bear witness to the faithful, who are often silenced even in our own stories. May we find the courage to speak their names. Amen.

Brian Shivers

NOVEMBER 10

Hebrews 11:32–38

What More Is There?

And what more should I say? For time would fail me to tell of [them].

Hebrews 11:32

There are people in our memories and living in our midst whose stories amaze us, whose dedication is a marvel, and whose faith is a wonder to behold. They have faced more than can be imagined, have overcome more than should be possible, and they have lived to bear witness to it all.

Yet if we were to sit with them to hear their stories from the inside out instead of the outside in, they would likely talk about raging doubt, overwhelming uncertainty, and agonizing faithlessness. They would talk of being unworthy of the manner in which we speak of them.

Why are they celebrated so?

Look at their hands, calloused from never giving up, no matter how tired they were. Look at the soles of their shoes, completely worn from taking the next step in front of them, no matter how treacherous it seemed. Look at the thin fabric on their knees, evidence of a life of faith, humility, and prayer.

And what more is there to say?

God of the journey, we celebrate those who have gone before us in faith. Grant us the courage to follow their way. Amen.

Brian Shivers

NOVEMBER 11

HEBREWS 11:39–40

Not without Us

God had provided something better so that they would not, apart from us, be made perfect.

Hebrews 11:40

It is so easy to consider ourselves as less than. It is so easy to think of ourselves as not as capable, not as faithful, not as committed as those we elevate as examples of faith and exemplars of life well lived. It's as if we believe the lived and flawed experience of others is more honorable than ours. As my friend Dan says, "We like to compare our blooper reel with everyone else's highlight reel."

We forget we are claimed by the same God who empowered the extraordinary ordinary lives of the saints. We forget that the same God who walked with them through the fire and the rivers walks with us through the flames and raging waters. We forget that it has never been about our amount of faith or depth of devotion. No, the stories of the saints remind us that this journey is about the faithful God who meets us in the midst of the mess and mire and promises to not leave us alone there. These saints will not, without us, be made perfect.

God of presence, may we remember your faithfulness within our extraordinary journey. Amen.

Brian Shivers

NOVEMBER 12

EZEKIEL 34:11–16, 20–24

I Myself Will Search

For thus says the Lord GOD: I myself will search for my sheep, and will seek them out.

Ezekiel 34:11

When problems arise, we look for clear guidance. In previous verses, God said that the nation was led by neglectful shepherds who did not protect, feed, or care for the flock, letting them wander alone into dangerous places. Leaders were self-serving and uncaring. God cares for each sheep. "I myself will search."

My mother was recently in and out of the hospital and rehabilitation systems. Each move was stressful and confusing. Doctors and nurses gave us contradictory information about her diagnosis and treatment as her health rapidly declined. We repeatedly questioned whom we should trust: a doctor who saw her five minutes daily or nurses who monitored her for hours? We felt lost in the system.

We can feel lost in spiritual and personal matters, trying to listen for God's voice. Social leaders, spiritual leaders, and the media scream at us to the point of confusion, making it difficult to hear God speak. But God woos and pursues us. God is personally searching for us.

Lord, guide my steps with clarity. Never stop searching for me. I want to be in your loving care. Amen.

B. Denise Adams

NOVEMBER 13

EZEKIEL 34:11–16, 20–24

I Myself Will Be Their Shepherd

I myself will be the shepherd of my sheep, and I will make them lie down, says the Lord GOD.

Ezekiel 34:15

While my mother was in the healthcare system, no one cared for or pampered her the way her children did. The aides, while nice, fed her too quickly. The physical therapist didn't massage her foot with the attention I did. She preferred it when we moved her in bed or fluffed her pillows. Her caregivers were professional and efficient, but we did the tasks with love and tender care because she was *our* mother. Our attention was reserved solely for her.

It is wonderful to have the promise of God saying, "I myself will be the shepherd of my sheep." The One who loves us most meets our every need. In our weakness, God is our strength. In our infirmity, God tends our wounds. When we are in danger, God provides protection. When we are distracted by confusion, God makes us lay down so that we can receive peace. God's care is not out of duty but out of deep love and concern for our personal needs.

Lord, your love, care, and protection leave us in awe. May we be willing to humbly accept all that you provide. Amen.

B. Denise Adams

NOVEMBER 14

EZEKIEL 34:11–16, 20–24

I Myself Will Judge

Therefore, thus says the Lord GOD to them: I myself will judge between the fat sheep and the lean sheep. Because you pushed with flank and shoulder, and butted at all the weak animals with your horns until you scattered them far and wide, I will save my flock.

Ezekiel 34:20–22

As much as I love and respect my son, I still recognize that he is not perfect. Like all of us, he has a few flaws. As his mother, I am allowed to occasionally mention a flaw when I am talking about him to friends or family. They are allowed to acknowledge my frustration and perhaps agree with me. But they should not agree too adamantly, nor bring up other flaws. I will quickly defend his honor. I have the right to judge him as no one else can because he is my son. I judge him through eyes clouded with love.

When God claims us as God's own, divine judgment is filtered through love. God knows our innermost motives and intent. God will defend our honor as only a parent can.

David was not perfect. Yet because of his loving and contrite heart, God honored him in spite of his sins. Love wins. Consider the results of being intentional in not judging others. It leaves us free to love that person unconditionally.

Lord of mercy and grace, teach me to live out of love instead of judgment. Amen.

B. Denise Adams

NOVEMBER 15

Psalm 100

You Are Mine

Know that the Lord is God.
It is he that made us, and we are his;
we are his people, and the sheep of his pasture.

Psalm 100:3

I am a bit of an artist and a crafter. I enjoy creating something with the skill of my hands. In one sense, I like to share my creations. At least, I like others to see and appreciate them. In another sense, it is difficult to part with pieces. It is easier when I create a piece specifically to give to someone, knowing it is for them. Once it leaves my home, I am content; the pieces that I give away remain special to me. When I create for the sheer joy of creating, the piece often lingers in my home. It becomes a part of my life and my soul. I no longer wish to live without it.

God has made us for God's own pleasure and purpose. We are divine works because the artist is divine. No matter where we go or what we do with our lives, we will always belong to our Creator. We will always be special to God.

Lord, we can be sure that because we are your special creations we matter to you. Help us to recognize others as yours also. Amen.

B. Denise Adams

NOVEMBER 16

PSALM 100

I Am Present with You

Make a joyful noise to the LORD, all the earth.
Worship the LORD with gladness;
come into his presence with singing.

Psalm 100:1–2

One summer day at church camp I was alone at the outdoor worship area. Tree lined, with a mountain vista, it is nature at its best. In the early afternoon sunshine, the crickets, cicadas, and squirrels were active and raising their voices in what seemed to be a song of combined praise and thanksgiving. Their song lifted and fell in unison, a chorus of worship to their Creator. I actually felt like the whole earth joined me in worshiping the Lord with gladness—on a perfect day, in a perfect place.

While not every day is perfect and not every place is teeming with singing creatures, we can always find reasons to worship the Lord. Even in the darkest moments of our lives, we can be thankful for the joyful times of the past or be hopeful for the future joys to come. We are aware of God's continued presence with us.

Lord, I stand among all your creation, and I am thankful for your presence within me and around me. Help me to recognize your presence in others. You, oh Lord, are worthy of our thanks. Amen.

B. Denise Adams

NOVEMBER 17

MATTHEW 25:31–46

I Was in Need

"'I was naked and you gave me clothing, I was sick and you took care of me, I was in prison and you visited me.'"

Matthew 25:36

Each of these unfortunates are prisoners of their circumstances, of poverty, of their failing bodies, alienated from mainstream society. My husband's cousin is incarcerated. I occasionally write him in the state prison. When he writes back, he always says, "This is a cold and lonely place." The crimes that led to his imprisonment also alienated him from his closest family. He says I am the only person in contact with him.

This world can be a cold and lonely place when you lack essentials like food, shelter, and justice. People treat you as if you do not matter, asif you do not even exist. So Christ instructs us to be present with the poor and lonely, to recognize them and care for them, to notice them. Each act of kindness we do is caring for Jesus himself. When we free the impoverished from their prisons, we free Christ's love in our own hearts and in our world.

Lord of abundance, help me to spread your grace and love today, especially with those who need your attention the most. Give me courage to extend your love. Amen.

B. Denise Adams

NOVEMBER 18

MATTHEW 25:31–46

I Was Rejected by You

"Then they also will answer, 'Lord, when was it that we saw you hungry or thirsty or a stranger or naked or sick or in prison, and did not take care of you?'"

Matthew 25:44

As a church secretary, I often have to turn desperate people away. It is difficult and heart-wrenching to look someone in the eyes and tell them I cannot help them with a utility shut-off notice. We cannot help everyone, but we must look for ways to help some. And we should certainly treat those in need with dignity and grace, like real people, as Christ did. Often, I refer people to other community resources. While this church might not have money for utilities, the ministerial alliance may. The church down the road has a food pantry, and another has a clothes closet. Sometimes a person just doesn't know how to access the help that is available.

Find the ministries in your area that provide direct services so that, even if you cannot give out money, you know where to send someone for assistance. Volunteer regularly for at least one service organization. Look for Christ in those rejected by the world.

Lord, we struggle to be your hands and your presence in a hurting world. Continue to challenge us to receive the "least of these" (v. 40) with your kind of love. Amen.

B. Denise Adams

NOVEMBER 19

PSALM 99

The God of Wonder, Who Is Near

They cried to the LORD, and he answered them.

Psalm 99:6b

Psalm 99 leads us to imagine the breathtaking splendor of God. God sits enthroned upon the cherubim, and God is exalted over all the peoples. And the phrase "holy is he" is repeated throughout the psalm. The beauty, majesty, and holiness of God are overwhelming. God is qualitatively different from humans.

But God does not choose to stay far from us because of this difference. With all God's awesome aspects, God comes near to us. Approaching us, God forgives our sins, listens to our cries, and answers them. About six hundred years ago, a king in Korea ordered a big drum to be put near the palace. Anyone who had suffered a false accusation or unjust damage could beat the drum. When the king heard the sound, he would come out to listen to the person's appeal. God hears our prayers and gives us God's royal support. The majestic God is our kind savior, who rejoices in sharing God's self with us, in boundless love for us.

Lord, both stunning glory and humble love belong to you. Amen.

Joon Ki Kim

NOVEMBER 20

MATTHEW 22:15–22

To God What Is God's

"Give therefore to the emperor the things that are the emperor's, and to God the things that are God's."

Matthew 22:21b

In order to get Jesus in trouble, the religious leaders asked him a tricky question: "Is it lawful to pay taxes to the emperor?" (v. 17). In those days, the land of Israel had been colonized by the Roman Empire. Facing the question, Jesus said, "Give therefore to the emperor the things that are the emperor's, and to God the things that are God's." Jesus admitted that, because Jews were living under the governance of Rome, it was not necessarily wrong for them to pay taxes. But Jesus also clarified a crucial point: "Give God what is God's," which could mean, *when you give back to the emperor what is his, never forget that he is not God, even though he pretends to be.*

From the Bible, we learn that all the earth belongs to God; the slain lamb of God will turn out to be the final victor over all the powers of the world. Through our words and actions that seek the justice and peace of God, the light of Christ shines in the midst of the world.

Empower us to testify to your goodness in our lives, both personal and public. Amen.

Joon Ki Kim

NOVEMBER 21

EXODUS 33:12–23

How God Listens

The LORD said to Moses, "I will do the very thing that you have asked; for you have found favor in my sight, and I know you by name."

Exodus 33:17

For many years, the image of God that I had in my mind was basically static. God knows all; God decides all by God's self, being somewhat aloof from what happens in the world. Nevertheless, when I looked at the Bible more carefully, I was startled by the dynamic nature of God, which many biblical texts attest to. God is deeply engaged with the realities of the world. Moreover, God is willing to converse with people, and the result of the interactions affects God!

Here is a good example. Moses knew that God had been stunned and grieved by the waywardness of his people, so he strongly asked God to continue to lead him and his people. God's response: God would do everything that Moses asked God to do. God listened to, pondered on, and incorporated requests from Moses in order to shape the latter part of their journey, the future of God's people. God gladly interacts with us to deepen God's relationship with us because of God's astonishing love.

Considering how you treat us in your love, may we learn to listen to you with all our hearts. Amen.

Joon Ki Kim

NOVEMBER 22

Exodus 33:12–23

The Inexhaustible Mystery

"You shall see my back; but my face shall not be seen."

Exodus 33:23b

I knew a teacher of theology who was a kind and thoughtful mentor to me when I was studying theology in Knox College in Toronto. One day, I came up to him and asked, "Today in your class, it sounded as if you intended to say that, essentially, God is a huge mystery. Is that right?" My concern was that if a crucial aspect of God might be a mystery, it would not be possible to give brilliant, clear answers to many challenging questions raised about the legitimacy of faith and the presence of God. Hearing what I said, my teacher said to me, "Yes, indeed. If God is not a mystery, I do not think that I can truly worship God. How can we worship a certain being, if the being can be thoroughly figured out by our human intellect and capabilities?"

As God is a mystery that we cannot perfectly understand, the Bible presents the matter of faith not in terms of certainty but in terms of trust. The biblical revelations point to the inexhaustible goodness and love of God, whom we can fully trust.

Your goodness stuns us with its mysterious depth. Amen.

Joon Ki Kim

NOVEMBER 23

1 THESSALONIANS 1:1–10

Gratitude for Everyone

We always give thanks to God for all of you and mention you in our prayers, constantly.

1 Thessalonians 1:2

Paul thanked God for all the people in the Thessalonian believing community. It is not that he enjoyed the presence of *some* particular members of the community, who were notably gifted, exceptionally kind, or outstandingly committed to God's ministry. All of them led him to his genuine gratitude for God. Interacting with diverse people in our believing communities, we may be elated and inspired, but also, at least sometimes, we may be frustrated or even hurt by the words or actions of other members of the communities. How can we be thankful for all of them?

Paul knew well that he was not to appreciate the people in the communities according to one's merits or lack thereof. All the people whom he served and worked with in Christ were parts of *one body*, whose head is Christ. All of them—as his brothers and sisters—were being nourished, challenged, and transformed together by the grace of God. That was his pivotal understanding of the church communities.

How beautiful it is for the people of God to live together in love and gratitude for one another. Amen.

Joon Ki Kim

NOVEMBER 24

1 THESSALONIANS 1:1–10

God's Presence in Suffering

In spite of persecution you received the word with joy inspired by the Holy Spirit.

1 Thessalonians 1:6b

When we experience troubles in life, we may think something that is not supposed to happen is happening. Paul's understanding of hardship in life is very different. He taught that, essentially, to live as a Christian entailed suffering of various forms. The suffering may be related to an outward oppression used for the purpose of deterring one's trust in God, challenges in faith communities, or pain in one's personal life.

When we face difficulties, our human instinct may prompt us to find a way to get out of them as soon as possible, no matter what. But the message from Paul helps us to understand that the troubles can open up opportunities to hear and receive the Word of God in inspiring, creative, and transformative ways—as the faithful people in Thessalonica did. In terms of our Christian life, there is new meaningful learning, growth, and change that we can have in spite of afflictions. In the midst of suffering, Paul and those Thessalonians were filled with the bountiful joy of God, to which all of us are gladly invited.

God, we celebrate your living presence in all situations of life. Amen.

Joon Ki Kim

NOVEMBER 25

LUKE 17:11–19

The Great Thanksgiving from an Abandoned One

He prostrated himself at Jesus' feet and thanked him. And he was a Samaritan.

Luke 17:16

In the time of Jesus, lepers were shunned to the very bottom of society. Physical disease, social alienation, and religious condemnation combined to make their lives painful in myriad ways. When a group of lepers called to Jesus for help, he let them know that God's presence and healing grace were fully given to them.

If we ever think that the troubles in life diminish the opportunities to offer our thanksgivings, Luke 17:11–19 shows that the truth is quite the opposite. It is not because the trouble itself is glorious. It is because in our suffering and brokenness, Christ is nearest to us. With the power of creating new heaven and earth, the Lord restores our joy and hope.

The punch line of the story is that the only person who came back to give thanks to Jesus was a Samaritan, who was doubly marginalized and hurt among the ten lepers. God creates the occasions of the most joyful thanksgiving even out of the most severe suffering. Thanks be to God!

God, you create and call forth the songs of joy even out of the depth of suffering. Amen.

Joon Ki Kim

NOVEMBER 26

Psalm 126

From Sorrow to Dancing

Those who go out weeping,
bearing the seed for sowing,
shall come home with shouts of joy,
carrying their sheaves.

Psalm 126:6

When I reflect on what I am thankful for each year, I frequently find myself grateful for the ways that God transforms us. I come back to this psalm year after year to appreciate the move from weeping to shouts of joy.

I frequently find myself in conversations with those who do not share my faith, and we often talk about the age-old question: If God is good, why is there suffering in the world? Did God cause that suffering? I believe that God does not cause suffering—suffering is inevitable if we have free will—but that God is present with us in our suffering. What's more, God transforms our suffering. Sometimes quickly, sometimes through years of heartache, we reach peace and even joy. I like to think of the Holy Spirit as an opportunist, entering horrible situations, pondering, "How can I bring about something good, even here?" As you think about what you are grateful for today, consider the transformations in your life since last year.

Generous God, thank you for all the ways you transform our lives. Amen.

Slats Toole

NOVEMBER 27

JOHN 18:33–37

Your Kingdom Come

Jesus answered, "My kingdom is not from this world."

John 18:36

When I was a child, I took this verse to mean that Jesus did have a kingdom, far off in space. It was probably like heaven, where my young mind imagined we would all walk on clouds and ride unicorns. I believed Jesus would eventually transport all of us to this magical kingdom when he came again. Of course, as I grew older, I grew out of these ideas, beginning to understand that Jesus meant that his kind of kingdom would be something completely at odds with how our world tends to function. Jesus, who promised that the first shall be last and the last shall be first, would not have a kingdom recognizable to any of us. He was always turning things upside down, going against the cultural norms; why would his kingdom be any different?

When we pray "your kingdom come" in the Lord's Prayer, we pray for our kingdoms to be toppled so that God's can thrive. It might mean we give up some of our own power, but wouldn't that be worth it to experience what God has in store?

O Christ, help us work for your kingdom to come. Amen.

Slats Toole

NOVEMBER 28

Psalm 132:1–18

Abide with Us

"This is my resting place forever;
here I will reside, for I have desired it."

Psalm 132:14

It is easy to think of God as being far off and away. When someone passes away, it is common to say that they have gone to be with God. While I surely hope that I experience God in a deeper and more immediate way when it is my time, this verse points us to another truth: God resides with us. God is not simply in heaven, disconnected from human affairs. God is with us, choosing to live among us. God actually desires to be with us on earth, and so God came to us in Jesus Christ and continues to dwell with us in the Holy Spirit.

The idea that the all-powerful Creator and Ruler of the universe, God, wants to spend time with us is one of the most awe-inspiring wonders of our faith. Psalm 8 says, "What are human beings that you are mindful of them?" (v. 4). Compared with the whole of creation, we are almost nothing, and yet God wants to be with us!

All-powerful God, thank you for your mindfulness of us. Amen.

Slats Toole

NOVEMBER 29

Psalm 25:1–10

Jesus, Remember Me

Do not remember the sins of my youth or my
transgressions;
according to your steadfast love remember me,
for your goodness' sake, O Lord!

Psalm 25:7

The memories I always want to forget are the ones I always seem to remember. I try to hold on to the details of wonderful days, but they turn into a haze in my mind. But I can recall every excruciating detail of times when I have been embarrassed, times when I have messed up, and conversations I wish I had never had. Shame still makes me blush when I remember these, and I desperately hope that these are not the moments other people remember when they think of me.

The psalmist's prayer is very relatable; we do not want God to think of us as a compilation of our worst moments. Rather, we pray that God remembers us through the lens of God's own steadfast love for us. Just as we tend to remember the best moments of those people whom we love, we pray that God thinks of us in a favorable light. The good news, of course, is that God comes to be with us while we are still sinners, offering us redemption and new life.

Merciful God, thank you for loving us even when we fall short. Amen.

Slats Toole

NOVEMBER 30

Luke 21:25–36

All Shall Fade

Heaven and earth will pass away, but my words will not pass away.

Luke 21:33

I have always been drawn to places and practices that feel ancient. I love to stand in cathedrals where the stone has darkened from years of weathering, marveling at windows and sculptures that have withstood centuries of wear. I order my life through the liturgical calendar because it helps me to feel connected with Christians throughout the ages, practicing traditions that have been practiced since far closer to the days when Jesus walked on this earth.

In times when things are too chaotic, when our lives are in shambles, when relationships are on the rocks, when grief overwhelms us, when our livelihoods are insecure, when the world around us is in upheaval, grounding ourselves in tradition can help us feel the truth of these words of Scripture. Everything else will pass away, but God's words will remain. God is here in chaos and loss. God is here in triumph and joy. God is here with us no matter what else happens.

Ancient of days, help me to feel grounded in you. Amen.

Slats Toole

DECEMBER 1

PSALM 25:1–10

Are We There Yet?

For you I wait all day long.

Psalm 25:5b

Patience is not a value our society tends to hold dear. We live in a time of instant gratification, of everything we need being available at our fingertips to order and receive in our mailboxes the next day. This is perhaps never clearer than during the holiday season. I say "holiday season" instead of Advent or Christmas because the holiday season starts far before either of these; stores rush to put out Christmas merchandise as soon as Halloween is over.

But I have come to treasure this time of waiting and preparing. It is a time to deepen our prayer life and practices, to reflect on what Christ's coming means so that when Christmas day finally arrives, we can greet it with the joy and celebration it deserves. Practicing Advent helps sustain me in other moments of my life when I feel as if I am stuck waiting. It helps me know that there is growth to be found even when I cannot immediately feel it.

Faithful God, give me the patience to wait for you. Amen.

Slats Toole

DECEMBER 2

JEREMIAH 33:14–16

Trusting God's Promises

The days are surely coming, says the LORD, when I will fulfill the promise I made to the house of Israel and the house of Judah.

Jeremiah 33:14

Advent is the beginning of the Christian year, when we once again commit ourselves to the story of Jesus Christ's birth, life, death, and resurrection. While Christmas gets the cultural spotlight, Advent brings with it the excitement and promise of a new year as we prepare to receive the Christ child into our world. Passages like this one speak to the promise of change and hope sung throughout Scripture.

At the same time, it can be hard to hear words that speak of fulfilled promises year after year. Advent comes every year, and still there is tragedy. Christmas comes every year, and there are still too many people who do not have enough to survive. Lent comes every year, and there are still so many ways we do not reflect God's image into the world. Easter comes every year, and there is still too much death.

But I am comforted every year knowing that God is present with us in our conflict and our mess. God continues to come to us, be with us, and fulfill the promises in our time.

Emmanuel, come to be with us again. Amen.

Slats Toole

DECEMBER 3

ROMANS 15:4–13

Dancing between Life and Death

For while we were still weak, at the right time Christ died for the ungodly.

Romans 5:6

This verse in Romans is jolting as a Scripture reading in Advent, as we anticipate the birth of Christ. Yet Advent is also about Christ's return at the end of time, which happens only after death and resurrection.

Advent reminds us that we live in this middle place between birth and death. We feel both fragile and resilient in this middle place. Christ promises to take our hand and lead us in the dance of life, be it a slow, rhythmic waltz, a fast-paced quickstep, or a free-for-all.

Death, it is often said, is the great equalizer. That doesn't make it any easier when the time comes. Death is inevitable, yes, but rather than living in dread of its inevitability, let us claim the promises of Advent. As Christians, we trust that death will not have the last word. The promise born in Jesus shall be fulfilled at the end of time.

Jesus, lead me through every step of the journey, from birth to death to new life. Amen.

Kathleen Long Bostrom

DECEMBER 4

ISAIAH 11:1–10

And the Elementary School Children Shall Lead Them

And a little child shall lead them.

Isaiah 11:6b

Exhausted by years of COVID-19, gun violence, and the war in Ukraine, a local artist and elementary school teacher found a way to bring joy to her community. This teacher and her class developed PepToc, a phone hotline with words of encouragement provided by the children. Call the hotline and you can choose words of positive advice, encouragement, or simply the laughter of children. Even the Grinch's heart would grow several sizes listening to any one of these options. My favorite is the laughing children. Is there any heart that does not melt at that sound, no matter how grim the moment?

Bringing hope and joy to others is that simple. It is delivered in a thirty-second pep talk in the cheerful voices of children, in the loving sound of your voice on the phone, in a thinking-of-you note in a mailbox filled with advertisements. It is often in the smallest voices that God speaks loudest.

God, in these in-between times, let my words and simple deeds bring your light into the darkness. Amen.

Kathleen Long Bostrom

DECEMBER 5

PSALM 72:17–19

An Everyday Doxology

Blessed be [God's] glorious name forever;
may [God's] glory fill the whole earth.
Amen and Amen.

Psalm 72:19

The book of Psalms consists of 150 psalms divided into five groups, or books. Psalm 72 concludes the second book and ends with a doxology (v. 19).

Doxology is an opinion or glory expressed vocally or in writing. In many denominations, the doxology is a song of praise that comes after the weekly offering. We praise God for our many blessings, now returned in part to support the work of the church.

I like the idea of singing a doxology to God at the end of each day. We thank God for the blessings we have received and those we have given. But even more, we thank God for the gift of life itself and God's presence in, with, and around us, no matter what the day has been.

As we live in this middle place, our doxology is a lovely way to praise God with a grateful heart.

I praise you God above, God on earth, and God in every time and place, including here, right now. Amen.

Kathleen Long Bostrom

DECEMBER 6

MATTHEW 3:1–12

A Gift That Keeps Giving

In those days John the Baptist appeared in the wilderness of Judea, proclaiming, "Repent, for the kingdom of heaven has come near."

Matthew 3:1–2

Here comes John the Baptist, a ragged fanatic clothed in animal skins, eating the insects that terrorized the Egyptians during Moses' day. John hangs out by the Jordan River, baptizing anyone he can, to prepare for the Messiah who has been hot on his heels from the start.

It is startling to find John hollering repent a few weeks before Christmas.

The Amplified Bible expands *repent* to: "change your inner self—your old way of thinking, regret past sins, live your life in a way that proves repentance; seek God's purpose for your life."

I'm going to add this to my Christmas list: to let go of past regrets and live the life that proclaims God's purpose for me. These are gifts I can give and receive, ones that never need to be exchanged after the holidays.

I seek to live a life that proclaims your glory and purpose for me, O God, and promise to encourage others to do the same. In your glorious name I pray. Amen.

Kathleen Long Bostrom

DECEMBER 7

ISAIAH 35:1–10

Desert Wildflowers

The wilderness and the dry land shall be glad,
the desert shall rejoice and blossom;
like the crocus it shall blossom abundantly.

Isaiah 35:1–2a

California suffers from ongoing drought that turns the desert landscape into a monochrome of rocks, gravel, and concrete clay. A few years ago, a rainy season caught everyone by grateful surprise. The parched earth slurped up the water greedily, rousing the hidden seeds from slumber into splendor. Acres of orange, yellow, and purple wildflowers spilled across the arid land. People thirsty for beauty came in droves to view the carpets of glorious color. Our spirits were rehydrated after an endless season of dryness.

Isaiah writes of the wilderness and dry land rejoicing in abundant blossom when the Lord comes. Like the desert bursting into bloom, the glory and majesty of God's promises shower our weary hearts. Christ shall overcome the endless drought of despair once and for all. This is the promise born on Christmas, the promise that all creation shall be restored to new life.

Shower your promises on us, Child of Bethlehem.
Fill our weary hearts with bouquets of glorious hope.
Amen.

Kathleen Long Bostrom

DECEMBER 8

LUKE 1:46B–55

A Song for All Seasons

[God has] lifted up the lowly;
[God] has filled the hungry with good things."

Luke 1:52b–53

Read the entire passage of Luke 1:46–55, known as *The Magnificat.*

Read it silently and then aloud.

The poetry of this passage is beautiful—stunning, really. Take your time with it.

The Magnificat is a canticle, a song of praise and of hope. The words have been put to music numerous times, but one can only imagine the melody sung in Mary's heart and voice.

This beautiful song sums up Advent. The promise of God to redeem God's people is born into the world through Mary. God promises that, one day, heaven and earth shall be as one and all creation shall be redeemed. That promise is born in Jesus Christ.

For the remainder of Advent, read these verses every day. Let the words, images, promise, anticipation, and glorious joy soak into your soul, your mind, your imagination.

When the Christmas tree is gone and the decorations are packed away for next year, read the verses again. Hold the music in your heart and soul.

My spirit rejoices in God my Savior. Amen.

Kathleen Long Bostrom

DECEMBER 9

LUKE 1:46B–55

Not So Meek and Mild

"Surely, from now on all generations will call
me blessed;
for the Mighty One has done great things for me."

Luke 1:48b–49

Mary is often painted as being meek, mild, and submissive. Shc is anything but.

Her first response when Gabriel busts into her life with astonishing news is to be greatly perplexed. She needs a little more information, a little more time to digest it all. Even then, she challenges Gabriel: "Impossible!" Gabriel must step it up and explain in mystifying detail how she will conceive, not at all how she had expected to be expecting. She finally acknowledges her agreement to God's preposterous plan, knowing pregnancy could cause all kinds of dangerous reactions. Still, she welcomes it.

Mary's song of praise is anything but meek. It is strong and jubilant, claiming the great things God has done, granting her the privilege of bearing the Savior into the world. "All generations will call me blessed," she sings aloud. The blessing comes with terrible sorrow, but she accepts it.

It takes courage to bear God's Word into the world. Only by the grace of God can we do so.

Almighty God, grant me the courage of Mary as I seek to bear your light into this world. Amen.

Kathleen Long Bostrom

DECEMBER 10

MATTHEW 11:2–11

Good News for All

> *When John heard in prison what the Messiah was doing, he sent word by his disciples and said to him, "Are you the one who is to come, or are we to wait for another?"*
>
> Matthew 11:2–3

What just happened? Not long ago, John baptized Jesus and preached the necessity of repentance. Now, in prison because of a jealous queen, John sends his disciples to ask Jesus if he is truly the Messiah that John foretold. Why does he question Jesus now? Has John lost his faith in Jesus because his own life is at risk?

Jesus' response is to send John's disciples back to him with the news that "the blind receive their sight, the lame walk, the lepers are cleansed, the deaf hear, the dead are raised, and the poor have good news brought to them" (v. 5). The Messiah brings justice to God's people but also hope to those who have been treated like nobodies because of conditions deemed unworthy by society. This is indeed good news for all.

Thank you, Jesus, that nobody is beyond the reach of your grace. Amen.

Kathleen Long Bostrom

DECEMBER 11

ISAIAH 11:1–10

Inward Appearances

He shall not judge by what his eyes see,
or decide by what his ears hear.

Isaiah 11:3b

Christians have long heard this Isaiah passage about Jesus, the Messiah. During Advent, Isaiah reminds us that Jesus was a descendent of King David and his ministry was one of peace and justice. Isaiah proclaims that the coming Messiah will be able to see deeper than mere outward appearances. When we strive to imitate Christ, we are likewise called to see others not by their outward appearances but inwardly.

Some years ago, I was making my weekly trip to the small dump near our cottage in northern Michigan. The dump was overseen by a semiretired man often dressed in dirty coveralls. He typically greeted dump visitors with slightly bawdy jokes. I had always seen him by these outward appearances, until the day I commented on the lovely day and he proceeded to recite a long and stunningly beautiful poem about fall weather.

Teach us, O Lord, not to judge others by outward appearances but to see them deeply. Amen.

Michael L. Lindvall

DECEMBER 12

Isaiah 11:1–10

Peace and Justice

With the breath of his lips he shall kill the wicked.

Isaiah 11:4b

When we hear this familiar Advent passage from Isaiah, the portion that begins, "The wolf shall live with the lamb" (v. 6) falls much more comfortably on our ears than "he shall kill the wicked" (v. 4b). We often put the qualities of peace and justice together, but in a sense they can be in tension with one another. Peace suggests freedom from coercion and violence. Justice hints at the judgment of others, even the punishment of evil, as in this verse.

Yet, in another sense, peace and justice are like two sides of one coin. Where there is rank injustice, peace will be uneasy, if not impossible. And where greater justice reigns, peace becomes a realistic possibility. Isaiah insists that God is a God of both peace and justice. We who would follow God are called to work and live for both peace and justice, remembering that each is needful and that one cannot thrive without the other.

O God, may our hearts burn for justice and yearn for peace. Amen.

Michael L. Lindvall

DECEMBER 13

ISAIAH 11:1–10

Are We There Yet?

They will not hurt or destroy
on all my holy mountain;
for the earth will be full of the knowledge of the
LORD
as the waters cover the sea.

Isaiah 11:9

Every parent who has made a road trip with children has heard that familiar question echo from the back seat, "Are we there yet?" The answer is always something like, "Not yet." The latter half of the eleventh chapter of Isaiah paints a rhapsodic picture of humanity's destination on the long road trip of history: the reconciliation of all creation and a world "full of the knowledge of the LORD." But open a newspaper today, and it's clear that we're not there yet.

We live our lives in the *meantime*, between the promise made and the promise made realized. The challenge of living in the meantime is to trust the promise, to work toward its fulfillment in small and large ways, and to maintain hope. The dream may always seem to lie before us, just out of reach. But with that ultimate destination shaping our dreams, we inch closer to getting there.

Creator God, fire our imagination of creation restored and save us from giving up hope. Amen.

Michael L. Lindvall

DECEMBER 14

PSALM 72:1–7, 18–19

Little Ones

May he defend the cause of the poor of the people,
give deliverance to the needy,
and crush the oppressor.

Psalm 72:4

Psalm 72 is a royal psalm, a prayer that the leader of the nation may live long, bring peace, and show particular concern for the poor, needy, and oppressed. Psalm 72 suggests that we are right to ask just as much of our political, business, and church leaders. They must also show particular concern for the most vulnerable among us.

I have a fondness for "died-and-went-to-heaven" jokes. One of my favorites imagines a famous minister at the pearly gates. He tells St. Peter about his great achievements, such as spell-binding sermons, scholarly books, and prominent congregations. St. Peter scans the book in front of him and says, "I don't find your name." The minister turns away, dejected. As he retreats from the pearly gates, St. Peter calls him back, "Wait. Are you the man who fed the little birds?" We often evaluate others and ourselves in terms of great things done or undone. God may care more about the mercies we have shown the "little birds" of the world.

Loving God, open our eyes and hands to the "little birds" of our world. Amen.

Michael L. Lindvall

DECEMBER 15

ROMANS 15:4–13

Who Is Your Gentile?

Welcome one another, therefore, just as Christ has welcomed you, for the glory of God.

Romans 15:7

Chasms separated different groups of people in the ancient world—slave and free, male and female, Jew and Gentile. In contrast, the early Christian church radically created a community in which distinctions were submerged into a new unity in Jesus Christ. Today, in our divided society, we are inspired to ask, "Who is 'the other' you find it difficult to welcome?"

I once heard a story about a disheveled and ill-clad young man who wandered into a very staid Protestant church one Sunday morning. He made it past the ushers and plopped himself on the floor at the front of the center aisle, waiting for worship to begin. One of the ushers, an older man in a suit and tie, came up to the young man and sat himself down on the floor next to him. Together they listened to the prelude and awaited the call to worship.

Give us love wide enough and courage deep enough to welcome one another as Christ has welcomed us. Amen.

Michael L. Lindvall

DECEMBER 16

MATTHEW 3:1–12

Changing Direction

In those days John the Baptist appeared in the wilderness of Judea, proclaiming, "Repent, for the kingdom of heaven has come near."

Matthew 3:1–2

Some years ago, I preached a sermon in which I repeated the word *repent* several times. On Monday morning, I found an unfriendly note in my mailbox about my sermon. I could understand the writer's resistance, but the fact is that these twelve verses from Matthew describe John the Baptist repeating the word *repent* again and again. John, an unlikely and definitely un-Christmaslike guest, yells "Repent!" and calls his desert congregation a "brood of vipers" (v. 7).

We tend to hear the word *repent* as an invitation to list our peccadillos and grovel in self-distain. But in Greek, the word *repent* actually means something more like change your direction or even turn around. God invites us time and again in life to turn around, to change direction. It's seldom easy and often requires us to hear words that fall uncomfortably on our ears.

Give us the courage, loving God, to change the direction in which we are headed. Amen.

Michael L. Lindvall

DECEMBER 17

MATTHEW 3:1–12

Pointing Away

"I baptize you with water for repentance, but one who is more powerful than I is coming after me; I am not worthy to carry his sandals. He will baptize you with the Holy Spirit and fire."

Matthew 3:11

Jesus and John the Baptist are often portrayed together in art as infants in their mothers' arms and at Jesus' baptism. Jesus is usually at the center of the painting, with John to one side. John is often portrayed pointing toward Jesus, whether with a chubby baby finger or a bony old prophet finger. With this action, John does one of the most difficult things for any human being to do. He points away from himself to another. "I am not worthy to untie the thong of his sandals," says John (Luke 3:16).

How often in life do we turn the attention toward ourselves! A friend speaks of her illness, and we chronicle our own woes. Someone speaks of an achievement, and we crow about something we did. Some call our proclivity to self-orientation "the original sin." Whatever we call it, nothing is more challenging, or more liberating, than turning away from ourselves to attend to another.

O God, free us from our little prison of self-focus so that we can hear you and others. Amen.

Michael L. Lindvall

DECEMBER 18

LUKE 1:46–55

Expectancy

"My spirit rejoices in God my Savior."

Luke 1:47

Had I been Mary when the angel Gabriel came to call and announce the expectancy of the Messiah, the Son of God, I may have panicked, said "no way," and run as fast as I could in the opposite direction! Not Mary. Relying on her strong Jewish faith, she not only accepted God's call but also proceeded to sing with great joy. We know her words as the Magnificat, one of the oldest and most beautiful passages in our Scriptures. But Mary was not naive. She knew her journey would be challenging and difficult.

Realizing the value of family support and encouragement at stressful times, she left her home and traveled from Nazareth to the hill country to visit her older cousin Elizabeth, who was pregnant with her son, John the Baptist.

It was a powerful reunion, with both women pregnant and at opposite ends of the age spectrum—a young teenager and an old woman. Through those ties that bind—faithfulness, family, mutual love, and understanding—they provided great comfort to each other while awaiting the births of their sons.

God, thank you for your loving presence and for supporting us particularly in our times of uncertainty and challenge while we wait. Amen.

Peggy Rada

DECEMBER 19

LUKE 1:57–68

The Naming

[Zechariah] asked for a writing tablet and wrote, "His name is John." And all of them were amazed.

Luke 1:63

Is there any decision more exciting for expectant parents than deciding on the name of their child? Elizabeth and Zechariah were not deterred when neighbors and friends insisted their son should be called Zechariah after his father. Zechariah, however, had learned a valuable lesson when he did not trust or believe the message of his son's birth from the angel Gabriel and thus was mute throughout Elizabeth's pregnancy.

When Zechariah wrote on the tablet "'His name is John.' . . . his mouth was opened and his tongue freed, and he began to speak, praising God" (vv. 63–64). Elizabeth and Zechariah trusted God and recognized that God would use their son in unimaginable ways. Indeed, God did have a plan for John's life.

And God has a plan for our lives if we but listen and trust!

All-knowing God, help me to hear your voice and respond with trust and faithfulness. Amen.

Peggy Rada

DECEMBER 20

PSALM 27

Light

The LORD is my light and my salvation.

Psalm 27:1

The Advent season is surely a season of light! Festive Christmas lights adorn the stores, streets, and our homes. Light radiates from Advent candles, love feast candles, and candles we light during "Silent Night." And then there is starlight that awes and inspires us, led the magi on their journey, and marked the stable in Bethlehem.

The psalmist declares God to be his light and salvation but hastens to add that dark days will come. There will be trials, tribulations, challenges, and threats to our security; however, the Lord will be steadfast, will show us God's way, and will protect us from our enemies. Dark days come for each of us, but there is never a day without God's light. At times, we may feel that the darkness overtakes the light and that we are surrounded by the darkness of grief, pain, depression, or heartbreak. But dawn comes every day. And with it comes the light that lifts us from despair. The light will most certainly come. God's light! Thanks be to God.

Dear God, may your way always be a light unto my path. Amen.

Peggy Rada

DECEMBER 21

Isaiah 43:1–7

Peace

Do not fear, for I am with you.

Isaiah 43:5

Today I attended a Sanctuary Inquiry Workshop. Our session is beginning to explore the possibility of supporting neighbors who are seeking sanctuary from deportation orders. We were told before the meeting that approximately two hundred people would attend; however, upon arrival we discovered that more than four hundred people from our relatively small city and surrounding area had gathered to learn how we as a faith community can reach out to our immigrant brothers and sisters in crisis and in need of sanctuary.

The season of Advent is indeed a time of waiting, expecting, hoping, and finding a sense of peace with the birth of our Lord and Savior, Jesus Christ. May we also remember Isaiah's words "Do not fear, for I have redeemed you; I have called you by name, you are mine" and be reminded of God's steadfast love for us (v. 1b).

How can we help our friends, neighbors, and family members who are facing frightful times? There are no easy answers or quick fixes. Thank God for the people who are working to help in this time of crisis.

God, help us to remember always your question: Who is our neighbor? Amen.

Peggy Rada

DECEMBER 22

1 Corinthians 12:4–6

Gifts

Now there are varieties of gifts.
1 Corinthians 12:4

Indeed, all gifts are important for God's work. Each should be utilized and affirmed. In my opinion, there is no more important person on a church staff than the Christian educator. Today it was my great joy and privilege to share lunch with my local church's Christian educator. Her very presence exudes love for God and all God's people. As we visited, I saw in her face a deep and compassionate concern for the children, the youth, the college students, and the adults in our congregation. Her gift for listening with ear, heart, and spirit warmed my soul and affirmed my great hope for our church and our denomination.

I thank God for all who have heard God's call to ministry and especially to Christian education. May God continue to bless us with these faithful educators, who teach us and enable us to be stronger disciples of Jesus, the Christ.

Dear God, thank you for all the Christian educators who hear your call to teach and to lead. Amen.

Peggy Rada

DECEMBER 23

PHILIPPIANS 3:12–16

Endurance

Not that I have already obtained this or have already reached the goal; but I press on to make it my own, because Christ Jesus has made me his own.

Philippians 3:12

In this day of quick fixes, with easy and even flippant answers to life's problems and challenges, we listen to Paul. He reminds us with his words to the converts in the church at Philippi that they have not arrived. Even Paul has not arrived. We are all pressing on, striving for a perfection that will not be attained in this life. Yet we keep at it, following the model that Christ Jesus has set for us.

Advent provides us the perfect opportunity to slow down, to reflect, to examine, and to practice endurance! Our culture does not allow us this time. We must carve out a niche for ourselves when we acknowledge our past mistakes and continue, in spite of our past, by focusing on what lies ahead. Runners understand this image of pressing forward, of enduring, and of not looking back. Let us look to the future, knowing that the prize has already been won because Christ Jesus has named, claimed, and made us his own. There is much work to do for our Lord. Let us get busy doing it!

God, help us to realize that we have not "arrived" but must endure to do your work here. Amen.

Peggy Rada

DECEMBER 24

Psalm 126

Joy

May those who sow in tears
reap with shouts of joy.
Psalm 126:5

Life is difficult, life is challenging, life is unfair, and life sometimes seems impossible. The Hebrews knew these truths from their days of living in captivity in Babylon. They had lost their homes, their lands, their temple, and their way of life. They, however, had not lost their God! They strongly believed that one day they would return to their homelands and that they would rebuild their temple.

This psalm must ring very true for our brothers and sisters who have escaped their homelands looking for refuge, for sanctuary, for a better life. Last year I visited refugee camps in Lebanon, Iraq, Hungary, Germany, and Greece. The refugees were most appreciative for the hospitality they were receiving from these countries; however, they still remembered the harshness and the cruelty that had prompted their having to flee their homelands. They truly were "sowing in tears" and hoping to "reap with shouts of joy."

Dear God, as we turn from Advent to Christmas, may we do all that we can to help bring about light, hope, joy, endurance, and peace to our brothers and sisters around the world. Amen.

Peggy Rada

DECEMBER 25

ISAIAH 9:2–7

Light for the Journey

The people who walked in darkness
have seen a great light;
those who lived in a land of deep darkness—
on them light has shined.

Isaiah 9:2

It is more than a little strange that we celebrate the coming of a great light on one of the shortest days of the year. The gift of Christmas light can seem like a glimpse of glory that will fade away all too soon, with only the memories of this day to give us comfort and hope as we weather the long winter nights ahead.

Yet Isaiah reassures us that a greater light is still to come. The days are surely coming when God's light will shine more brightly than ever before. We will rejoice as with joy at the harvest, set aside every yoke of our burdens, and destroy the marks of war and strife as fuel for the fires of peace and justice (vv. 3–5).

A child *has* been born for us, a son given to us. And his light will show us the path to justice, righteousness, and new life. Merry Christmas!

Eternal God, shine your light of justice, mercy, peace, and love on us today and every day. Amen.

Andy James

DECEMBER 26

Luke 2:1–14 (15–20)

Setting Out on the Way

When the angels had left them and gone into heaven, the shepherds said to one another, "Let us go now to Bethlehem and see this thing that has taken place, which the Lord has made known to us."

Luke 2:15

December 26 is almost always a travel day for me. The carols have been sung, the presents unwrapped, and the cookies consumed. The first celebration of Christmas is now over, and it is time to move on to the next stop. Based on the number of cars I see along the way, I am not alone in this!

After hearing the angels' proclamation about Jesus' birth, the shepherds set out on their own journey to meet this child. They "went with haste" (v. 16) to find Mary, Joseph, and Jesus. Even as they basked in the glow from the glorious heavenly choir, they needed to figure out the next stop on their journey. So they set out to go wherever else God might take them.

As you move on from Christmas this year, where are you headed? How are you asking God to lead you?

God of light, guide us along all the journeys of our lives. Amen.

Andy James

DECEMBER 27

LUKE 2:1–14 (15–20)

Setting Out on the Journey

Joseph also went from the town of Nazareth in Galilee to Judea, to the city of David called Bethlehem, because he was descended from the house and family of David. He went to be registered with Mary, to whom he was engaged and who was expecting a child.

Luke 2:4–5

When I travel at Christmas, I am usually alone with my thoughts and the open road. But none of us are really alone when we travel. Millions of others are making similar journeys at this time of year.

And as Christians, we all join the first Christmas travelers, Mary and Joseph, for they, too, were on a journey from Nazareth to Bethlehem when Jesus was born. Their trip was mandated by the Roman emperor, not by family traditions. It was a difficult journey, and yet they set out with all the hope and expectation that they could muster as they prepared to begin this new phase of life together.

As we drive, ride, or fly on our Christmas travels this year, may we remember that we journey with countless others—beginning with Mary and Joseph—who seek to embody God's hope and expectation anew.

God of all travelers, give us safety, hope, and joy wherever we travel this Christmas. Amen.

Andy James

DECEMBER 28

LUKE 2:1–14 (15–20)

New Life on the Journey

And she gave birth to her firstborn son and wrapped him in bands of cloth, and laid him in a manger, because there was no place for them in the inn.

Luke 2:7

Jesus was born to Mary at an unexpected time in an unexpected place. We don't know the exact circumstances surrounding his birth beyond the brief details of Luke 2:7. After Jesus was born, Mary "wrapped him in bands of cloth, and laid him in a manger, because there was no place for them in the inn." Even though nothing seemed ready, Jesus was ready.

Perhaps this is the greatest gift of Christmas: that Jesus arrives, ready or not. The world was turned upside down by the wonder of this new life. We cannot predict where and how Jesus will arrive, but we can trust that he is always ready to love us.

God of new life, help us to see Jesus in unexpected times and places. Amen.

Andy James

DECEMBER 29

PSALM 96

A Song along the Way

O sing to the LORD a new song;
sing to the LORD, all the earth.

Psalm 96:1

Each of the past three Christmases, I drove more than two thousand miles to visit family and friends. As I prepared to hit the road, I loaded up my phone with podcasts and audiobooks. I had great intentions to catch up on favorite shows, listen to a few new things, and learn and laugh a lot.

Inevitably, though, I left my podcasts behind and turned on Christmas carols and music of the season instead. All these songs along my way helped me celebrate this holy season by opening the meaning of these days in new ways.

The psalmist inspires me to join in singing a new song to the Lord. May you find new songs, and treasured old songs, on your journey of faith.

Lord Jesus, as we prepare to welcome you at Christmas, help us to sing a new song to you. Amen.

Andy James

DECEMBER 30

Luke 2:1–14 (15–20)

Sharing the Story—or Keeping Quiet

But Mary treasured all these words and pondered them in her heart.

Luke 2:19

How do you respond to good news? Maybe you shout glad tidings from the mountaintops so that everyone will hear. Maybe you hold the good news deep within yourself to let it sink into the depths of your being.

The Christmas story includes both of these responses to the birth of Jesus. After visiting the baby Jesus lying in the manger, the shepherds went forth to tell everyone they met what they had heard and seen. Jesus' mother, Mary, on the other hand, said very little as she let the experience of this birth settle into her being. Both of these very different reactions are deeply faithful echoes to the wonder of the birth of Jesus.

Loving God, help us to share your good news, both heartily and quietly. Amen.

Andy James

DECEMBER 31

TITUS 2:11–14

Encouragement for the Journey

For the grace of God has appeared, bringing salvation to all.

Titus 2:11

I often catch myself giving people instructions as we go our separate ways. "Let me know how it goes tomorrow." "Text me when you get home." "Tell your family I said hello." "Take care."

In this reading from the Pastoral Epistle Titus, Paul gives us instructions like these. With the gift of grace in Christ among us, we are invited to set aside the things that get in the way of showing this salvation to the world. We are encouraged to live in faithfulness as we wait for the fullness of God's glory in Christ to be revealed among us.

These words of hope, promise, and challenge remind us that God encourages us to be agents of love in a world that needs new life.

God of grace, help us to make your light visible each and every day. Amen.

Andy James